WILTON 1993 YEARBOOK
Cake Decorating!

Cakes for Special Occasions

Decorator's Mini Course

Products

✓ Time Savers

This symbol signals a cake idea that you can decorate in minutes. These cakes use fewer colors, fewer tips and time-saving Wilton products for those times when you need a great cake in a hurry!

POP GOES THE BIRTHDAY!

- 8, 12 in. Round Pans, p. 175, 179
- Tips 3, 4B, 5, 10, 16, 101, 103, 124, 125, 352, p. 134-139
- Kelly Green, Lemon Yellow, Creamy Peach, Pink, Violet Icing Colors, p. 124
- Flower Nail # 7, p. 130
- 9 in. Decorator Preferred Round Separator Plate, p. 173
- Hidden Pillars, p. 171
- '93 Pattern Book (Jack In The Box Pattern), p. 112
- Cake Dividing Set, p. 128
- Meringue Powder, p. 125
- 14 in. Ruffle Board, p. 133
- Celebration Jumbo Candle, p. 145
- Comical Clowns Set, p. 140
- Crinkle Cookie Cutters, p. 118
- Buttercream, Royal Icings, p. 93
- Roll-out Cookie Dough Recipe, p. 105

- Using royal icing, make 36 roses with tips 10 and 103. Make 36 sweet peas with tip 103.
- For cookie box and plaques: Tint half of cookie dough with pink and half with lemon yellow. Cut out box pattern in pink dough and crinkles shapes in yellow dough. Bake and cool. Attach all sides of box with royal icing and decorate with tip 16 stars.
- Ice both 2-layer cakes smooth with buttercream. Using cake dividing set, dot mark 12" cake into 10ths. Connect marks with tip 3 triple drop strings, leaving front side open. At bottom border, add tip 16 shells, then tip 125 ruffle topped with tip 16 rosettes and tip 3 multicolored dots. Pipe tip 124 ruffle top border, trimmed with tip 16 shells. Cut pillars to 5" length and position into 12" cake. Using cake dividing set, dot mark 8" cake into 8ths, leaving front side open. Repeat steps as for 12" cake.
- For crinkle cookie plaques, use royal or buttercream with tip 3 to outline and decorate with dots, name, age, etc. Attach with icing to cookie box, 8" and 12" cake.
- For clown, brush stripe (p.94) bag with yellow, pink and green. On top of box, pipe body and arms with tip 4B, hands with tip 5. Add tip 101 ruffle above hands in pink. Top with clown head.
- Arrange flowers on tops of both cakes. Add tip 352 leaves. To serve, position 8" cake on top of pillars and place cookie box directly on 8" cake. Serves 32.

HOPPY BIRTHDAY

- *Special Delivery Bunny Pan, p. 186*
- *Mini Balloon Pan, p. 192*
- *Tips 3, 16, 21, p. 134-139*
- *Lemon Yellow, Brown, Kelly Green, Peach, Violet, Pink, icing Colors, p. 124*
- *Cake Boards, Fanci-Foil Wrap, p. 132*
- *Buttercream Icing, p. 93*
- *Shoestring Licorice*
- For Balloons: Position cakes on individual foil-covered boards. Cover with tip 16 stars; use circular motion to pipe balloon tie to narrow end. Print tip 3 message on one balloon. Set aside.

- For Bunny: Ice cake background and sides smooth. Outline details, and pipe in facial features and pads of paw with tip 3. Pipe tip 16 stars on body and head, pull-out stars on tail. Add tip 21 shell border; trim with tip 3 dots.
- Position balloon with message on cake top, other balloons around. Attach licorice to balloon ends and to paw. *Cake Serves 12. Each Balloon Serves 1.*

NUMBER ONE KID

- *10 in. Round Pan, p. 175*
- *Tips 3, 21, p. 134-139*
- *12 in. Ruffle Board, p. 133*
- *Birthday Bears Cake Top Set, p. 144*
- *Numeral Candle, p. 146*
- *Buttercream Icing, p. 93*
- *Pastel Candy-coated Chocolates*
- Ice two-layer cake smooth. Edge top with tip 21 star border, base with tip 21 zigzag border.
- Position decorations on cake top and sides. Randomly add pastel candy-coated chocolates. Position candle.
- Write tip 3 name. *Serves 24.*

Time Saver

First Birthdays

Time Saver

BEAR ON BASE

- *Teddy Bear Stand Up Pan, p. 188*
- *Tip 4, p. 134*
- *Brown, Christmas Red Icing Colors, p. 124*
- *Cake Board, Fanci-foil Wrap, p. 132*
- *Buttercream Icing, p. 93*
- *Round coconut-covered snack cakes, candy-coated chocolates, cardboard*

- For tie, crimp center of double-folded Fanci-Foil strip.
- To make cap: with tip 4, outline down sides of round coconut-covered snack cake cap. Add tip 4 spiral bead at crown. Cut cardboard oval for cap brim and ice smooth. Position cap on brim.
- To make baseball: Pipe two tip 4 semicircles on round coconut-covered snack cake. Add tip 4 angled stitch marks above and below semicircles.
- Ice snout, bottom of paws, inside of ears smooth. Generously ice rest of bear, then fluff with fork to create fur effect.
- With tip 4 pipe nose, mouth, and pads of feet. Smooth with finger dipped in cornstarch. Add candy-coated chocolate eyes. Position baseball in front of bear. *Serves 12.*

PARTY-READY TEDDIES

- *Mini Bears Pan, p. 188*
- *Tip 4, p. 134*
- *Pink, Sky Blue Icing Colors, p. 124*
- *Candy Melts™* — *1 bag each Light and Dark Cocoa, p. 116*
- *Cake Board, Fanci-Foil Wrap, p. 132*
- *Buttercream Icing, p. 93*

- Make Mini Bear plaques out of melted Candy Melts (see p. 108). For the darker color bears, use dark cocoa melts; for the light color bears, use light cocoa melts. One recipe covers 6 bears.
- Ice sides and tops of bear cakes smooth. Position candy plaques on top. Pipe in tip 4 facial features, ears and paw prints. Add tip 4 bead border. *Each serves 1.*

*brand confectionery coating

4

Beary Happy Birthdays!

JUMPING FOR JOY

- Ballerina Bear Pan, p. 188
- Tips 3, 4, 16, 18, p. 134-135
- Pink, Brown Icing Colors, p. 124
- Cake Boards, Fanci-Foil Wrap, p. 132
- Buttercream Icing, p. 93
- Candy-coated chocolates, red shoestring licorice and licorice twists

- Ice cake sides and background area smooth. Outline bear with tip 4 strings. Fill in face, arms, legs, shoes, socks, shirt and shorts with tip 16 stars. Pipe in eyes, nose and mouth with tip 3; smooth with finger dipped in cornstarch.

- Add tip 3 outline shoestrings, bow and message. Cut licorice twists into pieces for jumprope handle; insert string licorice and position jumprope on hands; add candy-coated chocolates for eyes.

- Add tip 18 shell border at base; trim with tip 3 dots. *Serves 12.*

5

JIFFY THE CLOWN

- *Happy Clown Pan, p. 192*
- *Tip 18, p. 135*
- *Orange Icing Color, p. 124*
- *Cake Board, Fanci-Foil Wrap, p. 132*
- *Buttercream Icing, p. 93*
- *Sugar-Coated Candy Discs, Birthday Hat*
- Ice top and sides smooth.
- Pipe tip 18 eyebrows and elongated zigzags for collar and base.
- Position candies for hair, nose; cut candies in half for eyes and mouth. *Serves 12.*

THE FAST TRACK

- *14 in. Round Pans, p. 175*
- *Petite Doll Pan, p. 188*
- *Tips 1s, 1, 2, 4, 17, 20, 46, 225, 233, p. 134-139*
- *Golden Yellow, Lemon Yellow, Orange, Christmas Red, Kelly Green, Royal Blue, Brown Icing Colors, p. 124*
- *'93 Pattern Book (Sign and Track Pattern), p. 112*
- *Cake Dividing Set, p. 128*
- *Cake Boards, Fanci-Foil Wrap, p. 132*
- *Meringue Powder, p. 125*
- *Numeral Candle, p. 146*
- *Lollipop Sticks, p. 116*
- *Buttercream*, Royal Icings, p. 93*
- *Jelly Candies, Lollipop Sticks, Candy Sticks, Gumballs, Candy Mini Mints, Sweet/Sour Tart Candy*
- Using royal icing, make 100 tip 225 drop flowers (50 red, 50 orange) with tip 2 white dot centers.
- For passengers: With tip 1s and royal icing pipe facial features on tart candy before placing on bodies. Pipe tip 4 bodies on jelly candies, add tip 2 arms and tip 1 fingers. With royal icing, secure head on body and pipe tip 1 hair. Let dry.
- For sign: Trace sign pattern on cakeboard, ice and pipe tip 2 message and bead border. Attach to lollipop sticks. Let dry.
- Ice two layer cake smooth. Keep one petite doll mold actual size (to be used for back of rollercoaster), trim two medium height (for sides), and trim one to a short height (for front). Ice molds and place on cake. Build up icing at bottom of slopes so track will run smoothly.
- With toothpick, mark track pattern. Outline track and rails with tip 46.
- On sides of hills pipe tip 2 vertical and tip 4 horizontal lines. Finish with tip 4 "V" motion lines. Add tip 4 bead border to bottom of hills.
- At each rail, pipe tip 2 dot and insert mini mint for sides. Let dry until set.
- With royal icing use tip 4 to pipe two continuous lines around track for upper rails.
- Divide cake into 12ths, pipe tip 17 zigzag garland between marks. Secure gumball on candy stick with dot of icing.
- Edge cake top with tip 20 shell border. Position candy sticks between garlands. Add tip 233 grass on cake top and for bottom border.
- Position flowers, passengers on track, sign and numeral candle. *Serves 54.*

*Note: To reach desired shade of yellow icing used on cake, Lemon Yellow and Golden Yellow were mixed.
This exciting cake is also captured on our cover!

CAROUSEL ENCHANTMENT

- *Double-Tier Round Pan, p. 187*
- *Tip 21, p. 135*
- *Lemon Yellow Icing Color, p. 124*
- *Carousel Cake Top Set, p. 140*
- *Cake Boards, Fanci-Foil Wrap, p. 132*
- *Buttercream Icing, p. 93*
- *Candy-coated Chocolates*

- With spatula, ice cake smooth. Edge top and bottom borders and carousel with tip 21 stars. Trim with candy-coated chocolates. Position carousel. *Serves 12.*

ANIMAL TRACKS

- *11 x 15 in. Sheet Pan, p. 174, 179*
- *Tips 3, 10, 48, 57, 233, p. 134-139*
- *Violet, Wilton Red, Lemon Yellow, Leaf Green, Sky Blue Icing Colors, p. 124*
- *Circus Friends Cake Top Set, p. 144*
- *Cake Boards, Fanci-Foil Wrap, p. 132*
- *Buttercream Icing, p. 93*

- Ice 1 layer cake smooth- sides white, top blue and 2 ½ in. high area on bottom green.
- Using toothpick, mark roller coaster frame on cake top: Mark top track first; then criss-cross lines ¾ in. apart; add vertical support columns last, spacing 1 in. apart and intersecting every other criss-cross area. Outline in same order, using tip 48 for top track and tip 57 for criss-cross lines and support columns.
- Position animal cake tops above track, piping tip 10 cars with tip 3 wheels. Add tip 10 zigzag clouds in sky.
- Position elephant cake top, add tip 233 pull-out grass edging. Print tip 3 dot message. Pipe alternating color tip 10 bulb border at top and base. *Serves 20.*

Time Saver

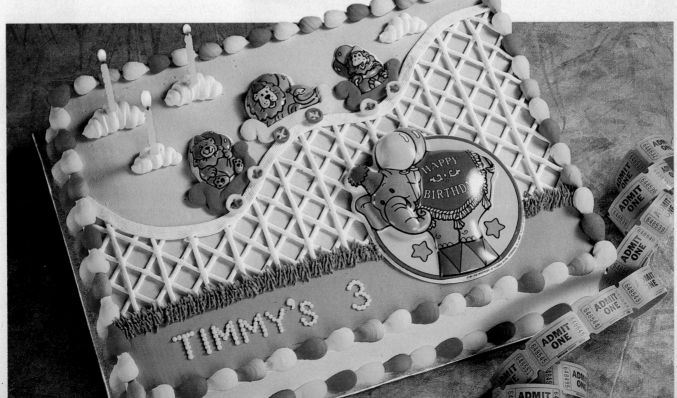

7

Balloons Balloons Balloons

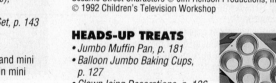

BIG BIRD'S BOUQUET OF BALLOONS

- 6 x 3 in. Round Pan, p. 175
- Mini Balloon Pan, p. 192
- Tips 3, 10, 18, p. 134-139
- Lemon Yellow, Wilton Red (No-Taste), Royal Blue Icing Colors, p. 124
- Big Bird With Age Birthday Topper Set, p. 143
- Cake Board, Fanci-foil Wrap, p. 132
- Black Shoestring Licorice

- Ice smooth the one-layer 6 in. cake and mini balloon cakes. Make spatula marks in mini balloons to create faceted look.

- On 6 in. cake pipe tip 18 top star border, leaving space for balloons every two stars. Add tip 18 bottom zigzag border. With tip 10, pipe balloons in alternating colors (smooth with finger dipped in cornstarch). Add tip 3 balloon necks and strings. Position Big Bird topper. Print tip 3 name.

- On mini cakes: Place on serving plate - then add balloon neck by piping a tip 3 dot, then a spiral around it. Add licorice strings. Print tip 3 names on all cakes. *Cake serves 12, each balloon serves 1.*

Sesame Street Characters © Jim Henson Productions, Inc. © 1992 Children's Television Workshop

HEADS-UP TREATS

- Jumbo Muffin Pan, p. 181
- Balloon Jumbo Baking Cups, p. 127
- Clown Icing Decorations, p. 126
- Sprinkle Decorations, p. 127
- Buttercream Icing, p. 93

- Ice cupcakes smooth, position "Clown Heads"; add sprinkles. *Each serves one.*

CLOWNS IN THE CLOUDS

- *6 in. Square Pan, p. 174*
- *Tips 2B, 3, 18, 32, 102, p. 134-139*
- *Brown, Lemon Yellow, Red-Red, Sky Blue, Orange Icing Colors, p. 124*
- *Comical Clowns Set, p. 140*
- *Florist Wire (2 lengths needed), p.130*
- *Flower Spikes (4 needed), p. 166*
- *Buttercream Icing, p. 93*
- *Helium Balloon, Ribbons, Drinking Straws*
- Ice 2-layer cake smooth with a thin layer of buttercream icing. Cover sides with tip 2B basketweave. Edge top and base with tip 18 rope border. Divide cake sides in half, dot mark with toothpick. Add tip 18 brush striped (p. 94) zigzag garland, using dot marks and corners as guidelines. Trim with tip 3 double drop strings and bows.
- Position flower spikes in corners of cake top. Pipe clown bodies and arms with tip 32; add tip 102 ruffle cuffs; pipe tip 3 hands and dot pompons. Insert heads.
- Shape wires to accomodate balloon. Insert wire ends into drinking straws cut in half, then into flower spikes. Add ribbon trim. *Serves 8.*

ALL ABOARD!

- *Little Train Pan, p. 189*
- *Tips 3, 4, 16, p. 134-139*
- *Wilton Red (No-Taste), Royal Blue, Lemon Yellow Icing Colors, p. 124*
- *Circus Balloons (2 packages), p. 140*
- *Cake Boards, Fanci-Foil Wrap, p. 132*
- *Buttercream Icing, p. 93*
- Ice sides, background areas, cab window smooth.
- Outline smokestack, cab, front of engine, back car, brake shift, wheels, roof, and cowcatcher with tip 4 strings.
- Pipe tip 16 zigzag on wheels and brake shaft.
- Cover engine, cowcatcher, smokestack and inner wheels with tip 16 stars.
- Pipe tip 16 star border. Print tip 3 message, add tip 16 outline number and rosette (light at front). Position circus balloons. *Serves 12.*

MAGICAL CARRIAGE RIDE

- Sports Ball Pan, p. 187
- 12 x 18 in. Sheet Pan, p. 174
- Tips 2, 2A, 3, 4, 7, 10, 16, 17, 18, 68, 101, 102, 225, p. 134-39
- Flower Nail #9, p. 130
- Teal, Pink, Violet Icing Colors, p. 124
- 6-pc. Nesting Round Cookie Cutter Set, p. 120
- Script Pattern Message Press Set, p. 128
- 4 mm Pearl Beading, 1 package needed, p. 167
- Carousel Separator Set, p. 140
- Wooden Dowel Rods, p. 172
- Mini Doll Pick Set, p. 188
- Meringue Powder, p. 125
- Celebration Jumbo Candles, p. 145
- Cake Board, Fanci-Foil Wrap, Tuk N' Ruffle, p. 132-133
- Roll-Out Cookie Dough Recipe, p. 105
- Sugar Mold Recipe, p. 108
- Buttercream, Royal Icings, p. 93

PREPARE CARRIAGE AT LEAST ONE DAY IN ADVANCE

- Using Sports Ball Pan and Sugar Mold Recipe, make Carriage (see p. 108)
- **FOR CARRIAGE WHEELS:** Roll out cookie dough, cut out two 3" and three 2" round cookies. Bake and cool. Ice smooth. With tip 4, outline spokes and rim and two 3" and two 2" cookies. Save one 2" cookie for seat in coach. Add pearls.
- Using royal icing and tip 225 make 80 drop flowers. (40 violet with tip 2 pink centers, 40 pink with tip 2 violet centers). Let dry. With royal icing, make 12 tip 102 roses with tip 10 bases (4 violet, 8 pink) and 5 tip 101 roses with tip 7 bases (4 pink, 1 violet).
- Ice cake sides and top smooth. Prepare cake for stacked construction, p. 106.
- Ice separator plate and place on dowel rod area. Trim with tip 3 zigzag.
- Use metal base from Sports Ball Pan for carriage base. Ice base with royal icing and trim with pearls, place on iced separator plate.

- Before assembling coach, make seat using 2" cookie. Outline cookie with tip 4 strings and edge with pearl beading. Set in bottom portion of coach, using royal icing to affix. Trim about 1" from pick portion of doll pick with craft knife. Pipe base for princess on seat with tip 2A. Position doll pick. Add tip 16 stars for dress, edge with tip 102 ruffle and tip 2 beads.
- With royal icing, assemble coach, add tip 68 ruffles. Trim with pearl beading. With tip 4, add scroll designs and top with pearl beading. Secure roses on top of carriage and wheels on sides with royal icing.
- Decorate horses with tip 2 strings and beads. Position in cake. Attach pearl beading "reins". Use message press and outline with tip 3. Edge top border with tip 17 reverse shell, bottom with tip 18 shell. Add roses and drop flowers. Trim all roses with tip 68 leaves. Position candles. *Serves 30.*

Happy Birthday Brittany

Fairy Tales

FANTASY FLIGHT
- *Wonder Mold Pan, p. 188*
- *9 in. Round Pan, p. 175*
- *Tips 2, 6, 102, 104, p. 134-139*
- *Pink, Violet, Teal Icing Colors, p. 124*
- *Teen Doll Pick, p. 188*
- *Pearl Stamens, p. 130*
- *Flower Spikes, p. 166*
- *Florist Wire, p. 130*
- *Cake Board, Fanci-Foil Wrap, p. 132*
- *Buttercream Icing, p. 93*
- *Pink Plastic Wrap, Cellophane tape*

- Fill and ice 9 in. round and Wonder Mold cakes together.
- Push doll pick into Wonder Mold. Ice bodice smooth (build up waistline with icing for a natural look). Trim neckline with tip 2 outline. Add tip 2 dot "buttons". With tip 102, add ruffles on bodice, edge with tip 2 beads.
- With tip 2, add scalloped string work to front of skirt, overpipe with dots. Edge base with tip 6 bead border.
- Pipe three rows of ruffles on skirt with tip 104, trim with tip 2 beads; add tip 102 bow at waist. Add dot trim to skirt with tip 2.
- For headband: place cellophane tape on hair where headband will go. With tip 6 pipe icing "headband". Randomly add pearl stamens. Position wings.
- For wings: Shape florist wire into four "wings" and cover with pink plastic wrap. Connect in middle and leave 3" florist wire to be wrapped with cellophane tape and inserted in floral spike. *Serves 32.*

ENCHANTED RIDE

- Carousel Horse Pan, p. 192
- Tips 3, 16, 21, 103, 129, 352, 362, p. 134-139
- Violet, Pink, Teal, Golden Yellow Icing Colors, p. 124
- Dowel Rod, p. 172
- Meringue Powder, p. 125
- Buttercream, Royal Icings, p. 93

- Using royal icing, make 14 tip 129 drop flowers (11 violet, 3 pink) with tip 3 yellow centers. Let dry.
- Ice background areas and sides smooth.
- Outline unicorn, facial features and hooves with pink tip 3 strings. Pipe in eye with tip 3 (smooth with finger dipped in cornstarch). Add tip 3 dots to eye and nose.
- Cover unicorn with tip 16 stars. Use tip 16 zigzag on hooves and inside ear. Add tip 3 strings for eyelashes and mouth; dot for nose.
- Pipe tip 21 spatula-striped (see p. 94) mane and tail.
- Trim base with tip 103 ruffle and add tip 21 shells with tip 3 dots.
- To make horn: cut dowel rod to 4" with craft knife. Hold one end and with tip 362 cover with a swirling motion. Leave top 1" empty. Push into cake. Finish trimming point of horn. Position flowers, trim with tip 352 leaves and print tip 3 message. *Serves 12.*

OPENING NIGHT

- 9 x 13 in. Sheet Pan, p. 174, 179
- Tips 3, 5, 8, 16, 127D, 129, p. 134-39
- Violet, Pink, Lemon Yellow Icing Colors, p. 124
- Candy Melts™ *— Pastel Mix, (Pink, Lavender, Blue), White, Light Cocoa, p. 116

- Ballerina Candy Lollipops Molds, p. 114
- '93 Pattern Book (Stage and Curtains), p. 112
- Make Any Message Letter Press Set, p. 128
- Decorating Comb, Decorator's Brushes Set, p. 128
- Cake Board, Tuk-N-Ruffle, Fanci-Foil Wrap, p. 132-133
- Meringue Powder, p. 125
- Buttercream, Royal Icings, p. 93

*brand confectionery coating

- Mold (see p. 108) 14 ballet slippers and 5 ballerinas out of melted Candy Melts; painting in areas of contrasting color.
- Using royal icing, make 21 drop flowers with tip 129, add tip 3 centers. Let dry.
- Ice sides and top center of 2-layer cake smooth. With a toothpick, lightly mark curtains and stage pattern. Ice stage area in violet, curtain area in pink. Use decorating comb to create folds in curtains. Add tip 127D ruffle above curtains.
- Print tip 3 message and edge stage with tip 3 bead border.
- Divide front and back of cake sides by 4. Divide sides by 3. With tip 16 add double drop strings on sides. Add tip 5 bead border on top; tip 8 bead border on bottom.
- Position flowers, ballerinas, and slippers. *Serves 28.*

HEART'S DELIGHT

- Heart Mini Cake Pan, p. 183
- 6 in. Heart Pan, 9 in. Heart Pan, p. 183
- Tips 3, 129, 224, 362, p. 134-139
- Pink, Teal, Violet, Golden Yellow Icing Colors, p. 124
- Cake Boards, Fanci-Foil Wrap, p. 132
- 8" Round Doilies, p. 132
- Dowel rods, p. 172
- Ballerina Candle Holder Set, p. 147
- Meringue Powder, p. 125
- Buttercream, Royal Icing, p. 93

- Using royal icing make 164 tip 224 and 70 tip 129 drop flowers. Add tip 3 centers. Let dry.
- Place doilies on cake board.
- Ice one layer and mini cakes smooth. Dowel rod and position 6 in. heart atop 9 in. heart.
- Print tip 3 message.
- Edge borders with tip 362 shells.
- Add tip 129 drop flowers to 9" heart and tip 224 drop flowers to 6" heart and mini hearts, alternating colors.
- Add ballerina candle holders. Insert candles. *Large cakes serve 12 (total). Mini cakes each serve one.*

Birthday Fantasy

HAPPY BIRTHDAY KATIE

Time Saver

Happy Birthday
Melissa
from
All of Us

Marie Lynn
Beth
Jane
Mary
Dianne

SLEEPOVER PARTY

- *7 x 11" in. Sheet Pan, p. 174*
- *Tips 1, 2, 2B, 3, 4, 7, 10, 14, 102, 125, p. 134-139*
- *Violet, Golden Yellow, Red-Red, Brown and Copper Icing Colors, p. 124*
- *Cake Boards, Fanci-Foil Wrap, p. 132*
- *1 pkg. each Scrolls, Filigree Swirls, p. 169*
- *Buttercream Icing, p. 93*
- *1 pkg. Large Marshmallows (5 needed)*
- For Pillows: Flatten marshmallows to make small pillows; edge with tip 102 ruffles.
- With tip 10, pipe faces on pillows; flatten with finger. Pipe tips 3 and 14 for hair, and tip 3 for facial features. Set aside.
- Ice white sheet area. Pipe tip 7 body and leg formations to position under "covers".
- Ice blanket area smooth. Pipe tip 2 Cornelli Lace (p. 97) effect on blanket. Edge blanket top with tip 2B. Add tip 125 blanket ruffle; trim with tip 4 beads.
- Pipe tip 7 beads at head of bed. Position pillows and faces. Pipe tip 2 and 3 hands holding covers. Position scrolls and filigree swirls for headboard.
- Pipe tip 2B birthday banner; add tip 3 message.
- Figure pipe cat with tips 1, 3 and 7 (see pg. 104). *Serves 12.*

14

QUINCEAÑERA

- 7, 8, 10, 12, and 16 in. Round Pans, p. 175
- Tips 2, 16, 18, 124, 125, 131, 224, 225, p. 134-139
- Violet, Pink, Golden Yellow Icing Colors, p. 124
- 6-Pc. Nesting Oval Cookie Cutter Set (3 1/2 in. x 2 1/4 in. used), p. 120
- Arched Tier Set, 4 1/2 and 6 1/2 in. Arched Pillars (1 pkg. each needed) p. 171
- 9 and 10 in. Round Separator Plates, (2 of each size needed), p. 173
- 4 and 6 mm Pearl Beading (2 pkgs. each needed), p. 167
- 2 pkgs. Mini Bouquets (5 needed) p. 153
- Kolor-Flo Fountain, Filigree Stairway, Flower Holder Ring, p. 169
- Cake Dividing Set, p. 128
- Meringue Powder, p. 125
- 12 and 18 in. Ruffle Boards, p. 133
- Cake Boards, Fanci-Foil Wrap, p. 132
- Designer Bridesmaids, Designer Groomsmen (7 pkgs. of each needed), p. 160
- Joyful Debut Ornament, p. 160
- Buttercream, Royal Icing, p. 93

Quinceañera means fifteen. . .this is a traditional design which honors a girl on her 15th birthday.

- Using royal icing, make 264 drop flowers — 100 each with tips 224 and 225; 64 with tip 131. Add tip 2 dot centers. Let dry.
- Prepare 2-layer cakes for pillar and stacked construction, (p. 106). Using Cake Dividing Set, dot mark 16 in. tier into 12ths, 12 in. tier into 10ths, 8 in. tier into 8ths, 10 in. and 7 in. satellite cakes into 8ths. For 12 in. and 10 in. cakes, use oval cookie cutter as guide for positioning flower sprays.
- For 16 in. bottom tier, 8 in. top tier and 7 in. satellite top tier, decorate as follows: Edge base with tip 18 shell border. Add 3 rows of tip 125 ruffles for 16 in. cake and tip 124 ruffles for 8 in. and 7 in. cakes. Pipe tip 18 reverse shell top border on 16 in. cake and tip 16 reverse shell top border for 8 in. and 7 in. cakes. Trim around separator plates with tip 16 e-motion shells. Position 6mm pearl beads* at top of ruffles on each cake; make bows with 4mm pearl beads, using 13 in. length for 16 in. cake and 7 in. lengths for 8 in. and 7 in. cakes. Position at each dividing point. Trim cakes with tip 131 drop flowers.
- For 12 in. middle tier and 10 in. satellite cake bottom tier, decorate as follows: Edge base with tip 18 shell border. Add 2 rows of tip 125 ruffles on each cake. Pipe tip 16 reverse shell top border. Add 6mm pearl beads at top of ruffles and over oval markers. Position flower sprays and tip 131 drop flowers.
- At reception: place Flower Holder Ring and Kolor-Flo Fountain on base plate. Add filigree stairway. Position bridesmaids, groomsmen mini bouquets and ornament. *Serves 234.*

*Remove pearls before serving.

A NOVEL BIRTHDAY

- Book Pan, p. 188
- Tips 3, 5, p. 134
- Pink Icing Color, p. 124
- Decorating Comb, p. 128
- Ready-To-Use Icing Roses, Buds, Leaves, p. 126
- Buttercream Icing, p. 93

- Ice sides and top of cake smooth.
- Add ribbed effect on sides with decorating comb. Write tip 3 message and names.
- Edge base and top border with tip 5 beads.
- Position roses, buds and leaves. *Serves 12.*

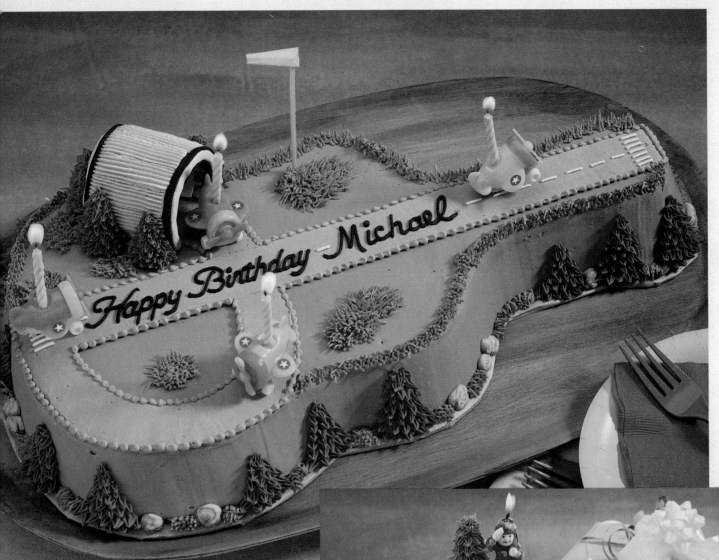

HAPPY LANDINGS

- Guitar Pan, p. 189
- Tips 2B, 3, 6, 15, 233, p. 134-139
- Black, Kelly Green, Leaf Green Icing Colors, p. 124
- Script Pattern Press Message Set, p. 128
- Airplanes Candle Holder Set, p. 147
- Cake Board, Fanci-Foil Wrap, p. 132
- Parchment Paper, p. 130
- Buttercream Icing, p. 93
- 2 Flat Bottom Ice Cream Cones, Straw

- Ice cake top and sides smooth. Using smooth edge of tip 2B, pipe 2 widths for runway. Smooth with spatula. Add tip 3 bead border to edge of runway, and tip 3 stripe markings.

- Imprint Happy Birthday with press on runway. Pipe tip 3 name.

- To make hangar: Trim off bottom of ice cream cones and trim off a small amount of side on each to sit flat. Secure the 2 cone tops together with icing. Positon on cake top at end of runway. Cover sides using ridged edge of tip 2B, outline openings with tip 3, fill in with tip 6.

- To make windsock: Ice straw, cut a small triangle from parchment, roll into windsock, attach to straw with icing.

- Pipe tip 233 pull-out grass, tip 15 pull-out trees, and tip 6 spatula-striped (p. 94) rocks randomly around cake top and base. Edge cake top with tip 233 pull-out grass. Position airplanes on runway. Insert candles. Push windsock into field. Serves 12.

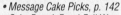

CAPTURING THE HILL

- Wonder Mold Pan, p. 188
- Horseshoe Pan, p. 187
- Tips 3, 12, 73, p. 134-139
- Brown, Moss Green Icing Colors, p. 124
- Hidden Pillars, p. 171
- 8 in. Separator Plate, p. 173
- Tree Formers Set, p. 130
- Parchment Paper, p. 130
- 4-pc. Army Set Candles, p. 146
- Cake Board, Fanci-Foil Wrap, p. 132
- Meringue Powder, p. 125
- Buttercream, Royal Icings, p. 93
- Granulated Light Brown Sugar

- For trees: Make 6 trees of various sizes with royal icing on tree formers and tip 73 pull-out leaves. Let dry.
- Ice horseshoe cake smooth. Cut 4 Hidden Pillars each to height of cake. Position 3 pillars in cake and one on board. Place separator plate on top. Position wonder mold cake on plate.

- Ice path on hill and horseshoe. Using parchment bag, sprinkle granulated light brown sugar over icing for road.
- Using tip 12, pipe tri-color camouflage effect. Smooth areas with parchment paper and heel of hand after icing has set slightly.
- With tip 73 add pull-out grass on bottom border. Print tip 3 message.
- Position trees and candles. *Serves 24.*

CAMP BIRTHDAY FUN!

- 4 Pc. Oval Pan Set, (13 x 9⁷/₈ in. pan is used), p. 180
- Tips 1, 2, 4, 6, 12, 13, 68, 233, 352, 403, p. 134-139
- Brown, Golden Yellow, Red, Kelly Green, Royal Blue, Black, Copper Icing Colors, p. 124
- Tree Former Set, p. 130

- Message Cake Picks, p. 142
- Cake Board, Fanci-Foil Wrap, p. 132
- Meringue Powder, p. 125
- Buttercream, Royal Icings, p. 93
- Pretzel Sticks
- Ice top and sides of cake smooth.
- To make deep green shade for the trees, combine Kelly Green and Royal Blue Icing Colors. Make trees of royal icing using tree formers and tip 352 for leaves/branches, tip 13 for pine cones. Let dry.
- To make campers: Combine Brown and Golden Yellow icing colors for sleeping bag color. Figure pipe 5 campers in sleeping bags, using royal icing and tips 403, 6, 12, 1 and 2 (see p. 104). Let dry. Position on cake top.
- With royal icing figure pipe dog using tips 6, 4 and 1. Let dry. Position on cake top.
- Position trees on cake top. To make bushes: Use tip 12 to build icing base, then add tip 233 pull-out grass or tip 13 pull-out stars. Pipe bushes on cake top around trees and randomly around cake base.
- Pipe tip 12 spatula-striped stones to cake top and base borders in random sizes. Add tip 6 snakes with tip 1 eyes. Print tip 1 message on pick, positon on cake top.
- Position pretzel sticks for firewood. Using spatula striping (p. 94) and tip 68, add campfire to cake top. *Serves 16.*

The Great Outdoors

Baseball Players!

Time Saver

18

SLUGGER ON DECK

- *Long Loaf Pan, p. 181*
- *Tips, 2, 5, p. 134*
- *Wilton (No Taste) Red, Lemon Yellow, Brown Icing Colors, p. 124*
- *Color Flow Mix, p. 125*
- *'93 Pattern Book (Alphabet and Star Pattern), p. 112*
- *Decorating Comb, p. 128*
- *Cake Board, Fanci-Foil Wrap, p. 132*
- *Buttercream, Color Flow Icings, p. 93, 105*
- *Baseball cards, protective plastic card covers*

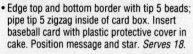

- For Message, Name and Star: With color flow icing, outline message, name and star pattern with tip 2. Flow in with thinned icing and let dry (see p. 105).
- Ice cake smooth, leaving 4 inches at one end to be open box effect. At this end, ice white on top and beige on sides. Use red for remainder of cake. With decorating comb make lines on top at "open" end.
- Edge top and bottom border with tip 5 beads; pipe tip 5 zigzag inside of card box. Insert baseball card with plastic protective cover in cake. Position message and star. *Serves 18.*

STAR PLAYER

- *Shining Star Pan, p. 187*
- *Sports Ball Pan, p. 187*
- *Tips 3, 5, 17, 233, p. 134-135*
- *Christmas Red, Kelly Green Icing Colors, p. 124*
- *Cake Board, Fanci-Foil Wrap, p. 132*
- *Buttercream Icing, p. 93*

- With spatula, ice sides of star cake smooth. Make one half of Sports Ball cake. Spread icing on flat side of ball and place on star cake.
- Cover ball with tip 17 stars, use tip 5 strings for seams, tip 3 strings for stitches and message.
- Cover top of star with tip 233 pull-out grass. Add tip 3 dots to dot sides.
- Pipe tip 17 shell border. *Serves 16.*

PLAY BALL!

- *10 in. Square Pan, p. 174, 179*
- *Tip 3, p. 134*
- *Kelly Green Icing Color, p. 124*
- *Softball Player Set, p. 142*
- *Message Pattern Press Kit, p. 128*
- *Cake Board, Fanci-Foil Wrap, p. 132*
- *Buttercream Icing, p. 93*
- *Brown Granulated Sugar*

- Ice 1-layer cake smooth. Swirl sides with spatula. Pipe tip 3 base lines and bases (smooth with finger dipped in cornstarch). Spread brown granulated sugar evenly along base lines and into center for "pitcher's mound." Lay strips of waxed paper over green icing to keep brown sugar on baselines.
- Imprint message with pattern press; print tip 3 message. Position players. *Serves 12.*

ROOKIE OF THE YEAR

- *Home Run Hitter Pan, p. 187*
- *Tips 3, 4, 12, 16, 21, p. 134-135*
- *Brown, Christmas Red, Royal Blue, Copper Icing Colors, p. 124*
- *Cake Board, Fanci-Foil Wrap, p. 132*
- *Buttercream Icing, p. 93*

- Ice cake sides and background smooth. Using tip 4, outline player and bat, pipe in eyes and mouth (smooth with finger dipped in cornstarch). Spatula stripe (see page 94) white icing with brown; pipe in bat with tip 12 and smooth. Cover player and helmet with tip 16 stars. Use Copper color for flesh tones. Add tip 4 zigzag trim on shirt.
- Edge base border with tip 21 shells, trim with alternating color tip 16 stars. Add tip 3 message encircled with beads. *Serves 12.*

HE'LL SHIVER YER TIMBERS

- Teddy Bear Stand-Up Pan, p. 188
- Tips 3, 4, 6, 17, 102, p. 134-139
- Black, Golden Yellow, Wilton Red (no taste), Copper Icing Colors, p. 124
- '93 Pattern Book (Hat Pattern), p. 112
- Cake Board, Fanci-Foil Wrap, p. 132
- Buttercream Icing, p. 93
- Trim ears off bear cake. Ice white eye area smooth. Outline coat, hands, pants, boots, eye patch, eye, nose with tip 4. Pipe-in boots, hooked hand, eye, and eye patch with tip 4, smooth with finger dipped in cornstarch.
- Fill in face, coat, pants, and hand with tip 17 stars (use copper color for flesh). Add tip 102 ruffle trim at chin and wrists. Use tip 17 pull-out stars for hair, beard, and shoulder trim. Add tip 17 swirled shell moustache. Add tip 3 dots and string trim for jacket buttons and braid; triple string trim on sleeves. Pipe tip 4 mouth; tip 6 hook. Cut hat from pattern book and position. *Serves 12.*

POLLY WANTS A PARTY

- Partysaurus Pan, p. 192
- Tips 2A, 4, 6, 16, 67, 104, p. 134-139
- Brown, Wilton Red (no taste), Royal Blue, Lemon Yellow, Orange Icing Colors, p. 124
- '93 Pattern Book (Parrot Pattern), p. 112
- Cake Board, Fanci-Foil Wrap, p. 132
- Buttercream Icing, p. 93
- Ice cake top and sides smooth. With toothpick, mark pattern on top. Outline with tip 4. Pipe in beak, tongue, and scarf top with tip 6, eye with tip 4; smooth with finger dipped in cornstarch. Pipe scarf knot using tip 6, smooth, add two pull-out scarf ends.
- Add tip 67 feathers to head and tail. Pipe tip 2A perch, add tip 6 claws. Fill in striped shirt with tip 16 stars. Add tip 104 ruffles to wings. Edge base with tip 16 rope border. *Serves 12.*

PINT-SIZED PIRATES

- Mini Gingerbread Boy Pan, p. 185
- Tips 3, 14, p. 134-135
- Copper, Wilton Red (no taste), Royal Blue, Brown, Black, Golden Yellow Icing Colors, p. 124
- Cake Boards, Fanci-Foil Wrap, p. 132
- Buttercream Icing, p. 93
- Using tip 3, outline areas on clothes; add piped-in details for belts, eye patch. Fill in with tip 14 stars (use copper color for flesh). Add tip 3 facial features, hair, bandana trim.
- For peg leg: Ice background area smooth. Pipe in leg with tip 3, smooth with finger dipped in cornstarch. *Each serves 1.*

SHIP AHOY!
- *2 pc. Oval Pan Set, p. 180*
- *Tip 21, p. 134-135*
- *Brown, Royal Blue Icing Colors, p. 124*
- *'93 Pattern Book (Flag and Sail Pattern), p. 112*
- *Decorating Comb, p. 128*
- *Cake Board, Fanci-Foil Wrap, p. 132*
- *Parchment Paper, p. 130*
- *Buttercream Icing, p. 93*
- *Pretzel Rods, Pretzel Sticks, Open-Center Hard Candies, Individual-Sized, Creme-Filled Sponge Cake.*
- Ice two-layer cake and small sponge cake smooth. Add ribbed effect to sides with decorating comb. Position sponge cake on large cake.
- Cut pretzel sticks into 1in. lengths. Insert into sponge cake for railing. Add hard candy steering wheel.
- Position pretzel rods on both cakes. Cut sail pattern from parchment paper; cut flag from pattern book. Secure flag and sails to pretzels with tape.
- Add tip 21 zigzag border and c-scrolls. Position candies for portholes.
Serves 12.

Time Saver

Party Pirates!

HE'S ABOUT TO POUNCE!

- *Six-Cup Standard Muffin Pan, p. 181*
- *Tip 32, p. 135*
- *Garfield Candy Molds, p. 114*
- *Garfield Baking Papers, p. 127*
- *White, Orange, Light Cocoa, Yellow Candy Melts™* (1 bag each), Lollipop Sticks, p. 116*
- *Decorator's Brushes Set, p. 128*
- *Rainbow Nonpareil Sprinkle Decorations, p. 127*
- *Buttercream Icing, p. 93*
- Mold a variety of Garfield lollipops (see p. 108).
- Using tip 32 and "c" motion, ice tops of cupcakes. Sprinkle with Rainbow Nonpareils. Position lollipops. *Each serves 1.*

*Brand confectionery coating
GARFIELD: ©1978 United FeaturesSyndicate, Inc.

PARTY ANIMAL

- *Mini Garfield Pan, p. 191*
- *Tips 4, 8, 14, p. 134-135*
- *Orange, Black, Golden Yellow, Pink, Teal Icing Colors, p. 124*
- *"93 Pattern Book (Bow Tie Pattern), p. 112*
- *Tree Formers, p. 130*
- *Cake Boards, Fanci-Foil Wrap, p. 132*
- *Meringue Powder, p. 125*
- *Buttercream, Royal Icings, p. 93*
- *Black Licorice*
- Tape bow tie pattern to flat surface, tightly cover board with waxed paper. With royal icing outline tie with tip 4. Fill in with tip 14 stars. Let dry. For hat, use royal icing,waxed paper-covered tree former and tip 4 to pipe swirl lines to hat top. Fill in with tip 14 stars. Add tip 4 pull-out strings for pom-pom.
- Ice cakes smooth with spatula. Outline facial features and ears with tip 4. Pipe in eyes and nose with tip 4, yellow cheek area with tip 8 (flatten with finger dipped in cornstarch). Add tip 4 dots on cheeks.
- Position black licorice whiskers, hat and bow tie. Pipe tip 4 bead border. *Each serves one.*

GARFIELD: ©1978 United FeaturesSyndicate, Inc.

BEAUTIFUL BARBIE®

- Barbie Pan, p. 191
- Tips 3, 4, 7, 10, 16, 101, 102, 103, 352, p. 134-135
- Peach, Pink, Violet Icing Colors, p. 124
- Cake Board, Fanci-Foil Wrap, p. 132
- Flower Nail No. 9, Edible Glitter, p. 130
- Meringue Powder (for royal icing), p. 125
- Buttercream, Royal Icing, p. 93
- Graham Cracker (trimmed to 3 1/2 x 1 1/2 in.) for gift
- With stiffened buttercream or royal icing, make 5 tip 101 roses with tip 4 bases for top of dress. Make 6 (3 pink, 3 violet) tip 102 roses with tip 7 bases. Make 4 peach roses with tip 103 and tip 10 bases.
- Ice graham cracker. Pipe tip 3 bow and print tip 3 message.
- Ice side of cake smooth. Position Barbie facemaker (included with pan). Outline dress with tip 3. Cover dress with tip 16 stars and sprinkle with Edible Glitter. Pipe tip 103 waistband.
- Position roses; add tip 352 leaves. Position "gift". Serves 12.

BARBIE'S ACCESSORIES

- Barbie Candy Mold, p. 114
- Decorator's Brushes Set, p. 128
- Candy Melts ™ *--Spring Mix, White, Yellow, Red (1 bag each), p. 116
- Mold a variety of candies (see p. 108). Position around Barbie cake.

*Brand confectionery coating

Your birthday girl will love the fact that her "Beautiful Barbie" cake looks just like the real Birthday Barbie doll! Our Barbie pan also includes exciting decorating suggestions which match the fashions of Dream Bride Barbie and Sparkle Eyes Barbie. You can invite all three Barbies to the party!

Famous Faces

BATMAN RETURNS

- *Batman Pan, p. 190*
- *Tips 2, 4, 16, 21, p. 134-135*
- *Royal Blue, Black, Lemon Yellow, Copper Icing Colors, p. 124*
- *Cinnamon Sprinkle Decorations, p. 127*
- *Cake Board, Fanci-Foil Wrap, p. 132*
- *Buttercream Icing, p. 93*
- Ice background areas (including face and eyes) and sides smooth.
- Outline Batman with tip 4, emblem and mouth with tip 2. Print tip 4 message.
- Pipe in bat emblem and belt with tip 4 (smooth with finger dipped in cornstarch).
- Cover Batman with tip 16 stars. Add tip 21 pull-out stars at wrist area on gloves.
- Edge base with tip 21 rosettes, position cinnamon decorations on rosettes. *Serves 12.*

TM and © 1992 DC Comics, Inc. All Rights Reserved.

Party Pals

WILD WABBIT

- *Bugs Bunny Pan, p. 191*
- *Tips 3, 4, 16, 21, p. 134-135*
- *Black, Lemon Yellow, Peach, Terra Cotta, Brown Icing Colors, p. 124*
- *Rainbow Jimmies Sprinkle Decorations, p. 127*
- *Cake Board, Fanci-Foil Wrap, p. 132*
- *Buttercream Icing, p. 93*
- Ice sides and background area on cake top smooth.
- Outline face, facial features and ears with tip 4.
- Pipe in eyes, nose, teeth, tongue, mouth, inside ears with tip 4 (smooth with finger dipped in cornstarch).
- Cover Bugs Bunny with tip 16 stars. Add tip 16 pull-out star for tuft of hair.
- Print tip 3 message. Pipe tip 4 outline eyebrows and whiskers.
- Edge base with tip 21 star border.
- Add rainbow jimmies to cake top and sides. *Serves 12.*

LOONEY TUNES, characters, names and all related indicia are trademarks of Warner Bros. Inc. © 1991

WWF SUPERSTARS®

For Hulk Hogan:

- WWF® Superstars Pan, p. 190
- Tips 3, 16, 21, p. 134-135
- Golden Yellow, Christmas Red, Copper, Brown, Royal Blue, Ivory Icing Colors, p. 124
- Cake Board, Fanci-Foil Wrap, p. 132
- 6-Pc. Nesting Star Cookie Cutter Set (second largest cutter used), p. 120
- Buttercream Icing, p. 93
- Roll-Out Cookie Dough Recipe, p. 105

- Cut star out of cookie dough, bake and cool. Place cookie on rack, pour on thinned icing, let set. Use tip 3 to pipe name and number on cookie. Set aside.
- Ice background areas and sides of cake smooth. Outline body details, facial features, wristbands, headband, waistband with tip 3.
- Cover body, face, and waistband with tip 16 stars. Use tip 3 for the following: Pipe-in headband and eyes (smooth with finger dipped in cornstarch); add dots for eye centers and teeth; pipe-in zigzag wristbands.
- Add tip 16 pull-out stars for moustache, reverse shells for eyebrows and stripes for hair. Edge base with tip 21 star border trimmed with tip 16 stars. Position star cookie on cake top. *Serves 12.*

AND IN THIS CORNER...COOKIES!

- WWF® Cookie Cutter Set, p. 119
- 6-Pc. Nesting Star Cookie Cutter Set, p. 120
- Tip 2, p. 134
- Brown Icing Color, p. 124
- Buttercream Icing, p. 93
- Roll-Out Cookie Dough Recipe, p. 105

- Cut cookies out of dough and bake. Cool completely. Outline WWF® cookies with tip 2.
- Place stars on cooling rack. Pour on thinned icing.

You can make a tag team of WWF® favorites with the WWF® Superstars Pan! Included are ideas and patterns for Hulk Hogan™, Big Boss Man™, and Macho Man Randy Savage™ cakes. Kids can celebrate with WWF® over and over again.

Rock 'n Roll

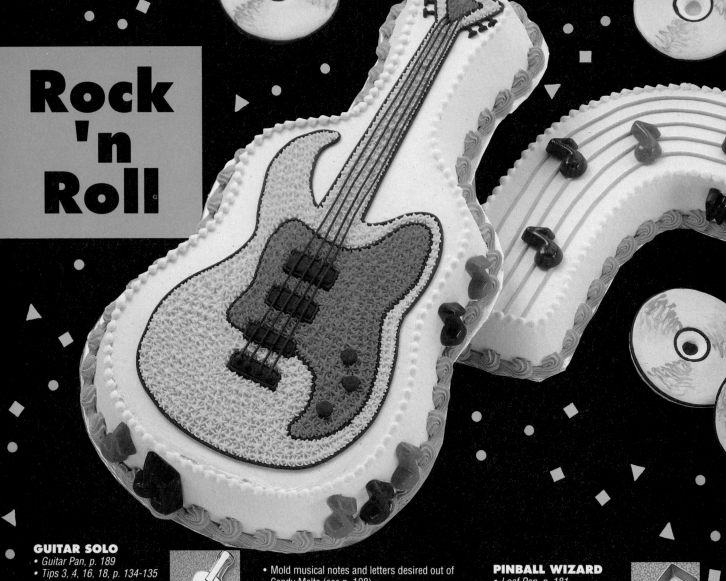

GUITAR SOLO
- Guitar Pan, p. 189
- Tips 3, 4, 16, 18, p. 134-135
- Christmas Red, Teal, Black, Lemon Yellow Icing Colors, p. 124
- Candy Melts*™ — Red, Dark Cocoa, p. 116
- '93 Pattern Book (Guitar Pattern), p. 112
- Musical Notes Candy Mold, p. 114
- Cake Board, Fanci-Foil Wrap, p. 132
- Buttercream Icing, p. 93

*brand confectionery coating

- Mold musical notes out of Candy Melts (see p. 108).
- Ice cake top and sides smooth. With toothpick, mark guitar pattern on cake top. Outline guitar and body details with tip 4.
- Fill in guitar with tip 16 stars. Pipe-in tip 3 tuning knobs, circles and bars (smooth with finger dipped in cornstarch). Add tip 3 guitar strings. Edge top of cake with tip 4 bead border. Edge base with tip 18 C-shells.
- Attach musical notes to sides with dots of icing. Serves 12.

SWEET MUSIC
- Horseshoe Pan, p. 187
- Tips 4, 18, p. 134-135
- Teal Icing Color, p. 124
- Candy Melts*™ — Red, Dark Cocoa, p. 116
- Musical Notes, Alphabet Candy Molds, p. 114
- Cake Board, Fanci-Foil Wrap, p. 132
- Buttercream Icing, p. 93

*brand confectionery coating

- Mold musical notes and letters desired out of Candy Melts (see p. 108).
- Cut cake in half. Invert one side and position end-to-end on cake board as shown.
- Ice cake top and sides smooth. Add tip 4 lines on cake top. Edge top with tip 4 bead border, base with tip 18 C-shells.
- Attach musical notes and name to cake top and sides with dots of icing. Serves 12.

CD SINGLES
- Round Cookie Cutters, p. 120
- Tip 4, p. 134
- Pink, Teal, Lemon Yellow, Black Icing Colors, p. 124
- Color Flow Mix, p. 125
- Parchment Triangles, p. 129
- Roll-Out Cookie Dough Recipe, p. 105
- Color Flow Icing, p. 105

- Cut desired number of CD's out of cookie dough using largest round cookie cutter. Cut center holes using large open end of any decorating tip. Bake and cool.
- Using color flow icing, outline cookies with tip 4.
- Have parchment bags filled with light grey, teal, pink, lemon yellow and white color flow icings ready to use. Flow-in light grey icing on cookie, (see pg. 105). Immediately make 3 zigzag lines of pink, teal and lemon yellow; feather colors together with a pin. Flow-in white icing at center to cover. Dry on rack so excess icing drips through hole, leaving an opening. Decorate one cookie at a time. Each serves 1.

PINBALL WIZARD
- Loaf Pan, p. 181
- Tips 4, 7, 16, 47, p. 134-139
- Lemon Yellow, Black, Teal Icing Colors, p. 124
- '93 Pattern Book (Pinball Backboard and Table Top Patterns), p. 112
- 5 in. Spiked Grecian Pillars (2 sets needed), p. 171
- Party! Party! Cake Top Set, p. 144
- Cake Board, Fanci Foil Wrap, p. 132
- Buttercream Icing, p. 93
- Multi-color Gum Squares, Candy Discs, Colored Candy Nonpareils

- For pinball machine backboard, cut cake board according to pattern. Cover with foil. Ice top half smooth, add cake top set piece. Trim edge with tip 4 strings. Let dry.
- Ice cake smooth. Trace table top pattern with toothpick. Trim pattern with tip 4 strings; edge top with tip 47 stripes.
- Pipe tip 7 balls of icing for "bumper" bases and top with candy discs.
- Fill in front corners of playing board with tip 16 stars; add tip 4 strings.
- For coin slot and knob backplate, pipe in tip 4 fill-in and pat with cornstarch. Use tip 4 to add coin slot and knob.
- Pipe tip 4 flippers. Position gum square barriers. Add colored candy sprinkles.
- Trim bottom border with tip 7 beads.
- Cover pillars with Fanci-Foil Wrap.
- Position remaining cake top set pieces on sides and attach backboard to cake. Serves 12.

THE ENTERTAINER
- *Handsome Guy Pan, p. 189*
- *Tips 1D, 3, 7, 16, 21, p. 134-139*
- *Copper, Black, Golden Yellow, Sky Blue Icing Colors, p. 124*
- *Cake Board, Fanci-Foil Wrap, p. 132*
- *Buttercream Icing, p. 93*
- Ice background area on top and sides smooth. Outline dancer with tip 3. Pipe in eyes and buttons on cuffs with tip 3 (smooth with finger dipped in cornstarch).
- Add tip 1D striped cummerbund. Cover dancer with tip 16 stars. Pipe-in tip 7 tie (smooth with finger dipped in cornstarch).
- Cover hair with tip 16 side-by-side stripes.
- Add tip 3 dots, confetti and streamers on cake. Edge base with tip 21 shells. Add tip 3 dots between shells. *Serves 12.*

A SWEET SWING
- *Handsome Guy Pan, p. 189*
- *Tips 3, 7, 16, 47, 233, p. 134-139*
- *Sky Blue, Copper, Leaf Green, Kelly Green, Black Icing Colors, p. 124*
- *Cake Boards, Fanci Foil Wrap, p. 132*
- *Uncooked, thick Spaghetti, Black Licorice, Golf Ball*
- For golf club handles: Break spaghetti into 5 in. pieces (above hand), and 3 in. pieces (below hand) Insert 5 in. pieces into black licorice. Coat pieces of spaghetti using buttercream icing and tip 7 (see p. 103).
- Ice background areas on cake top and sides smooth.
- With tip 3, outline facial features and golfer. Use smooth side of tip 47 to pipe belt on pants.
- Cover golfer (except for hand holding golf clubs) with tip 16 stars.
- Pipe in tip 3 eyebrows; outline tip 7 sunglasses; fill in with tip 7 (smooth with finger dipped in cornstarch).
- Position golf clubs (longer handles above hand, shorter below) and overpipe tip 3 outline on fingers, fill in with tip 16 stars.
- Add tip 47 ribbed stripes for golf club heads.
- Add tip 16 pull-out stars for hair.
- Add tip 233 pull-out grass at base. Position golf ball. *Serves 12.*

CENTER OF ATTENTION
- *Handsome Guy Pan, p. 189*
- *Tips 3, 4, 6, 16, 21, p. 134-139*
- *Brown, Kelly Green, Lemon Yellow, Terra Cotta Icing Colors, p. 124*
- *'93 Pattern Book (Basketball, Number, and Hands Patterns), p. 112*
- *Cake Board, Fanci-Foil Wrap, p. 132-133*
- *Buttercream Icing, p. 93*
- Ice cake background and sides smooth. Using toothpick, mark patterns for basketball, number, and hands on cake top. With tip 4, outline body, suit details and basketball. Using tip 3, outline and fill in facial features. Pipe-in tip 4 suit trim and number; tip 6 basketball; smooth with finger dipped in cornstarch.
- Cover body and suit with tip 16 stars; pipe tip 16 reverse shell ears and zigzag wristband. Pipe tip 4 C-motion curly hair.
- Edge base border with tip 21 stars. Trim with tip 3 dots. *Serves 12.*

WALLY CAUGHT THE BIG ONE

'65

WHOPPER OF A DAY

- *Handsome Guy Pan, p. 189*
- *Tips 1, 3, 4, 13, 16, 21, 125, p. 134-139*
- *Brown, Sky Blue, Kelly Green, Black, Terra Cotta Icing Colors, p. 124*
- *Message Cake Picks (1 needed), p. 142*
- *'93 Pattern Book (Fisherman and Fish Pattern), p. 112*
- *Cake Board, Fanci-Foil Wrap, p. 132*
- *Buttercream Icing, p. 93*
- Ice background area on top and sides smooth. Lightly ice area where fisherman will go. Mark fisherman and fish pattern with toothpick.
- Outline fisherman and fish with tip 4, facial features with tip 3. Cover body with tip 16 stars.
- Pipe in tip 4 face, hands, hat and fish (flatten with finger dipped in cornstarch). Pipe tip 125 brim on hat.
- Pipe tip 13 pull-out stripes for hair, eyebrows and moustache. Pipe in eyes, buttons, hat vent holes with tip 3 dots. Outline glasses with tip 3.
- Edge base with tip 21 spatula-striped (p. 94), reverse shells.
- Print tip 4 message on pick and number on fish. Position Pick. *Serves 12.*

ANCHORS AWEIGH!

- *Handsome Guy Pan, p. 189*
- *Tips 1D, 3, 8, 16, 21, 103, 127, p. 134-139*
- *Royal Blue, Christmas Red, Brown, Copper, Black Icing Colors, p. 124*
- *'93 Pattern Book (Sailor Pattern), p. 112*
- *Cake Board, Fanci-Foil Wrap, p. 132*
- *Buttercream Icing, p. 93*
- Ice background areas on top and sides smooth. With toothpick, mark Sailor Pattern (for easier marking, lightly ice area first).
- Outline details with tip 3. Pipe in eyes and eyebrows with tip 3 (flatten with finger dipped in cornstarch).
- Cover face, uniform, hands with tip 16 stars. Use tip 127 to pipe collar, add tip 103 ties; pipe tip 8 center knot (flatten with finger dipped in cornstarch).
- For hat: pipe back brim using tip 1D; pipe center of hat with tip 8 in one line just below back brim; pipe front brim with tip 1D. Add tip 3 lines and dot on center of hat.
- Add tip 3 dots for hair. Add tip 3 striped trim to cuffs, collar and arm "patch". Edge base with tip 21 shell border. *Serves 12.*

Introducing our Handsome Guy — the original Renaissance Pan! This guy does it all — serving his country, leading his team to victory, or simply relaxing with his favorite hobby. Choose him for your next party.

Meet our new Pretty Lady — a pan which brings a lot of decorating options to the party! This Lady can play just about any role from corporate executive to athletic champion.

ALOHA!

- *Pretty Lady Pan, p. 189*
- *Tips 2, 4, 16, 129, p. 134-135, 137*
- *Copper*, Brown*, Golden Yellow, Pink, Black Icing Colors, p. 124*
- *Meringue Powder, p. 125*
- *Cake Board, Fanci-Foil Wrap, p. 132*
- *Buttercream, Royal Icings, p. 93*

*These colors mixed produce the shade shown.

- With royal icing, make approximately 85 tip 129 drop flowers with tip 2 centers. Let dry.
- Ice cake background and sides smooth. With tip 4, outline body and suit details; pipe tip 2 facial features, mouth and eyes (flatten with finger dipped in cornstarch).
- Cover bathing suit and body with tip 16 stars. Add tip 16 side-by-side stripe hair.
- Position drop flowers with dots of icing around base border, and on cake top. *Serves 12.*

CORPORATE WOMAN

- *Pretty Lady Pan, p. 189*
- *Tips 3, 4, 16, 18, p. 134-135*
- *Black, Royal Blue, Golden Yellow, Sky Blue, Copper Icing Colors, p. 124*
- *'93 Pattern Book (Corporate Woman Pattern), p. 112*
- *Cake Board, Fanci-Foil Wrap, p. 132*
- *Buttercream Icing, p. 93*

- Ice background area on top and sides smooth. With toothpick, mark Corporate Woman pattern (for easier marking, lightly ice area first). Outline suit, blouse and facial features with tip 4. Overpipe blouse collar to give added dimension.
- Pipe tip 3 eyeliner and eyebrows, eyes and teeth (smooth with finger dipped in cornstarch).
- Cover face, suit, handbag and hands with tip 16 stars.
- Pipe tip 3 dot earrings, necklace and buttons. For hair, pipe tip 16 side-by-side stripes, using spatula striping (p. 94)
- Edge cake with tip 18 star bottom border. *Serves 12.*

Pretty Ladies

GOAL-ORIENTED GIRL

- *Pretty Lady Pan, p. 189*
- *Tips 3, 16, 21, p. 134-135*
- *Lemon, Copper, Black, Sky Blue, Terra Cotta, Orange Icing Colors, p. 124*
- *'93 Pattern Book (Soccer Player and Ball), p. 112*
- *Cake Board, Fanci-Foil Wrap, p. 132*
- *Buttercream Icing, p. 93*

- Ice background areas on top and sides smooth. With toothpick, mark Soccer Ball Pattern.
- Outline body, ball and facial features with tip 3. Pipe in eyes and ball with tip 3 (flatten with finger dipped in cornstarch).
- Cover player with tip 16 stars. Add tip 16 side-by-side stripes for hair and zigzags for collar and cuffs. Edge base with tip 21 shell border. *Serves 12.*

STAYING IN SHAPE

- *Pretty Lady Pan, p. 189*
- *Tips 3, 16, 21, p. 134-135*
- *Purple, Pink, Teal, Copper, Black, Terra Cotta, Royal Blue Icing Colors, p. 124*
- *Cake Board, Fanci-Foil Wrap, p. 132*
- *Buttercream Icing, p. 93*

- Ice background areas and sides of cake smooth. With tip 3, outline body, facial features, headband, leotard details and wristbands; pipe-in eyes and mouth (flatten with finger dipped in cornstarch).
- Cover body, face, leotard, and wristbands with tip 16 stars.
- Add tip 16 side-by-side stripe hair and tip 3 eyebrows. Edge cake base with tip 21 star border. *Serves 12.*

PARTY PRESCRIPTION

- *Pretty Lady Pan, p. 189*
- *Tips 2, 3, 4, 16, 18, 47, p. 134-135, 139*
- *Sky Blue, Black, Copper, Red-Red Icing Colors, p. 124*
- *'93 Pattern Book (Nurse Pattern), p. 112*
- *Cake Board, Fanci-Foil Wrap, p. 132*
- *Show 'N Serve Board (4 in. x 6 in. piece needed for clipboard), p. 133*
- *Parchment Triangles (4 needed), p. 129*
- *Buttercream Icing, p. 93*

- **For clipboard:** Cut 4 in. x 6 in. from Show 'N Serve Cake Board, place laminated side down. Using pattern, cut clip from Show 'N Serve Board and cover with foil. Cut 3 1/2 in. x 5 1/2 in. piece from parchment paper to "clip" to board. Write message with marker.
- **For cap:** Cut pattern from double thickness of parchment paper.
- Ice top and sides of cake smooth. With toothpick, mark nurse pattern.
- Outline nurse and cap with tip 4 strings. Pipe in tip 3 eyes and mouth (smooth with finger dipped in cornstarch). Cover nurse with tip 16 stars. Add tip 16 swirls for hair. Position cap. Add tip 3 cross and trim on cap.
- Pipe tip 47 name plate, cuffs and pocket on uniform. Pipe in tip 2 pen and thermometer. (Print name of birthday girl on name plate if desired.)
- Edge cake base with tip 18 reverse shell border.
- Position clipboard. *Serves 12.*

HAPPY Rx from all of the Gang!

A BUTTERFLY DROPS BY

- *12 in. Round Pan, p. 179*
- *Tips 1, 2, 3, 15, 18, 32, 101, 101s, 352, p. 134-139*
- *Burgundy, Violet, Royal Blue, Kelly Green, Golden Yellow Icing Colors, p. 124*
- *Flower Nail No. 9, p. 130*
- *4 mm White Pearl Beading* (1 pkg. needed), p. 167*
- *Bomboniere!™ Gathering Ribbon, 2" with Lurex and Picot Edge (20 in. needed), p. 150*
- *Pearl Stamen (1 pkg. needed), Florist Wire, Flower Formers, p. 130*
- *Meringue Powder, p. 125*
- *Buttercream, Royal Icings, p. 93*

- Using royal icing, make 15 apple blossoms using tip 101 with tip 1 centers, 30 forget-me-nots using tip 101s with tip 2 center dots, and approximately 150 lilacs using tip 101s. Note: Make extras of all flowers to allow for breakage. Let dry.
- Make ribbon butterfly. For wings: Divide gathering ribbon into two 10 inch lengths. Gather, tie together at center of each with florist wire. For body: Twist wire around 8 inch strand of pearls, shape to form body. Tie or glue pearl stamen onto wire for antenna. Attach body to wings by twisting wires together.
- Ice 2-layer cake smooth. Write tip 3 message. Edge top border with tip 18 swirled shells. Pipe

tip 32 upright shells around base. Trim with tip 15 zigzag garland around bottom and tip 15 rosettes at top of shells. Position pearls on top and base borders.
- Attach flowers to cake top. To attach lilacs, pipe an elongated shell with tip 32, position flowers over shell. Trim with tip 352 leaves. Position butterfly. *Serves 30.*
  *Caution—Remove pearls before cutting cake.

WE'LL ALL HAVE TEA

- *Sport Ball Pan, Mini Ball Pan, p. 187*
- *Tips 2, 5, 10, 16, p. 134-135*
- *Royal Blue, Burgundy, Brown, Kelly Green Icing Colors, p. 124*
- *'93 Pattern Book (Teapot and Cup Handle Patterns), p. 112*
- *6-pc. Nesting Round Cookie Cutter Set, p. 120*
- *Angled Coupler, p. 129*
- *Plastic Dowel Rod, p. 172*
- *Cake Boards, Fanci-Foil Wrap, p. 132*
- *Roll-Out Cookie Dough Recipe, p. 105*
- *Buttercream Icing, p. 93*

- Using Handle Patterns, cut four small handles and one large handle out of cookie dough; with 4" round cutter, cut four saucers. Bake and cool.
- For cups: Ice saucers and place mini balls on top. Ice top of each mini ball in brown. Outline cup tops with tip 10. Push handle into cake. Cover with tip 16 stars. Add tip 2 beads to bottom edge of cups and saucers. Add tip 2

vines. Make flowers with tip 2 using a series of five-dot petals and one dot center.
- For teapot: Cut dowel rod to 4" with craft knife. Attach angled coupler to dowel rod, then position for spout in cake. Use a dab of icing to attach mini ball to top of sports ball. Push large handle into side. Cover pot with tip 16 stars. Add tip 10 bead border on teapot lid and tip 10 ball on lid top. Edge spout opening with tip 5 beads. Add tip 2 vines. Make tip 2 vines and flowers as on cups. Write tip 2 message. *Cake serves 12. Each "cup" serves 1.*

FRESHLY PICKED FLOWERS

- *Mini Balloon Pan, p. 192*
- *Tips 7, 127, 190, p. 134-139*
- *Burgundy, Royal Blue, Kelly Green Icing Colors, p. 124*
- *Cake Boards, Fanci-Foil Wrap, p. 132*
- *Buttercream Icing, p. 93*

- Place cakes on individual plates or serving platter.
- Cover cakes with tip 190 drop flowers (do right on cake). Add tip 7 pull-out stems and tip 127 leaves. *Each serves 1.*

Garden Party

Happy Birthday Martha

HAPPY BIRTHDAY BOB

Paul

For Gents

Time Saver

STAR BILLING

- Star Pan, p. 187
- Tip 4, p. 134
- Brown Icing Color, p. 124
- Alphabet Cookie Cutter Set, p. 119
- Cake Board, Fanci-Foil Wrap, p. 132
- Chocolate Jimmies Sprinkle Decorations, p. 127
- Buttercream Icing, p. 93
- Ice top and sides of cake smooth. Press jimmies on sides of cake.
- Place cookie cutters in position; spoon jimmies through cutter openings. Lift away cutters and press jimmies lightly to secure.
- Print tip 4 message. Add tip 4 top zigzag and bottom ball border. *Serves 12.*

PICKED FOR PRAISE

- 4-pc. Oval Pan Set (10 ³/₄ x 7 ⁷/₈ in. pan used), p. 180
- Tips 3, 17, 103, 104, 199, 352, p. 134-139
- Moss Green, Golden Yellow, Brown, Orange, Icing Colors, p. 124
- 15 Pc. Decorator Pattern Press Set, p. 128
- Yellow Stamens (1 pkg. needed), p. 130
- Lily Nail Set, Flower Former Set, Flower Nail No. 7, p. 130
- Cake Boards, Fanci-Foil Wrap, p. 132
- Meringue Powder, p. 125
- Buttercream, Royal Icings, p. 93
- Granulated sugar
- Using royal icing: Make 4 California Poppies (p.102) using tip 104 and 1 ⁵/₈ in. lily nail. Pipe tip 3 center and add stamens. Using Daisy instructions (p. 102), make 4 tip 104 and 10 tip 103 Brown-Eyed Susans using flower nail no. 7. Pipe tip 3 dot center and pat with granulated sugar that has been tinted brown. Dry on flower formers. **Note:** Make extras of all flowers to allow for breakage.
- Ice 2-layer cake smooth. With toothpick, mark 3 in. up from base, at 2 ¹/₂ in. intervals around cake. Pipe tip 199 upright columns at marks. Connect columns with tip 3 double drop strings. Add tip 17 stars with tip 3 dot centers to top of each column. Pipe tip 17 stars at base between columns.
- Imprint scrolls from Pattern Press Set on cake top as shown. Cover with tip 17 piping. Write tip 3 message. Edge top of cake with tip 17 shell border; add tip 103 flutes between shells. Position flowers on cake top, trim with tip 352 leaves. *Serves 22.*

HANDYMAN

- Ballerina Bear Pan, p. 188
- Tips 3, 4, 8, 16, 20, 127, 127D, p. 134-139
- Brown, Orange, Golden Yellow, Royal Blue Icing Colors, p. 124
- '93 Pattern Book (Handyman Pattern and Tool Patterns), p. 112
- Cake Board, Fanci-Foil Wrap, p. 132
- Buttercream Icing, p. 93
- Uncooked spaghetti, cardboard (for tools)
- Cut tool patterns from cardboard and cover with Fanci Foil Wrap. For nails, pipe over spaghetti using tip 4 (see p. 103). Set aside "tools".
- Ice sides of cake smooth. With toothpick, mark Handyman Pattern on cake top. (For easier markings, lightly ice top of cake before tracing pattern.) Outline handyman and facial features with tip 3.

- Cover face, hands, shirt, pants and shoes with tip 16 stars. Fill in eyes, ears, nose and mouth with tip 3 pipe-in. (Smooth with finger dipped in cornstarch.)
- For hat: Smooth top with spatula. Edge brim using tip 127. Add tip 3 strings on top.
- Add tip 3 shoelaces. Pipe in tip 3 socks. Smooth with finger dipped in cornstarch.
- For tool belt: Pipe across waist with tip 127D, then overpipe vertical bars for pockets. Position "tools". Overpipe hammer with tip 8. (Smooth with finger dipped in cornstarch.)
- Pipe tip 4 nail heads. Overpipe saw handle with tip 20. Mark measurement lines on carpenter's square with tip 3.
- Add tip 16 zigzag moustache and eyebrows. Edge cake with tip 20 star border. *Serves 12.*

SCANDAL SHEET

- *11 x 15 in. Sheet Pan, p. 174,179*
- *Tips 1, 2, 4, 7, 10, p. 134*
- *Royal Blue, Red-Red, Black, Burgundy, Golden Yellow, Leaf Green Icing Colors, p. 124*
- *Cake Board, Fanci-Foil Wrap, p. 132*
- *'93 Pattern Book (Newspaper Columns 1, 2, and 3 Patterns), p. 112*
- *Decorating Comb, p. 128*
- *Candy Melts™*— Pink, Light Cocoa, White, Red (1 bag each needed), p. 116*
- *Alphabet Set, Create-A-Face Set Candy Molds, p.114*
- *Buttercream Icing , p. 93*

*Brand confectionery coating.

- Ice cake top and sides smooth. Comb sides of cake, using decorating comb. Let icing set up.
- Cut out waxed paper stencil of column patterns. Place stencil on cake; ice green, burgundy, blue area smooth. Remove stencil carefully and let icing dry.
- Measure 3 ½ in. down from top of cake and ice area yellow.
- Mold (see p. 108) face, hair, features and "National Insider" out of melted Candy Melts. Unmold when set. Position candy on cake top.

- Using tip 10, (see figure piping on p. 104) pipe body in zigzag motion, smooth with spatula. Use tip 10 and pipe arms and legs; tip 7 to pipe shoes, tip 2 for fingers. Add tip 2 dots and zigzags on dress.
- Print "the" and 75¢ using tip 2. Print tip 4 head-lines; use tip 1 to print message in color panels. Outline all panels and top border with tip 7 . *Serves 20.*

TIME SLIPS AWAY

- *10 ½ in. Ring Mold Pan, p. 182*
- *Tips 1A, 2, 10, 225, 233, p. 134,137*
- *Copper, Kelly Green, Brown, Black, Christmas Red, Violet, Pink, Royal Blue, Golden Yellow Icing Colors, p. 124*
- *Cake Board, Fanci-Foil Wrap, p. 132*
- *"Over the Hill" 40 candle, p. 146*
- *Make Any Message Letter Press Kit, p. 128*
- *Buttercream Icing, p. 93*
- Using stiffened buttercream, make 50 tip 225 drop flowers (assorted pink, yellow, violet, blue) with white tip 2 centers. Let dry.

- With spatula, ice outside of cake smooth; inside fluffy.
- Using figure piping instructions (p. 104), pipe tip 1A head and body, tip 10 arms and legs, tip 2 fingers, hair and facial features. Add tip 233 pull-out hair.
- Press message on cake side with message press, print with tip 2.
- Add tip 233 pull-out grass to top and on bottom border. Position drop flowers.
- Position candle. *Serves 14.*

24-KARAT CELEBRATION

- *Mini-Loaf Pan, p. 181*
- *Tip 2, p. 134*
- *Candy Melts *—Yellow (3 pkgs. needed); Candy Colors Kit, p. 116*
- *Numeral Picks Set, p. 141*

*brand confectionery coating

- Melt candy, add orange and yellow candy color for gold shown.
- Place cakes on wire rack over drip pan. Pour melted candy over cakes. When dry, use tip 2 and pipe "24 kt" on front and back ends of each cake. Let dry completely, stack, position picks. *Serves 5.*

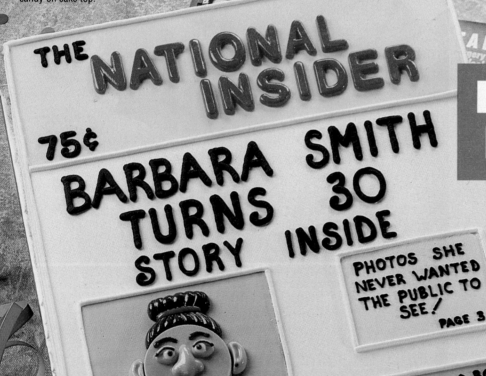

Big News Birthday

Here Lies My Youth
40

HAPPY BIRTHDAY
JACKIE

50

24 KT 24 KT

24 KT 24 KT 24 KT

Happy Golden 50th Birthday Annie

GUEST LIST

- 10 in. Round Cake Pans, p. 175
- Tips 1, 1s, 1D, 2A, 3, 4, 7, 12, 44, 101s, 127, 349, p. 134-139
- Christmas Red, Kelly Green, Golden Yellow, Black Icing Colors, p. 124
- Tiny Toddlers Cake Toppers (2 needed), p. 141
- Meringue Powder, p. 125
- Christmas Trees Icing Decorations (10 needed), p. 126
- Royal, Buttercream Icings, p. 93

- Transform the Tiny Toddlers into Santa and Mrs. Claus using royal icing. **For Mrs. Claus:** Paint on dress and shoes using thinned red royal icing. Using regular consistency royal icing: Pipe hat in circular motion using tip 3, smooth with finger dipped in cornstarch; add tip 127 dress ruffle; add tip 101s hat ruffle, cover bottle using tip 349 to make tree; add tip 1 hair, eyebrows, dots on dress, shoe cuffs and dress trim. **For Santa:** Paint with thinned royal icing—all of body red, boots black, and gloves kelly green. Using regular consistency royal icing: Pipe tip 2A hat, tip 1D list with tip 1s names, add tip 44 belt; add tip 1 belt buckle, hair, beard, eyebrows, coat trim, pants and hat. Set Santa and Mrs. Claus aside to dry completely.
- Ice 2-layer cake smooth. Add tip 1D band ribbed side up on top and bottom edges; trim with tip 7 dots. Print tip 4 message. Edge top and base with tip 12 bead border.
- Attach tree icing decorations to sides of cake with dots of icing. Position Santa and Mrs. Claus on top of cake. *Serves 24.*

SANTA'S GIFT

- Santa Bear Pan, p. 185
- Tips 3, 16, 18, 68, p. 134-139
- Christmas Red, Kelly Green, Golden Yellow Icing Colors, p. 124
- '93 Pattern Book (Package Pattern), p. 112
- Cake Board, Fanci-Foil Wrap, p. 132
- Buttercream Icing, p. 93
- 2 Candy-coated Chocolate Pieces

- Ice cake sides and package area smooth. With toothpick, mark Package Pattern. Outline face, mouth, nose, hat, arms, gloves, and package with tip 3 strings. Fill-in mouth and nose; smooth with finger dipped in cornstarch.
- For fleshtone on face and hands, add small amount of Christmas Red to white icing. Fill-in coat, hat, face, hands, and package ribbon with tip 16 stars. Pipe a bow with tip 16. Add tip 16 eyebrows; pull-out fur on hat and cuffs, rosette swirl for pompon. Pipe tip 18 pull-out hair, beard and stripe moustache. Position candy for eyes.
- Add tip 68 shell motion base border trimmed with tip 3 dots. *Serves 12.*

Special Santas

THE BOSS

- Gingerbread Boy Pan, p. 185
- Tips 1A, 1D, 4, 7, 17, p. 134-39
- Christmas Red, Kelly Green, Golden Yellow, Copper, Black Icing Colors, p. 124
- '93 Pattern Book (Santa Face Pattern), p. 112
- Cake Board, Fanci-Foil Wrap, p. 132
- Buttercream Icing, p. 93
- Ice face smooth and mark Santa Face Pattern with toothpick.
- With smooth side of tip 1D trim boot tops. With ribbed side of tip 1D add belt. Outline 2 in. x 1 1/2 in. buckle with tip 4 strings, pipe-in buckle with tip 7 (flatten with finger dipped in cornstarch).
- Cover face, body, boots, hat and gloves with tip 17 stars.
- Outline tip 4 crease in Santa's hat. Add tip 17 zigzag trim on hat, cuffs and eyebrows. Pipe-in tip 7 eyes and mouth. Add tip 1A nose. Pipe tip 17 swirled stripes for beard and moustache.
- Add tip 17 swirl pompon on hat. *Serves 12.*

ELF HELP

- Mini Gingerbread Boy Pan, p. 185
- Tips 2, 2A, 3, 6, 16, 104, p. 134-139
- Christmas Red, Kelly Green, Black, Copper Icing Colors, p. 124
- '93 Pattern Book (Elf Pattern), p. 112
- Cake Boards, Fanci-Foil Wrap, p. 132
- Buttercream Icing, p. 93
- Silver Dragees
- Lightly ice cakes and mark Elf Pattern with toothpick.
- Outline tip 3 strings on ankles, sleeves, and mouths.
- Cover face, body, arms and shoes with tip 16 stars. For shoetips, pipe tip 16 pull-out stars.
- For ears, use wide side of tip 104. Squeeze and move up simultaneously to form ears. Add tip 2 pull-out hair, sideburns and beard; mix dark copper with a little Christmas Red for color.
- Add tip 6 eyes, mouth and nose, pat with cornstarch. For hat make a flattened circle with tip 2A, then pull out for tail. Add silver dragees for buttons. *Each serves 1.*

SPEEDY GREETINGS

- Six-cup Standard Muffin Pan, p. 181
- Santa Claus Standard Baking Cups, Christmas Trees Standard Baking Cups, p. 127
- Santa Icing Decorations, Christmas Trees Icing Decorations, p. 126
- Green and Red Crystal Sprinkle Decorations, p. 127
- Buttercream Icing, p. 93
- Ice tops. Add crystal sprinkle decorations.
- Position icing decorations. *Each serves 1.*

SENSATIONAL SANTA

- Jolly Santa Pan, p. 185
- Tips 3, 16, 105, 234, p. 134-39
- Candy Melts™*, White (1 bag needed), Candy Colors Kit, p. 116
- Christmas Red, Black, Royal Blue Icing Colors, p. 124
- Buttercream Icing, p. 93
  *brand confectionery coating
- Mix a small amount of red candy color into melted white Candy Melts. Pour into pan to make candy face plaque (see pg. 108). Refrigerate or freeze to set. Unmold; place on cake top.
- Ice sides of cake smooth. Outline eyes and fill-in using tip 3. Smooth with finger dipped in cornstarch.
- Fill-in hat with tip 16 stars. Add tip 105 rosette swirl hat tassel trim, tip 234 pull-out beard and zigzag eyebrows and moustache.
- Edge base border with tip 105 rosettes. Add tip 3 dots to rosette centers and cake sides. *Serves 12.*

Christmas Critters

OPEN HOUSE

- Treeliteful Pan, p. 185
- Tips 2, 3, 5, 6, 13, 17, 57, 74, 233, p. 134-139
- Brown, Kelly Green, Leaf Green, Golden Yellow, Black, Royal Blue and Christmas Red Icing Colors, p. 124
- '93 Pattern Book (Window, Shutter, Door and Animal patterns), p. 112
- Meringue Powder, p. 125
- Cake Boards, Fanci-Foil Wrap, p. 132
- Buttercream, Royal Icings, p. 93
- **For Shutters:** Using royal icing, trace waxed paper-covered pattern with tip 3 outline. Fill in with tip 13 stars. Let dry.
- **For Raccoons:** Using royal icing, figure pipe raccoon with tips 2, 3, 6 and 13. See p. 104 for figure piping. Let dry.
- **For Squirrels:** Using royal icing, figure pipe squirrel with tips 2, 3, 5, 6, 13 and 233. See p. 104 for figure piping. Let dry.
- **For Lights:** Using royal icing and tip 5, pipe bead for light sockets. Use tip 6 and royal icing to pipe light bulbs. Let dry. (These could also be made directly on the cake later in buttercream icing.)
- Ice window and door areas of cake smooth. With toothpick, mark window and door patterns. Outline windows and door with tip 57.
- Using tip 17, cover trunk with elongated zigzags.
- Cover tree with tip 74 pull-out leaves. Cover door wreath with tip 13 pull-out stars.
- Place animals in windows; attach shutters with dots of icing.
- Add tip 5 string garlands, position lights with dots of icing. Add five lights on top to form star. Pipe tip 3 wreath bow; tip 3 bead for doorknob. *Serves 12.*

PENGUIN PAL

- Snowman Pan, p. 185
- Tips 4, 8, 14, 16, p. 134-135
- Black, Kelly Green, Wilton No-Taste Red, and Golden Yellow Icing Colors, p. 124
- '93 Pattern Book (Penguin Face Pattern), p. 112
- Cake Board, Fanci-Foil Wrap, p. 132
- Buttercream Icing, p. 93
- Ice cake smooth. With toothpick, mark Penguin Face pattern. Outline details using tip 4. Build-up beak using tip 8, fill-in eyes using tip 4, smooth with finger dipped in cornstarch.
- Star fill-in hat, face, scarf, torso/wings using tip 16; holly using tip 14. Add tip 4 holly berry dots. Print tip 4 message. *Serves 12.*

JOYFUL TIMES

- Holiday House Pan, p. 185
- Tips 2, 349, 352, p. 134-139
- Kelly Green, Christmas Red, Ivory, Brown Icing Colors, p. 124
- '93 Pattern Book (Eaves, Bird and Shutters, Leaves, Acorns, Pinecones, Mouse and Clock Face Patterns), p. 112
- 4mm. Pearl Beading (1 pkg.), two 3" lengths needed, p. 167
- Cake Boards, Fanci-Foil Wrap, p. 132
- Color Flow Mix, p. 125
- Buttercream and Color Flow Icing, p. 93, 105
- Using color flow icing, outline eaves, bird and shutters, leaves, acorns, pinecones, mouse and clock face patterns with tip 2. When dry, flow in designs with thinned icing (see Color Flow, p. 105). Let dry.
- For Pull Chain: Paint two 3" pearl beading lengths with thinned icing. Let dry.
- For Pendulum Bar: Cover 1" x 4 1/2" cardboard with foil; paint with thinned icing or with buttercream. Let dry. You may also use a wide craft stick for pendulum, without foil.
- Ice cake smooth with buttercream. With toothpick run lines through clock to resemble wood grain.
- Position pendulum, pull chain and color flow* designs.
- Add tip 349 leaf edging on eaves and clock face.
- Edge cake with tip 352 shell border. *Serves 12.*

* Note: Since buttercream icing will break down color flow, position on a piece of plastic wrap cut to fit; set atop sugar cubes or mini marshmallows.

IT'S RUDOLPH!

- Rudy Reindeer Pan, p. 185
- Tip 21, p. 135
- Brown Icing Color, p. 124
- Cake Board, Fanci-Foil Wrap, p. 132
- Buttercream Icing, p. 93
- Candy trims: red string licorice, candy-covered chocolate dot candies, cherry ball candy, cinnamon dots
- Ice cake top and sides smooth. Build-up knot on bow with icing.
- Star fill-in head, eye and inside ear using tip 21. Add tip 21 pull-out star antlers and eyebrow.
- Outline bow and mouth with red string licorice, add cinnamon dots to bow, position cherry ball for nose, place candy-covered chocolate dot in eye, and trim base border with alternate color chocolate dots. *Serves 12.*

Time Saver

41

CELESTIAL SYMPHONY

- 9 in., 12 in. Hexagon Pans, p. 180
- Tip 6, p. 134
- Cake Boards, Fanci-Foil Wrap, p. 132
- 1 pkg. Scrolls (12 needed), p. 169
- 7 in. Disposable Pillar (1 needed), Dowel Rods, p. 172
- 3 pkgs. White Pearl Stamens, p. 130
- 3 pkgs. 1 7/8" White Artificial Leaves, p. 165
- 4 Heavenly Harpists, p. 168
- 4 mm, 6mm White Pearl Beading* (2 pkgs. of each needed), p. 167
- Meringue Powder, p. 125
- Buttercream, Royal Icings, p. 93
- 9" white candle

- **To make poinsettias:** (Make 18) With royal icing and tip 3, pipe mound of icing on waxed paper. Insert 6 leaves. Pipe another mound of icing and insert 6 more leaves. To achieve finished look, pipe tip 6 dot of icing in center and position 20 stamens trimmed to 1/4 in.). Let dry.
- **For both tiers:** Ice two layer cakes smooth. To prepare cakes for stacked construction, see pg. 106. Position one row of 6 mm pearls on top and bottom of cakes. Place two rows of 4 mm pearls on bottom of cakes. Add a row of 4 mm pearls, 1/2 in. from tops of both cakes. DIvide each side of 9 in. cake in halves; 12 in. cake in thirds. Drape 4 mm pearls 1 inch from horizontal line of 4 mm pearls. Position scrolls on edges; harpists, pillar, candle on top. Attach poinsettias to cake with dots of buttercream icing. *Serves 44.*

*Remove pearls before serving.

SNOW-TRIMMED TREES

- Mini Christmas Tree Pan, p. 185
- Edible Glitter, p. 130
- Cake Boards, Fanci-Foil Wrap, p. 132
- Buttercream Icing, p. 93
- Peppermint candy canes (crushed)
- Ice cakes fluffy. Sprinkle with edible glitter. Decorate with crushed candy canes. Each serves 1.

FUN-TIME FROSTIES

- Mini Snowman Pan, p. 185
- Tips 2, 4, 47, p. 134-139
- Christmas Red, Kelly Green, Royal Blue, Black Icing Colors, p. 124
- Edible Glitter, p. 130
- Cake Boards, Fanci-Foil Wrap, p. 132
- Buttercream Icing, p. 93
- Ice cakes fluffy. Sprinkle with edible glitter. Use tip 4 to pipe in hat. Smooth with finger dipped in cornstarch. With smooth side of tip 47, add bottom brim to hat. Add tip 2 pull-out pompon.
- Pipe tip 4 dot buttons. Use tip 2 dots for facial features.
- WIth ribbed side of tip 47, add scarf. Each serves 1.

THE BLESSED EVENT

- 4-pc. Oval Pan Set (13 x 9 $^7/_8$ in. pan used), p. 180
- Tips 2, 3, 14, 32, p. 134-135
- Wilton Royal Blue Icing Color, p. 124
- '93 Pattern Book (Nativity Pattern), p. 112
- Color Flow Mix, p. 125
- Cake Boards, Fanci-Foil Wrap, p. 132
- Buttercream Icing, Color Flow Icing, p. 93, 105
- Using Nativity Pattern and Color Flow Icing, outline pattern with tip 2. When dry, flow in design with thinned icing (see Color Flow, p. 105). Let dry.
- Ice 2-layer cake smooth. Edge top with tip 32 crown border (See p. 103). Add tip 3 double overlapped drop strings. Trim top of strings with tip 14 stars.
- Edge bottom border with tip 32 shells. Pipe tip 14 curved zigzag over shell. Randomly pipe tip 14 stars on cake top. Position color flow*. Serves 32.

*Note: Since buttercream icing will break down color flow, position on a piece of wax paper cut to fit, sugar cubes or mini marshmallows.

Time Saver

White Christmas

43

TASTY TREE AND TRAIN

- 4 pc. Christmas Favorites Cookie Cutter Set, p. 121
- 4 pc. Circus Train Cookie Cutter Set, p. 118
- Tips 2, 5, p. 134
- Christmas Red, Kelly Green, Icing Colors, p. 124
- 2 Recipes Roll-out Cookie Dough, p. 105
- Meringue Powder, p. 125
- Floral Scroll Base, White, p. 166
- Royal Icing, p. 93
- Styrofoam cone, 12 in. high x 5 in. wide at base; toothpicks; foil; ribbon bow, candy canes, candy jellies

- From cookie dough, cut out assorted Christmas cookies, 2 of each circus train car, eight 1 in. x 1½ in., and four 1 in. x 2 ¼ in. support pieces, and approximately 50 Santa, snowman, reindeer and tree cookies to fill tree. Thin down ½ cup red tinted cookie dough with milk or water 1 tsp. at a time until thin enough to pass through tip; also thin ½ cup green tinted dough as above. Using this thinned down cookie dough, add tips 2 and 5 outlines and details to cookies; on circus train cars flip over one set and decorate back side (finished train will be three dimensional); on each set add wreath to lion car, ribbon and bow to elephant car, stocking to giraffe car as shown. Make a hole in top of each Christmas cookie using tip 2. Bake and cool.

- Cover cone with foil, place on Floral Scroll Base , attach Christmas cookies from holes with toothpicks. Attach ribbon bow to toothpick; place on top of tree.
- Assemble circus train cars: Use matched train car pieces and one long and two short supports for each. Attach supports to back side of first train piece using royal icing; position long support piece horizontally about 1 in. from bottom edge of train car. Position short pieces one at each end of long piece creating a long-bottomed "u" shape. Attach matched train piece to supports. Let dry.
- Position train around tree. Fill with candies.

LETTER PERFECT TREE

- 10-pc. Christmas Collection Cookie Cutter Set, p. 121
- 26-pc. Alphabet Cookie Cutter Set, p. 119
- Tip 2, p. 134
- Kelly Green, Christmas Red Icing Colors, p. 124
- 8 in. Ruffle Board, p. 133
- 3 Recipes of Roll-Out Cookie Dough, p. 105
- Styrofoam Cone, 12 in. high x 5 in. wide at base; Colored Toothpicks, Silver Foil

- Cut out assorted Christmas cookies and letter messages. Thin ½ cup each — red, green, and untinted cookie dough with 1 tsp. milk or water.

- Decorate cookies with colored cookie dough, following instructions for Tasty Tree and Train and using tip 2. Make hole in top of each cookie (except stars) with tip 2. Bake and cool.
- To make tree: Cover styrofoam cone with silver foil and attach to Ruffle Board with dots of icing. Randomly push in toothpicks to hold hanging cookies. Add 2 star cookies to top, securing with dabs of icing.

BIG TIME FUN

- Large Gingerbread Boy Cookie Cutter, p. 121
- Large Teddy Bear Cookie Cutter, p. 118
- Tip 3, p. 134
- Ivory, Brown, Red-Red, Icing Colors, p. 124
- Buttercream Icing, p. 93
- Grandma's Gingerbread Recipe, p. 105
- Candy-coated chocolate pieces, cinnamon candies, sprinkle-covered chocolate chips, red ribbon

- Cut out desired number of Gingerbread Boy and Teddy Bear cookies from gingerbread dough. Bake and cool.
- With tip 3, outline facial features, shirt and shoes on gingerbread boy. Add tip 3 random dots to shirt. Add candies for eyes and buttons. For teddy bear, use tip 3 to pipe paws, ears and facial features. Add candies for eyes and buttons, tie ribbon around neck. *Each serves 1.*

Holiday Cookies

PEACEFUL VILLAGE

- *Gingerbread House Kit, Mini Gingerbread House Kit, p. 120*
- *Tips 1, 3, p. 134-139*
- *Brown Icing Color, p. 124*
- *Cake Boards, Fanci-Foil Wrap, p. 132*
- *Meringue Powder, p. 125*
- *Royal Icing, p. 93*
- *Grandma's Gingerbread Recipe (1 recipe), p. 105*
- *Pretzel sticks, nonpareils*

NOTE: *To achieve darker brown color in dough, either use dark molasses in recipe or add brown icing color.*

- Using patterns in gingerbread house kits, cut out and bake church (make an extra steeple base that will be used for eaves over door), and 2 mini houses. While still warm, cut church door in half. Let remainder of house cool.
- When completely cooled, use toothpick to etch in window outline. Pipe tip 1 lines in waffle pattern on windows.

- Attach walls, roof and steeple together with icing. Position door halves on either side; attach eaves with icing. Pipe tip 3 strings around doors, windows and seams of buildings; position pretzels, trimmed to desired lengths, on strings of icing. Trim eaves, roof lines and bases with nonpareils.

Gingerbread Heights

GINGERBREAD DREAM HOUSE

- Gingerbread House Kit, Mini Gingerbread House Kit, p. 120
- Tips 2, 3, 46, 47, 55, 233, 349, 352, p. 134-139
- Kelly Green, Christmas Red, Black, Golden Yellow, Ivory Icing Colors, p. 124
- Tree Former Set, p. 130
- Cake Boards (20 x 28 in. size needed), Fanci-Foil Wrap, p. 132
- Meringue Powder, p. 125
- Royal Icing, p. 93
- Grandma's Gingerbread Recipe (2 recipes needed), p. 105
- Large Marshmallows, Mini Shredded Wheat, Crisped Rice Cereal, Cotton

NOTE: Directions for this house refer to the three following areas, according to height: The Main House is the tallest portion, at the center. It has the front canopy door, a dormer and the large chimney. The Side Sections are those of medium height, to the right and left of the Main House. They each have a smaller chimney and large windows. The Mini Sides are the shortest sections. They have side windows and no chimneys.

- Make gingerbread, following recipe.
- Cut and bake pieces out of gingerbread dough, using pattern included in Gingerbread House Kit making the following changes:

For Main House: add 4 in. height to front, back and side pieces. **For dormer:** omit scallops on side pieces, cutting straight line between ends. **For chimney:** following pattern F, cut 2 short notched side and 1 long notched front pieces; following pattern F, cut a 4th long front piece into rectangle, without a notched bottom edge.

For front canopy entryway: cut only 1 roof section; divide in half vertically. Add 1 in. to height of 1 front and 1 side section. Divide front piece in half vertically cutting 1 in. wide x 3 in. high piece out of center of each. Cut arched door out of side piece.

For door: use pattern H in Gingerbread House Kit.

For Side Sections: cut roof, front and back pieces in half vertically.

For chimney of Side Sections: following pattern F, cut 4 notched short side pieces; cut 2 long front pieces into rectangles, without notched edges. Cut each long piece in half vertically. Using window pattern divided in half, cut shutters.

For Mini Sides: Cut pieces out of gingerbread dough, following instructions in Mini Gingerbread House Kit, making the following changes. Add 1 in. to height of front, back, and side pieces; cut front, back, and roof pieces in half vertically.

- Assemble gingerbread house on foil-covered base, following Building Basics instructions included with kit.
- Ice windows, pipe tip 3 curtains, (combine black and red icing colors to get maroon curtains) add tip 55 window crossbars. Outline window frames using tip 46. Ice shutters and trim with tip 2. Attach with dots of Royal Icing. Edge Main House door with tip 55, add tip 3 around window, tip 349 wreath and tip 2 trim and door handle.
- Trim house using tip 47. Attach shredded wheat shingle roof, starting at the bottom and working up, overlapping rows slightly.
- For garland and wreath trim, pipe tip 349 leaves and tip 2 bows, dots and trim.
- Ice base—green for ground, ivory for sidewalk. Add crisped rice cereal for stones in sidewalk.
- Cover large marshmallows with tip 233 short grass pull-outs. Make tip 352 trees on tree formers. Position around house. Add powdered sugar snow. Place cotton in chimneys.

LOCKED IN LOVE!

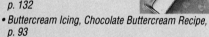

- *Heart Ring Pan, p. 183*
- *Jumbo Muffin Pan, p. 181*
- *Tips 2, 4, 8, 14, p. 134-135*
- *Pink, Copper, Brown, Icing Colors, p. 124*
- *Meringue Powder, p. 125*
- *Jumbo Baking Cups, p. 127*
- *Cake Board, Fanci-Foil Wrap, p. 132*
- *Buttercream, Royal Icing, p. 93*
- *Uncooked, thick spaghetti*

- Carefully break 5 pieces of spaghetti into lengths to fit across opening of cake. Using thinned royal icing, paint each piece. Let dry.
- Level and ice a jumbo cupcake smooth. Pipe tip 14 reverse shells for hair, tip 4 dot eyes and string mouth.
- Ice heart cake smooth. Position cupcake in center. Outline top edge of inner heart using tip 8 strings.
- Lay spaghetti across opening. Edge opening with tip 8 bead border.
- Print tip 2 message. Edge base with tip 8 bead border, top with tip 8 double bead border. *Serves 24.*

LONG ON ROMANCE

- *Long Loaf Pan, p. 181*
- *Tip 32, p. 135*
- *1 Red Floral Spray Set, p. 126*
- *Cake Board, Fanci-Foil Wrap, p. 132*
- *Buttercream Icing, Chocolate Buttercream Recipe, p. 93*

- Torte cake making three 1 in. layers. Spread layers with chocolate buttercream. Ice cake top and sides smooth.
- Arrange floral spray on cake top.
- Edge top and base borders with tip 32 shells. *Serves 18.*

HERE'S MY HEART

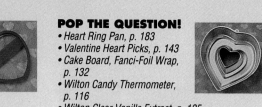

- *Giant Heart Cookie Cutter, p. 122*
- *Tip 3, p. 134*
- *Red-Red Icing Color, p. 124*
- *Red Crystal Sprinkles, p. 127*
- *Roll-out Cookie Dough Recipe, p. 105*

- Cut heart out of cookie dough. Sprinkle crystal sugar along edge. Bake and cool.
- Add tip 3 message. *Serves 1.*

THREE OF HEARTS

- *Heart Mini Tier Pan Set, p. 183*
- *Tips 16, 32, p. 135*
- *Strawberry Cake and Pastry Filling, p. 125*
- *Stabilized Whipped Cream Icing, p. 93*
- *Fresh Strawberries*

- Level cakes. Position 5 in. and 7 ½ in. tiers on separator plates, 9 in. tier on serving plate.
- **NOTE:** Pipe tip 16 dam of icing ½ in. from cake edge to hold filling. Spoon strawberry filling onto tops.
- Edge top of 5 in. tier with tip 32 c-scroll shell border. Slice a large strawberry to the stem, but not all the way through. Fan out and position on tier top. Edge top of 7 ½ in. and 9 in. tiers with tip 32 c-scroll shell border, placing ½ strawberry between each shell. Assemble tiers. *Serves 12.*

POP THE QUESTION!

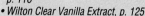

- *Heart Ring Pan, p. 183*
- *Valentine Heart Picks, p. 143*
- *Cake Board, Fanci-Foil Wrap, p. 132*
- *Wilton Candy Thermometer, p. 116*
- *Wilton Clear Vanilla Extract, p. 125*
- *Bomboniere!™ Instant Bow Ribbon, 5/16 in. Pink, (6 yards needed) p. 150*
- *Holiday Shaped Popcorn Recipe (below)*

- Spray Heart Ring Pan with vegetable oil pan spray. Prepare popcorn recipe, press into heart ring pan, packing firmly. Wait 15 minutes, and invert on foil-covered board. Position bows and heart picks at top of heart.

Holiday Shaped Popcorn

12 cups popped corn
1 cup granulated sugar
1 cup light corn syrup
½ cup water
2 tablespoons butter
2 teaspoons Wilton Clear Vanilla Extract

Butter the inside of a large bowl, fill with popped corn. Combine sugar, syrup and water in a 3-quart heavy saucepan. Add butter, cut in thin slices. Place over medium heat and stir with a wooden spoon until all sugar crystals are dissolved. Wash down sides of pan with a pastry brush dipped in hot water. Clip on thermometer and continue cooking until temperature reaches 240° F. Remove from heat and stir in vanilla.

Pour syrup over popcorn and toss with two forks until corn is evenly coated. When mixture is cool enough to handle, press into pan, packing firmly.

Lovely Valentines

MESSAGE OF LOVE

- *11 x 15 in. Sheet Pan, p. 174, 179*
- *Tips 3, 5, 30, 104, p. 134-136*
- *Pink, Creamy Peach, Violet, Willow Green Icing Colors, p. 124*
- *6-Pc. Nesting Heart Cookie Cutters, p. 120*
- *Cake Board, Fanci-foil Wrap, p. 132*
- *Buttercream Icing, p. 93*
- *Roll-out Cookie Dough Recipe, Cookie Icing Recipe, p. 105*
- With 3 ¼ in. heart cutter, cut 7 hearts from cookie dough. Bake and cool. Ice, let dry, and print tip 3 messages.
- Ice sheet cake smooth. Position cookies on cake top. Pipe tip 5 stems and leaves, and tip 104 bow.
- Edge top border with tip 30 reverse shells. Between shells, pipe tip 104 flutes. Edge base with tip 30 puff border. Between puffs pipe tip 5 hearts. *Serves 20.*

DRAWN TO YOU

- *Heart Dessert Pan, p. 183*
- *Doily, p. 132*
- *Confectioners Sugar Glaze, p. 93*
- *Favorite coffee cake recipe or streusel-type coffee cake mix*
- Bake cake, cool; position on doily.
- Using confectioners glaze, drizzle a freehand heart and border design on cake top (or use a cut bag with a small opening). *Serves 12.*

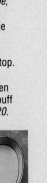

Time Saver

Time Saver

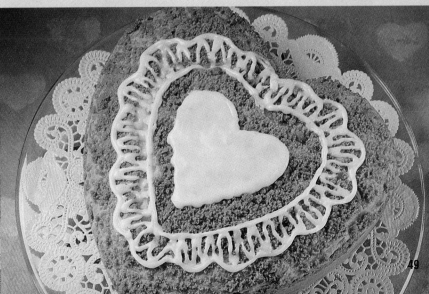

49

CUPID'S BOW
- *12 In. Heart Pan, p. 183*
- *Pink, No-Taste Red Icing Colors, p. 124*
- *Cake Board, Fanci-Foil Wrap, p. 132*
- *Rolled Fondant (1 ½ recipes needed), p. 94*
- *Buttercream Icing, p. 93*

- Following recipe instructions, color fondant with 4 dots pink icing color. Lightly ice one-layer cake with buttercream icing. Cover with rolled fondant. For base border, roll fondant into a rope approxi mately ½ in. diameter and edge base of cake.
- Knead red icing color into remaining fondant by hand. Roll out ⅛ in. thick and cut as follows: one 17 in. x 1 in. strip, five 6 in. x 1 in. strips, one 3 in. x 1 in. strip. Position long strip on cake top. Shape remaining strips into bow loops, pinching the fondant to close each loop. Turn on sides and allow to dry completely.
- Assemble loops together, with shortest in center, using stiffened buttercream icing to hold. *Serves 16.*

LOVE NOTES
- *True Love Candy Molds, p. 115*
- *Candy Melts™*-White, Red, Pink, Light Chocolate, Green, p. 116*
- *Lollipop Sticks, p. 116*
- *Disposable Decorating Bags, p.129*

*brand confectionery coating

- Mold a variety of candies using "painting' or "layering" method, (see p. 108). For lollipops, insert sticks into guides on molds and turn to coat entirely. Refrigerate to set. Unmold.

LUSCIOUS LACE
- *Mini Heart Pan, p. 183*
- *Light Cocoa Candy Melts™* (two bags needed), p. 116*
- *'93 Pattern Book (Lace Heart Pattern), p. 112*
- *Parchment Triangles, p. 129*
- *Ice cream (flavor of your choice)*

*brand confectionery coating

- Mold candy heart shells, p. 108. Refrigerate pan for 7 to 10 minutes, depending upon the thickness of shell desired. Pour out excess chocolate, smooth edge with knife, and refrigerate once again for 30 minutes. Unmold shells.
- Follow "Piping Decorations with Candy" instructions (p. 109) to pipe hearts and borders.
- For Lace Hearts: Cut disposable bag tip opening to tip 1 size; using lace heart pattern, pipe lace hearts. Set aside.
- Cut bag tip opening to tip 2 size and pipe bead borders around shells. Let set. When ready to serve, fill with ice cream and position lace hearts. May be made several days ahead and stored at room temperature. *Each serves 1.*

HEARTS AND FLOWERS
- *Double Tier Heart Pan, p. 183*
- *Tip 22, p. 135*
- *Candy Melts™*—White, Green, and Pink (1 pkg. each needed), p. 124*
- *Roses'N Buds Candy Mold, p. 114*
- *Cake Board, Fanci-Foil Wrap, p. 132*
- *Buttercream Icing, p. 93*

*brand confectionery coating

- Mold roses and candy plaque hearts out of melted Candy Melts™ (p. 108).
- Ice tops of cake. Position hearts on top. Cover sides of hearts with tip 22 stars. Position candy roses. *Serves 12.*

IN A HEARTBEAT
- *9 in. Heart Pans, p. 183*
- *Tip 70, p. 136*
- *Red Rose Floral Spray (2 pkgs. needed), p. 126*
- *Kneeling Cherub Fountain, p. 168*
- *Cake Board, Fanci-Foil Wrap, p. 132*
- *Buttercream Icing, p. 93*

- Ice two-layer cake smooth. Pipe tip 70 borders in a shell motion.
- Position floral sprays and cherub. *Serves 16.*

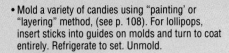

Winning Hearts

Time Saver

Easter Parade

EGG EXPRESS
- Special Delivery Bunny Pan, p. 186
- Tips 3, 4, 18, 47, 233, p.134-39
- Pink, Violet, Leaf Green, Golden Yellow Icing Color, p. 124
- Easter Treats and Egg Classic Candy Molds, p. 115
- Candy Melts™* — White, Light Cocoa, Spring Mix, p.116
- Candy Colors Kit, p. 116
- Cake Board, Fanci-Foil Wrap, p. 132
- Buttercream Icing, p. 93

*brand confectionery coating

- Mold a variety of candies (see p. 108). For yellow, green or orange, add candy colors to white melted coating.
- Ice sides of cake smooth. Outline bunny, facial features and basket handle with tip 4.
- Fill in basket with tip 47 basketweave. Cover handle with tip 18 stars. Use tip 18 and "e" motion or zigzag border to cover basket top and bottom edge.
- Pipe in ear, nose, eyes, mouth and button on basket with tip 4 (smooth with finger dipped in cornstarch). Cover bunny with tip 233 pull-out fur; inside of basket with tip 233 pull-out grass. Pipe in whiskers, eyelashes, eyebrows with tip 3.
- Edge base with tip 18 "c" motion border.
- Position candies. *Serves 12.*

COMING OUT OF HIS SHELL
- Great Eggs! Kit, p. 115
- Tips 1, 3, 5, 233, p. 134
- Sky Blue, Leaf Green, Violet, Pink, Teal, Lemon Yellow, Creamy Peach Icing Colors, p. 124
- 1 Yd. Bomboniere!™ 2 1/4 in. Gathering Ribbon, Striped Iridescent (for each egg), p. 150
- 2 Yds. Bomboniere!™ 5/16 in. Instant Bow Ribbon, White (for each egg), p. 150
- Meringue Powder, p. 125
- Royal Icing, p. 93
- Granulated sugar

- Following instructions included in Great Eggs! Kit, make Large Stand Up Sugar Egg with Window in color desired. Let dry.
- Mold bunny, eggs and basket of eggs out of sugar using candy mold included in kit. Let all dry.
- Add the following details: Pipe tip 1 string grass on basket of eggs. Pipe tip 1 eyes and mouth; and tip 3 nose, inside of ears, and zigzag bow and dot on bunny. Attach basket to bunny with dot of icing. Let dry.
- Join large egg halves with royal icing. Pipe a small mound of green icing on inside bottom of egg; add tip 233 pull-out grass. Position eggs and bunny.
- With tip 5 zigzag, cover seam where egg halves are joined. Pipe tip 5 dots around window opening. Cover egg with tip 3 dots.
- Make an Instant Bow and a Gathering Ribbon Ruffle following ribbon package directions. Attach bow to top of egg with dot of icing; position egg on ruffle.

SPEEDY LAMB

- Little Lamb Pan Set, p. 186
- Leaf Green Icing Color, p. 124
- Baby Jellies Sprinkle Decorations, p. 127
- Boiled Icing, p. 105
- Tinted shredded coconut, p. 103
- Generously ice cake fluffy with spatula. Fill in ears and desired facial features with Baby Jellies. Place tinted coconut along bottom edge of cake, add assorted Baby Jellies. *Serves 12.*

ENCHANTING EASTER TREE

- 12 in. Round Pan, p. 175, 179
- Tips 3, 8, p. 134
- Lemon Yellow Icing Color, p. 124
- Bomboniere!™ Wired Shaping Ribbon, Lavender (1 pkg. needed), Instant Bow Ribbon, ³⁄₁₆ in. White (7 pkgs. needed) p. 150
- Florist Wire (1 pkg. needed), p. 130
- Wooden Dowel Rods (1 needed), p. 172
- Tall Tier 14 in. Plate, Bottom Column Bolt, Glue-on Plate Legs (4 needed), 6 ½ in. Column, Cake Corer Tube, p. 170
- 12″ Cake Circle, p. 132
- Candy Melts™ *—Yellow, Light Cocoa, Pastel Mix, Green, White, (1 bag each needed) p. 116
- Playful Bunny Candy Mold, Whole Eggs Easter Mold, p. 115
- Lollipop Sticks, p. 116
- Rolled Fondant, Buttercream Icing, p. 93-4
- White florist tape

*brand confectionery coating

- Assemble Tall Tier Plate: Glue 4 legs onto the bottom.
- Cut hole the width of column in center of cake circle. Position 2-layer cake on circle and cut core out of cake center using Cake Corer Tube. Ice cake lightly with buttercream, then cover with rolled fondant. Insert 6 ½ in. column in center, being sure it screws into the bottom bolt. Wrap Wired Shaping Ribbon around cake, placing ribbon ends at back; secure with dots of icing. Using separate piece of Wired Shaping Ribbon, make a tailed bow. Pipe tip 3 dots on cake; edge base with tip 8 bead border. Attach ribbon at front of cake with florist wire.
- Using Candy Melts and molds, make a variety of bunnies (see p. 108). When set, attach sticks to backs with melted candy. Make 12 whole eggs with ribbon hangers: Cut twelve 5 in. lengths of Instant Bow Ribbon, remove strings. Place ribbon pieces inside of egg mold so ½ in. lays inside egg. Mold eggs. Set all aside.
- Make tree. Note: When wrapping wires, it is very important to wrap tightly with florist tape, especially at points where tree branches out. **For trunk:** Place 40 florist wires evenly around whole dowel rod, positioning even ends of wire 4 in. from top of rod. Tape the entire 4 in. length securely and compactly; check to see that rod will fit into center column of cake. Position an additional 35 wires evenly 3 in. up from bottom edge of the 40 wires. Tape 4 in. up; 7 in. should now be taped. **For branches:** Gather the bare wires into groups of 15 each and tape into 5 main branches. Wrap the entire tree with Instant Bow Ribbon, wrap the base of the tree with remaining Wired Shaping Ribbon. Position tree in column, pushing dowel end down to bottom.
- Make Instant Bows following package directions: 22 using 2 ft. ribbon for each and 4 using 2 yds. ribbon for each. Place 4 large bows around tree base. Tie 4 smaller bows onto trunk above wrapped area. Tie eggs randomly on tree 2-3 in. from branch ends. Tie remaining bows to branches. Position bunnies on cake top by pushing in sticks. *Serves 30.*

EGGS-TRAORDINARY!
- Egg Pan Set, p. 186
- Tips 3, 16, 129, p. 134-39
- Brown, Lemon Yellow, Pink, Violet Icing Colors, p. 124
- Easter Bunny Ready-To-Use Icing Decorations, (1 pkg. needed), p. 126
- Meringue Powder, p. 125
- Baby Jellies Sprinkle Decorations, p. 127
- Buttercream, Royal Icings, p. 93
- Shredded Tinted Coconut
- Using royal icing, make 16 tip 129 drop flowers with tip 3 dot centers. Let dry.
- Fill and position egg halves together, divide egg into 1½ in. wide sections, dot mark with icing. Pipe tip 16 scallops along division lines. Fill-in sections with tip 16 stars.
- Position Baby Jellies, flowers and icing decorations on cake. Place on a bed of shredded coconut. (see p. 103). Serves 12.

HARE STYLED EGG
- 4-Pc. Oval Pan Set (16" x 12 ³/₈" used), p. 180
- Cottontail Bunny Pan, p. 186
- Tips 1D, 2B, 789, p. 139
- Pink, Leaf Green, Lemon Yellow, Violet Icing Colors, p. 124
- Candy Melts™*—2 bags White, 1 bag Pastel Mix, p. 124

54

Easter Joy

- Decorator's Brush Set, p. 128
- Buttercream Icing, p. 93
- Shredded Tinted Coconut
*brand confectionery coating
- Mold candy plaque bunny out of Candy Melts™ (see p. 108 multi-color effect). Refrigerate plaque for at least ½ hour, until completely chilled. Unmold and set aside.
- Cover cake top and sides with tips 1D, 2B and 789 zigzags and stripes. Spread tinted coconut (see p. 103) around cake base. Position candy plaque on cake top. *Serves 35.*

MOM'S BUNNY BROOD

- Peek-A-Boo Bunny Pan, Mini Bunny Pan, p. 186
- Tips 3, 4, 16, 47, 125, 233, p. 134-139
- Pink, Lemon Yellow, Violet, Leaf Green, Black Icing Colors, p. 124
- Light Cocoa Candy Melts™* (1 bag needed), p. 116
- Egg Classic Candy Mold, p. 115
- Cake Boards, Fanci-Foil Wrap, p. 132
- Buttercream Icing, p. 93
*brand confectionery coating
- Mold candy eggs (see p. 108); set aside.
- For Mom Bunny and Basket: Ice background areas and sides of cake smooth. Outline head, hat, ears, paw with tip 4. Outline and pipe in facial features using tip 3. Fill in with tip 16 stars. Trim hat with tip 125 ruffle, add tip 4 outline at edge of ruffle. Cover basket with tip 47 basketweave. Add tip 16 rope border around basket and for handle.
- For Mini Bunnies: Outline and pipe in facial features with tip 3. Cover with tip 16 stars. Trim with tip 3 bows and piped-in bow ties.
- Position Mini Bunny. Fill basket with tip 233 pull-out grass. Edge base with tip 16 rosette and star border. Position candy eggs. *Cake serves 12. Mini Bunnies each Serve 1.*

EASTER BOUQUETS

- Egg Mini-Cake Pan, p. 186
- Tips 1, 2, 3, 16, 101s, 349, 501 (tip 501 included in Deep-Cut Stellar Star Set #502), p. 134-39
- Violet, Leaf Green, Pink, Lemon Yellow Icing Colors, p. 124
- Meringue Powder, p. 125
- Flower Nail No. 9, p. 130
- Poured Fondant, Royal Icings, p. 93
- Prepare cakes for poured fondant (see p. 93). Divide prepared fondant into 4 parts and add color. Pour over cakes and let set.
- Use royal icing for the following: Make tip 101 and tip 101s apple blossoms with tip 1 centers; tip 101 rosebuds and roses with tip 3 bases; tip 16 drop flowers with tip 2 centers. Set all aside.
- Position flowers, add tip 2 vines and tip 349 leaves. Edge base borders with tip 501 C-motion shells, tip 16 shells. *Each serves 1.*

DON'T TRICK HIM!

- Boo Ghost Pan, p. 184
- Tips 1, 2A, 3, 4, 6, 17, 233, p. 134-135
- Terra Cotta, Black, Brown Icing Colors, p. 124
- 2 Pc. Halloween Variety Candy Mold Set, p. 115
- Candy Melts™* —1 bag each White, Orange and Light Cocoa; Candy Colors Kit, p. 116
- '93 Pattern Book (Werewolf Pattern), p. 112
- Cake Board, Fanci-Foil Wrap, p. 132
- Buttercream Icing, p. 93
- 2 bendable plastic drinking straws
- Halloween candy — Candy Corn and Foil-Covered Chocolate Coins

* brand confectionery coating

- Mold a variety of candies (see page 108). For yellow or green candy, add candy colors to white melted coating. Set aside.
- Ice cake sides and top smooth. With toothpick, mark werewolf pattern on cake top.
- Build up top and opening of bag using tip 2A.
- Trim straws to 3" below bend; position at sides of cake top for "ears". Outline eyes, nose, mouth, shirt, arms and fingers with tip 4. Pipe-in tip 6 whites of eyes to appear "bulging"; pipe-in tip 4 nose, mouth, pupils of eyes and smooth with finger dipped in cornstarch. Pipe-in ears with tip 4 zigzags.
- Cover shirt with tip 17 stars. Add tip 233 pull-out hair.
- Add tip 6 teeth and fingernails; tip 1 bloodshot lines in eyes. Print tip 3 message. Position candy on cake top. *Serves 12.*

CAN'T SCARE CROWS!

- Wicked Witch Pan, p. 184
- Tips 3, 4, 12, 16, 17, 21, 127, p. 134, 135, 138
- Brown, Orange, Black, Golden Yellow Icing Colors p. 124
- '93 Pattern Book (Crow and Scarecrow Face Patterns), p. 112
- Cake Boards, Fanci-Foil Wrap, p. 132
- Buttercream Icing, p. 93
- Ice cake background, top and sides, and face area smooth. With toothpick, mark face and crow patterns on cake top.
- Outline hat details, eyes, nose, mouth and cheeks with tip 4. Fill-in outlined areas with tip 12; smooth with finger dipped in cornstarch.
- Outline crow with tip 3, fill-in eye and beak; smooth with finger dipped in cornstarch. Cover crow with tip 16 stars.
- Fill-in hat, face and neck with tip 17 stars. Add tip 127 neck ruffle and tip 21 bow tie.
- Spatula stripe bag (p. 94) with golden yellow and orange. Pipe tip 16 pull-out stars for hair.
- Edge base border with tip 17 shells. *Serves 12.*

MINI MONSTERS

- Mini Ghost Pan, p. 184
- Tips 2, 3, 5, 14, 16, 102, p. 134-135
- Black, Orange, Leaf Green, Violet, Christmas Red Icing Colors, p. 124
- '93 Pattern Book (Vampire and Witch Patterns) p. 112
- Cake Boards, Fanci-Foil Wrap, p. 132
- Buttercream Icing, p. 93
- Pretzel Stick
- Ice sides and tops of cakes smooth. With toothpick, mark vampire and witch patterns on cake tops.
- Fill-in bodies with tip 14 stars. Add tip 2 facial features, tip 5 witches' hat with tip 102 brim. Position pretzel stick for broom, add tip 3 pull-out broom bristles. Pipe tip 3 hands, bow ties, hair and filled-in areas (smooth with finger dipped in cornstarch).
- Edge each cake with tip 16 star border. *Each serves 1.*

PARTY WITH THE FRANKENSTEINS

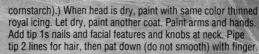

- *10 in. Square Pan, p. 174, 179*
- *Tips 1s, 2, 3, 6, 46, 134, 233, 789, p. 134-139*
- *Leaf Green, Black, Brown Icing Colors, p. 124*
- *Teenage Doll Picks (2 needed), p. 141*
- *Cake Boards, Fanci-Foil Wrap, p. 132*
- *Dowel Rods, p. 172*
- *Decorator's Brushes Set, p. 128*
- *'93 Pattern Book (laboratory pattern), p. 112*
- *Piping Gel, Meringue Powder, p. 125*
- *Rolled Fondant, (1 recipe needed), p. 94*
- *Buttercream, Royal Icings, p. 93*

- Cut cake in half to make slabs. Add a small amount of Black Icing color to buttercream for grey color icing. Ice smooth. Edge bottom border with tip 6 beads, top border with tip 3 beads.
- Before decorating doll picks, trim 1" from the bottom with craft knife.
- **For Bride:** Apply piping gel to doll pick hair. Fold hair back to be half the original length. Place on waxed paper and let dry. Paint face and arms with thinned royal icing. Let dry and apply second coat. When hair is dry, ice smooth with royal icing.
- Cover hair with tip 134 zigzags. Add tip 1s fingernails, facial features and knobs on neck. Ice body smooth. With tip 789, pipe front and back of body, add piping on shoulders and smooth (with finger dipped in cornstarch) to have front meet back of dress. For ruffled effect on sleeves use tip 46 to continually pipe on arms. Let dry.
- **For Frankie:** Cut hair off doll pick. With royal icing, pipe tip 6 zigzag for top of forehead (pat smooth with finger dipped in cornstarch) to create built-up look. With tip 6, overpipe nose and chin for square-jawed effect; add ears. Continuing with tip 6 and royal icing, complete piping zigzag formation down to neck. (Smooth with finger dipped in

cornstarch).) When head is dry, paint with same color thinned royal icing. Let dry, paint another coat. Paint arms and hands. Add tip 1s nails and facial features and knobs at neck. Pipe tip 2 lines for hair, then pat down (do not smooth) with finger.
- For shirt and vest: With royal icing, ice body and arms. Pull-out tip 233 vest. Let dry.
- Insert bodies into cake, supporting with 2 ½" dowel rod in back.
- For Bodies: Use fondant to form legs and feet. Lay on cake.
- For Sheets: Cut two sheets of fondant, each 8 ¾" x 6 ¾" and position.
- Cut "laboratory" from pattern book. Tape or glue onto cake boards, cut to fit.
- Pipe tip 6 spiders and mice, tip 1s webs. Add tip 101s for mice ears. Position Laboratory wall. *Serves 14.*

Raising Spirits

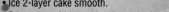

- Cats and Bats Icing Decorations, p. 126
- Buttercream Icing, p. 93
- Black candy dots
- Ice 2-layer cake smooth.
- Edge top and bottom border and cake edges with tip 17 stars.
- Position cake top decoration and icing decorations on top and sides.
- Add black dot candies to sides. *Serves 16.*

FRIGHTFULLY GOOD!
- 6-Cup Standard Muffin Pan, p. 181
- Orange, Brown Icing Colors, p. 124
- Halloween Standard Baking Cups, p. 127
- Cats and Bats Icing Decorations, p. 126
- Buttercream Icing, p. 93
- Ice cupcakes smooth. Position icing decorations. *Each serves 1.*

SCARECROW SANDWICH
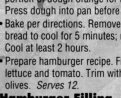
- Scarecrow Pan, p. 184
- Orange Icing Colors, p. 124
- Hamburger Filling recipe, below
- 1 pkg. favorite hot roll mix or frozen bread dough; lettuce, tomato, cheese, black olives
- Grease Scarecrow pan with vegetable shortening. Prepare hot roll dough according to directions on package or defrost bread dough. Color a small portion of dough orange for hat, hands and feet. Press dough into pan before second rising.
- Bake per directions. Remove from oven and allow bread to cool for 5 minutes; remove from pan. Cool at least 2 hours.
- Prepare hamburger recipe. Fill and garnish with lettuce and tomato. Trim with cheese and black olives. *Serves 12.*

Hamburger Filling
3 lbs. ground chuck
Salt and pepper to taste
Preheat broiler. Line scarecrow pan with plastic wrap. Pack meat into pan. Invert meat on broiler pan; remove wrap. Broil 3-4 inches from heat for 7-8 minutes per side. Use a cookie sheet as a large spatula to turn hamburger. Broil second side until brown.
Split bread horizontally; toast in broiler if desired.

Happy Halloween

HAUNTING HALLOWEEN!

- Jack-O-Lantern Pan, p. 184
- Tips 1, 4, 8, 12, 17, 21, p. 134-135
- Orange, Black, Kelly Green Icing Colors, p. 124
- Cake Board, Fanci-Foil Wrap, p. 132
- Buttercream Icing, p. 93
- Candy corn
- Ice mouth, nose and eyes smooth. Add tip 4 outlines. Cover cake top and sides with tip 17 stars. Pipe tip 21 stripes and rosette to form stem. Add tip 4 "carved" message.
- To make ghosts, figure pipe tip 12 head and body, tip 8 arms and tip 1 facial features (see page 104).
- Add tip 17 stars for base border and position candy corn as shown. *Serves 12.*

TRY THESE TREATS

- Halloween Favorites Cookie Cutters Set, p. 122
- Tips 1, 2, 14, p. 134-135
- Orange, Black Icing Colors, p. 124
- Roll-out Cookie Dough Recipe, p. 105
- Buttercream Icing, p. 93
- Cut out cookies, bake and cool.
- Outline cookies with tip 2. Fill in with tip 14 stars, or pipe-in using tip 2 (smooth with finger dipped in cornstarch). Add tip 1 details.

THE OLD HAUNT
- 9" Hexagon Pan, p. 180
- Tip 17, p. 135
- Orange Icing Color, p. 124
- Cake Boards, Fanci-Foil Wrap, p. 132
- Halloween Cake Top Set, p. 144

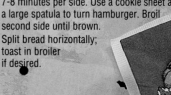

FLYING FELINE

- Scary Cat Pan, p. 184
- Orange, Black Icing Colors, p. 124
- Tips 2, 3, 105, 124, p. 134, 138-139
- Cake Board, Fanci-Foil Wrap, p. 132
- Candy Melts™*— 2 bags Light Cocoa, p. 116
- Plastic Dowel Rods (1 needed), p. 172
- Buttercream Icing, p. 93
- Raffia paper (orange)
- Make cat plaque from melted Candy Melts (see p. 108)
- Ice dowel rod and sugar cone in black. Let dry.
- Ice cake smooth. Add tip 105 shell border.
- Overpipe with tip 2 to add contrasting strings to shells.
- Place dowel rod broomstick on cake top. Build up around broomstick with icing to secure position. Put a small amount of buttercream in dowel rod. Fold back strands of Raffia paper and attach to dowel rod.
- Position candy plaque. With tip 3 outline cat body and facial features. Cover body with tip 2 five-petal flowers using shell technique.
- Position hat. Add tip 124 ruffle, tip 3 beads to hat. *Serves 12.*
  *brand confectionery coating

TOP OF HER CLASS

- Round Tier Set (2-mix), p. 180
- Tips 3, 16, 131, 224, 349, p. 134-139
- Ivory, Golden Yellow, Violet Icing Colors, p. 124
- Glowing Girl Graduate, p. 143
- Cake Dividing Set, p. 128
- Cake Boards, p. 132
- Meringue Powder, p. 125
- 12 in. Ruffle Board, p. 133
- '93 Pattern Book (Letter Pattern), p. 112
- Buttercream, Royal Icings, p. 93
- Using royal icing, make approximately 75 tip 131 and 160 tip 224 drop flowers. Add tip 3 dot centers. Let dry.
- Ice one layer cakes smooth. Prepare cakes for push-in leg construction, following directions on package. Using cake dividing set, divide top and bottom tiers into 8ths. Dot mark middle tier every 2 inches around top.
- On bottom tier: Edge base with tip 16 shell border. Pipe tip 16 zigzag garlands between marks. Position drop flowers on garlands. Build up icing on top of cake using tip 16, cover with drop flowers. Trim with tip 349 leaves. Edge top border with tip 16 reverse shells.
- On middle tier: Edge base with tip 16 zigzag puffs. Add tip 3 double drop strings around cake top between 2 in. marks, omitting 2 double strings at cake front. Add tip 3 name at front. Build up icing on top of cake using tip 16, cover with drop flowers, trim with tip 349 leaves. Attach drop flowers between puffs and at ends of double strings with dots of icing. Edge top with tip 16 reverse shells.
- On top tier: Edge base with tip 16 shells. Pipe tip 16 zigzag garlands and tip 3 triple strings between marks. Attach drop flowers where garland meets top. Edge top with tip 16 reverse shells. Cover with drop flowers, trim with tip 349 leaves. Position Glowing Graduate.
- Assemble tiers on pillars; edge pillar bases with tip 16 shells. Write tip 3 name using lettering pattern as a guide. *Serves 24.*

Time Saver

GREAT GOING GRADUATE!

- 9 x 13 in. Sheet Pan, p. 174, 179
- Tips 3, 17, 21, p. 134, 135
- Wilton Red (no-taste) Icing Color, p. 124
- Decorating Comb, p. 128
- Red and Yellow Floral Spray Set (2 pkgs. each needed), p. 126
- Make Any Message Letter Press Set, p. 128
- Cake Board, Fanci-Foil Wrap, p. 132
- Glad Graduate, p. 143
- Buttercream Icing, p. 93
- Ice 1-layer cake smooth. Comb sides of cake using decorating comb.
- Imprint message on cake top using letter press set. Pipe-in tip 3 message. Edge base border with tip 21 shells, top border with tip 17 c-shells. Position roses, leaves and graduate on cake top and front. *Serves 14.*

Honor Roll

WELL-DESERVED BOUQUETS

- Pretty Lady Pan, p. 189
- Tips 3, 4, 7, 16, 21, 102, 104, 352, p. 134-139
- Flower Nail No. 9, p. 130
- Royal Blue, Kelly Green, Red-Red, Copper, Black, Brown Icing Colors, p. 124
- '93 Pattern Book (Grad Cap Pattern), p. 112
- Cake Board, Show 'N Serve Cake Board, Fanci-Foil Wrap, p. 132-133
- 4mm White Pearl Beading*, p. 167
- Meringue Powder, p. 125
- Buttercream, Royal Icings, p. 93
- Gold cord

- Using royal icing or stiffened buttercream, make 12 tip 102 full roses and 6 tip 102 5-petal roses. Use tip 7 for bases. Let dry.
- To make graduation cap: Cut pattern from Show 'N Serve cake board. Working on laminated side, outline with tip 4 and fill-in with tip 16 stars. Attach a length of gold cord with dot of icing. Set aside.
- Ice sides and background area of cake smooth. Outline gown, collar, and hat bottom edge with tip 4. Outline facial features with tip 3. Pipe-in eyes and mouth with tip 3 (smooth with finger dipped in cornstarch).
- Cover face and gown with tip 16 stars. For hair, use tip 16 stripes. Position roses, add tip 352 leaves and tip 3 strings for stems. Using tip 3, outline hands holding flowers, fill-in with tip 16 stars.
- Add tip 104 bow around bouquet.
- Cut pearl beading to fit. Position on cake. Edge base border with tip 21 shells. Position hat. Serves 12.

*Remove pearl beading before cutting cake

HONORS BESTOWED

- Handsome Guy Pan, p. 189
- Tips 3, 4, 16, p. 134, 135
- Royal Blue, Black, Copper, Terra Cotta Icing Colors, p. 124
- Cake Board, Show 'N Serve Cake Board, Fanci-Foil Wrap, p. 132

- Parchment Roll, p. 130
- '93 Pattern Book (Grad Cap Pattern), p. 112
- Buttercream Icing, p. 93
- Gold cord
- Ice background areas and sides of cake smooth.
- To make graduation cap: Cut pattern from Show 'N Serve cake board. Working on laminated side, outline with tip 4 and fill-in with tip 16 stars. Attach a length of gold cord with dot of icing. Set aside.
- Outline gown, shirt collar, tie, hands, hat bottom edge, with tip 4. Outline facial features with tip 3. Pipe-in tie, eyes, and mouth with tip 3 (smooth with finger dipped in cornstarch).
- Fill-in face, body, gown with tip 16 stars. Add tip 16 swirls for hair.
- For diploma, roll parchment paper from both ends to middle to achieve a scroll look. Print message with marker.
- Edge base with tip 16 shell border. Position hat and diploma on cake. Serves 12.

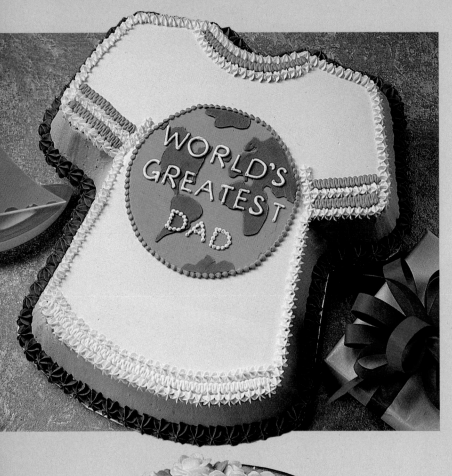

DAD'S SPECIAL-TEE
- T-Shirt Pan, p. 187
- Tips 3, 16, 21, p. 134-135
- Brown, Sky Blue Icing Colors, p. 124
- '93 Pattern Book (Globe Pattern), p. 112
- Cake Board, Fanci-Foil Wrap, p. 132
- Make Any Message Letter Press Set, p. 128
- Buttercream Icing*, p. 93

- Ice cake smooth on cake board cut to fit; let icing set until it is firm to the touch.
- Cut out waxed paper stencil from circle portion of Globe Pattern only. Place stencil on cake, ice area smooth. Remove carefully and let icing set up once again. Cut out continents (land) portions from stencil and position stencil over dried Globe Pattern on cake. Ice smooth, remove stencil pattern carefully, let dry.
- Imprint message with press, print with tip 3. Trim "world" with tip 3 beads.
- Add tip 3 zigzag border on shirt sleeves and neckline.
- Trim top border with tip 16 stars; bottom border with tip 21 stars. *Serves 12.*
- * Must use buttercream icing that crusts over easily. (If not using stiffer buttercream, trace pattern in cake with toothpick and fill in with tip 16 stars.)

MOM'S A WINNER!
- Up 'N Away Balloon Pan, p. 189
- Tips 3, 4, 7, 16, 18, 102, 104, 352, p. 134-136, 138
- Golden Yellow, Leaf Green Icing Colors, p. 124
- '93 Pattern Book (Award Ribbon Pattern), p. 112
- Meringue Powder, p. 125
- Flower Nail No. 7, p. 130
- Cake Board, Fanci-Foil Wrap, p. 132
- Buttercream, Royal Icing, p. 93
- Using royal icing or stiffened buttercream make 7 tip 7 and tip 102 roses and 14 half roses; make 1 tip 7 and tip 104 large half rose.
- Ice top and sides of cake smooth. Using toothpick, mark Award Ribbon Pattern on cake top. Outline with tip 4. Fill in with tip 16 stars. Edge top with tip 16 and base with tip 18 shell borders.
- Write tip 4 message, overpipe using tip 3.
- Position tip 102 roses and half roses around cake base. Place tip 104 half rose on cake top, pipe tip 4 stem. Trim all with tip 352 leaves. *Serves 12.*

UNINVITED GUESTS
- 9" x 13" Insulated Sheet Pan, p. 177
- Tips 1, 3, 6, 13, 21, 47, p. 134-139
- Brown, Black, Golden Yellow, Christmas Red, Leaf Green, Sky Blue Icing Colors, p. 124
- '93 Pattern Book (Basket, Strawberry, Apple, Olive, Bread, Banana Patterns), p. 112
- Buttercream Icing, p. 93
- Ice cake smooth, top half blue; bottom half green.
- With spatula, ice tree trunk smooth; fluff icing for leaves.
- With toothpick, trace patterns in icing.
- For picnic basket: Cover basket pattern with tip 47 basketweave. Add tip 6 pipe-in handles and lids; make tip 6 bottom rope border and top bead border.
- Outline fruits with tip 1; fill in with tip 13 stars. Add tip 1 dots on strawberries. Use tip 3 to outline bread and fill in with tip 13 stars.
- Pipe tip 3 ants with tip 1 legs and antennae.
- Print tip 3 message. Add tip 21 reverse shell border. *Serves 14.*

Family Occasions

FAMILY ALBUM

- Two-Mix Book Pan, p. 188
- Tips 1s, 2, 2B, 4, 6, p. 134, 139
- Leaf Green, Sky Blue, Brown, Black, Christmas Red, Golden Yellow, Copper Icing Colors, p. 124
- Color Flow Mix, Meringue Powder, p. 125
- '93 Pattern Book (Photograph Pattern), p. 112
- Decorating Comb, p. 128
- Buttercream, Royal Icing, Color Flow Icing, p. 93, 105
- Candy discs

- Using Photograph Pattern and Color Flow Icing, outline 8 panels with tip 4 (see Color Flow, p. 105). Let dry. Have parchment bags filled with Leaf Green, Sky Blue, White and Brown color flow icings ready to use. Color flow sets up quickly; finish decorating each photograph background before starting next one.
- Start by piping a small section of grass into outline. Immediately add sky and trees. Pipe clouds and background elements (tip 1s fences, mountains, roads, etc.) immediately after. Let dry completely.
- Using royal icing and tip 2, pipe block picture holders on each corner using zigzag motion; pat smooth with finger dipped in cornstarch.
- On candy discs, pipe tip 2 hair and tip 1s facial features. Secure in position on panels with dots of royal icing and add tip 2 strings for bodies and tip 1s names. Set aside to dry.
- Ice cake smooth. Comb sides with decorating comb to resemble pages. Add tip 2B (brown) flat edging around base. Print tip 4 message on cake top. Trim outside edge of flat border with tip 2 bead border. Add tip 6 beads along cake edge on top of flat border. Edge top of cake with tip 4 bead border.
- Position color flow*. Serves 24.

*Note: Buttercream icing will break down color flow. Position immediately before serving; or on a piece of plastic wrap cut to fit, on sugar cubes, or on mini marshmallows.

Christening & Communion

BLESS THE COMMUNICANT
- *7 x 11 in. and 9 x 13 in. Sheet Pans, p. 174*
- *Tips 3, 12, 104, 172, 199, 352, 362, p. 134-139*
- *Golden Yellow, Kelly Green Icing Colors, p. 124*
- *Cake Boards, Fanci-Foil Wrap,Tuk-N-Ruffle, p. 132-133*
- *Bomboniere!™ Party Favors Book (Big Debut instructions and materials, p. 26), p. 112*
- *Dowel Rods, p. 172*
- *Flower Nail No. 9, p. 130*
- *Meringue Powder, p. 125*
- *Communion Altar, (Boy); Shining Cross, p. 141*
- *Buttercream, Royal Icings, p. 93*

- Make desired number of favors, following instructions in Bomboniere!™ Party Favors Book. (Safety pin shown in book is not added.) Set aside.
- Using royal icing and tip 12 for bases, make 16 tip 104 gold roses and 20 rosebuds; and 13 tip 104 white roses and 20 rosebuds. Let dry.
- Ice one layer cakes smooth; prepare for stacked construction (see p. 106). Pipe tip 3 message.
- Add tip 362 reverse shell borders to tops of both cakes. Edge bases with shell borders: tip 172 on 9 x 13 in. cake; tip 199 on 7 x 11 in. cake.
- Position Communion Altar and Shining Cross. Attach roses and rosebuds with dots of icing. Add tip 352 leaves. Position favors. *Serves 25.*

SWEET BLESSINGS
- *Cross Pan, p. 186*
- *Tips 2, 5, 10, 103, 127, 352, p. 134-139*
- *Flower Nail No. 9, p. 130*
- *Pink, Leaf Green Icing Colors, p. 124*
- *Cake Board, Fanci-Foil Wrap, p. 132*
- *Buttercream Icing, p. 93*

- *Bomboniere!™ Party Favors Book (Sweet Little One instructions and materials, p. 26), p. 112*
- Make desired number of favors, following instructions in Bomboniere!™ Party Favors Book. Set aside.
- Use stiffened buttercream or royal icing to make 6 tip 103 roses with tip 10 bases. Let dry.
- Ice cake smooth. Cover cake top with tip 2 Cornelli lace. Add tip 127 bottom ruffle border. Pipe tip 2 dots on sides of cake. Add tip 5 bead borders around cake edges as shown.
- Position roses. Add tip 352 leaves. Position favors. *Serves 12.*

WELCOME TO THE FOLD
- *Two-Mix Book Pan, p. 188*
- *Tips 3, 12, 13, 16, 21, 79, 131, 352, p. 134-139*
- *Pink, Lemon Yellow, Leaf Green Icing Colors, p. 124*
- *Make Any Message Letter Press Set,15-pc. Decorator Pattern Press Set, Decorating Comb, p. 128*
- *Bomboniere!™ Party Favors Book (Lovely Lamb instructions, p. 26), p. 112*
- *Scrolls (1 pkg. needed), p. 169*
- *Cake Board, Fanci-Foil Wrap, p. 132*
- *Royal, Buttercream Icings, p. 93*

- Make Lovely Lamb favors according to instructions in Bomboniere!™ Party Favors Book. Set aside.
- With royal icing, make 46 (10 pink, 36 yellow) tip 131 drop flowers, with tip 3 dot centers. Let dry.
- Ice cake smooth. Comb sides with Decorating Comb to resemble pages. Insert scrolls into bottom of cake.
- Press in message, outline with tip 3.
- Edge top border with tip 16 shells; edge base with tip 21 shells.
- Use "scrolled look" press from Decorator Pattern Press Set for design. Overpipe with tip 13 strings.
- Position drop flowers and add tip 352 leaves.
- To make lamb: Using medium consistency buttercream and tip 12, hold bag at a 90° angle and, using heavy pressure, pipe a line of icing for body; add head. Cover body and top and sides of head with tip 16 reverse shells. Add tip 79 ears, and tip 3 feet. Add tip 3 dot eyes.
- Position favors. *Serves 24.*

GOD'S
BLESSINGS
ON
COURTNEY

PILLOW OF DREAMS
- *Double Tier Heart Pan, p. 183*
- *Tips 1s, 2, 5, 18, 127D, p. 134-138*
- *Golden Yellow Icing Color, p. 124*
- *Cake Board, Fanci-Foil Wrap, p. 132*
- *Floral Puff Accent, White, p. 165*
- *Bomboniere!™ Party Favors Book (Lavish Love instructions materials, p. 18), p. 112*
- *Bomboniere!™ Anniversary Bands, Gold, p. 152*
- *Bomboniere!™ Instant Bow Ribbon 3/16 in. White, p. 150*
- *Buttercream Icing, p. 93*
- Make desired number of Lavish Love favors, following instructions in Bomboniere!™ Party Favors Book. Set aside
- Make ornament: Cut a 11 in. length of Instant Bow Ribbon, remove string; tie one anniversary band onto each end. Tie onto Floral Puff Accent. Set aside.
- Ice cake top and sides smooth.
- Pipe tip 127D ruffle along edge of top heart. On ruffle, pipe tip 1s "S" shapes and small dots, add tip 2 flowers. Trim outside edge of ruffle with tip 2 dots. Pipe tip 5 bead border on inside edge of ruffle.
- Edge base with tip 18 reverse shell border. Position ornament on cake top and favors around cake. *Serves 12.*

HEARTY FARE
- *6-pc. Nesting Heart Cookie Cutter Set (3 in. size used), p. 120*
- *Golden Yellow, Kelly Green Icing Colors, p. 124*
- *Tips 4, 101, 349, p. 134-138*
- *Flower Nail No. 9, p. 130*
- *White and rye bread, cream cheese, lettuce, luncheon meat, American cheese, chicken salad, fresh dill*
- Use 3 in. size heart cookie cutter to cut desired amount of bread in heart shapes. Fill with assortment of meats, salads, cheeses and condiments. (Also use cookie cutter to cut cheese slices.)
- Pipe tip 101 roses with tip 4 bases using softened, tinted cream cheese. Pipe rosebuds with tip 101. Position on bread and add tip 349 leaves. *Each serves 1.*

LOVE BLOSSOMS
- *Six-Cup Standard Muffin Pan, p. 181*
- *Tips 12, 16, 113, 126, p. 134-139*
- *Peach, Kelly Green Icing Colors, p. 124-125*
- *Floating Tiers Cake Stand Set, p. 170*
- *Sweet Symphony Musical Ornament, p. 158*
- *Bells and Ribbons Baking Cup Liners (Standard Size), p. 127*

- Ruffle Boards (one each
  8 in., 10 in., 14 in., needed), p. 133
- Bomboniere!™ Party Favors Book (Basic Tulle
  Puff, p. 30; Tailed Bow, p. 33), p. 112
- Bomboniere!™ Wired Shaping Ribbon, Peach
  (6 pkgs. needed), p. 150
- Bomboniere!™ Pearl Sprays (3 pkgs. needed),
  p. 152
- Bomboniere!™ Tulle Circles, White Scalloped-
  Edge Organza (1 pkg. needed), p. 151
- Buttercream Icing, p. 93
- Ice cupcakes smooth. Make tip 126 roses with
  tip 12 bases on each cupcake. Edge with tip 16
  shell border. Add tip 113 leaves to roses.
- Place Ruffle Boards on separator plates.
- To make decorative bows for floating tier, follow
  directions in Bomboniere!™ Party Favors book
  for Basic Tulle Puff and Tailed Bow. Combine
  1 puff, 1 bow and 2 Pearl Sprays; hold together
  with florist tape.
- Trim floating tier with decorative bows. Place
  cupcakes on boards. Position Sweet Symphony
  Ornament. *Each serves 1.*

SHOWERS OF HAPPINESS

- 18 in. Half Round Pan
  (3 in. high), p. 179
- Tips 1, 3, 10, 12, 16, 21, 103,
  104, 127, 352, p. 134-139
- No. 9 Flower Nail, p. 130
- Creamy Peach, Violet*, Pink, Kelly Green, Golden
  Yellow Icing Colors, p. 124
- Bomboniere!™ Party Favors Book (Shelter Our
  Love instructions and materials, p. 16), p. 112
- Bomboniere Wired Shaping Ribbon (1 pkg.
  Lavender neeed), p. 150
- 6 mm Pearl Beading** (1 pkg. needed), p. 167
- Plastic Dowel Rods (1 pkg. needed), p. 172
- Flower Spikes (1 pkg. needed), p. 166
- Lacy Hearts (1 pkg. needed), p. 169
- Cake Board, Fanci-Foil Wrap, p. 132
- Meringue Powder, p. 125
- Buttercream, Royal Icings, p. 93

*To achieve violet shade, add pink icing color to violet.

- Make desired number of Shelter Our Love favors,
  following instructions in Bomboniere!™ Party
  Favors Book. Set aside
- Using stiffened buttercream or royal icing, make 6
  tip 103 roses with tip 10 bases and 3 tip 103 buds
  in violet. Also make 3 tip 104 roses with tip 12
  bases and 10 tip 103 buds in creamy peach. Let dry.
- Ice sides and top of one-layer cake smooth. Ice 5
  Lacy Hearts and position firmly on top straight edge
  of cake. Cover cake top and lacy hearts with tip 1
  sotas (p. 103). Pipe tip 127 ruffle on edge of hearts.
  Top ruffle with tip 16 shell border.
- Position pearl beading on cake top. Edge bottom
  border with tip 21 shells.
- Place flower spike into top of cake for umbrella tip.
- Wrap pearls and ribbon around dowel rod, add bow
  at bottom. (Secure trims with glue gun.) Push into
  sides of cake.
- Write tip 3 message. Position roses and buds. Add
  tip 352 leaves. Position favors. *Serves 18.*

**Remove pearls before serving.

A TRELLIS OF LOVE

- 4 Pc. Oval Pan Set
  (13 x 9 ⅞ in. size used), p. 180
- Tips 2, 5, p. 134
- Burgundy, Willow Green Icing
  Colors, p. 124
- 6 in. White Separator Plate
  (from Crystal-Clear Cake Divider Set), p. 170
- Hidden Pillars, p. 171
- Parchment Triangles, p. 129
- Cake Boards, Fanci-Foil Wrap, p. 132
- Color Flow Mix, Glycerin, Almond Extract, p. 125
- Glucose, p. 130
- Bomboniere!™ Party Favor Book ("So Fancy"
  Instructions and Materials, p. 18), p. 112
- 1993 Pattern Book (Rose, Top and Base Plate
  Floral Collar Patterns), p. 112
- Mary and Charles Couple, p. 159

- Buttercream, Color Flow Icings, p. 93, 105
- Rolled Fondant (2 recipes needed), p. 94
- Cardboard or pressboard
- ⅜ in. ribbon to trim plate and board
- Make desired number of "So Fancy" favors,
  following instructions in Bomboniere!™ Party
  Favor Book. Set aside.
- Using Top Floral Collar and Base Plate Floral Collar
  Patterns and color flow icing, outline pattern using
  tip 2. When set, flow in with Color Flow in cut
  parchment bag (see Color Flow, p. 105). Add tip 2
  dots on edge of collar. Note: When working with
  large Color Flow pieces, tape patterns down on
  sturdy board, tape wax paper over pattern, then
  lightly spray with no-stick cooking spray for easy
  release. Allow to dry at least 48 hours.

- Cut triple thick cardboard or pressboard to 15 x 19
  in. oval size (use pan as guide, or use base plate
  pattern cut ½ in. larger). Cover with foil.
- Cut a cardboard to fit the size of cake, place two
  layer cake on board, ice with buttercream and
  cover with rolled fondant. Cover separator plate
  and larger board with remaining rolled fondant.
- Trim board edge and plate edge with ribbon,
  secure with dots of icing. Trim and push hidden
  pillars into cake.
- Using toothpick, mark Rose patterns on cake side.
  Outline using tip 2.
- Position Color Flow Base Plate Floral Collar on
  prepared board. Carefully position cake in center.
  Pipe tip 5 bead border.
- At reception: Carefully position Color Flow Top
  Floral Collar. Position plate and ornament on cake
  top. Place favors around cake. Serves 30.

Bright Future

STRINGS ATTACHED

- 10 in. Square Pan, p. 174, 179
- 6 in. Round Pan, p. 175, 179
- Tips 1, 2, 8, 104, 352, 502, 504, p. 134-139
- Lemon Yellow, Violet, Moss Green Icing Color, p.124
- Cake Boards, Fanci-Foil Wrap, Tuk-N-Ruffle, p. 132-133
- Cake Dividing Set, p. 128
- Decorator's Brushes Set, p. 128
- Bomboniere!™ Party Favors Book (Precious Times Instructions and Materials, p. 4), p. 112
- Flower Nail No. 7, p. 130
- Dowel Rods, p. 172
- Reluctant Groom Couple, p. 165
- Seed Pearl Heart, p. 169
- Meringue Powder, p. 125
- Buttercream, Royal Icings, p. 93

- Make desired number of Precious Times party favors, following instructions in Bomboniere!™ Party Favor Book. Set aside.
- Using royal icing, make 18 tip 104 pansies (p. 102) with tip 1 loop centers (make extras to allow for breakage). Set aside.
- Ice 2-layer cakes smooth. Prepare cakes for stacked construction (see p. 106).
- On 6 in. Round Cake: Dot mark 1 in. down from top edge at 1 1/2 in. intervals around cake. Using 1 in. mark as a starting point, make tip 2 double dropstrings. Pipe tip 8 fleurs-de-lis (see p. 98) at string tops. Edge base with tip 504 "c" motion shell border and top with tip 502 shell border.
- On 10 in. Square Cake: Divide sides into 3rds. Drop tip 2 string 1 1/4 in. down and half the width of the marked side section. Continue dropping strings 1/4 in. apart until 6 are completed to fill each section. Pipe tip 8 fleurs-de-lis between string sections. Pipe tip 504 upright shell at base center of each side. Pipe tip 504 fleurs-de-lis at each corner, edge base with tip 504 "c" motion shell border and top with tip 502 shell border.
- Add flowers, trim with tip 352 leaves. Position heart and couple on cake top. Position favors around cake. Serves 32.

DANCING DOWN THE AISLE

- Ballerina Bear Pan, p. 188
- Tips 1, 3, 4, 16, 21, 101, 101S, 127D, 349, p. 134-139
- Brown, Teal Icing Colors, p. 124
- Flower Nail No. 9, p. 130
- Bomboniere!™ Party Favor Book (Wedded Bliss instructions and materials, p. 22), p. 112
- Bomboniere!™ White Tulle Circles (1 pkg. needed for veil), p. 151
- Bomboniere!™ Pearl Sprays (3 pkgs. needed for veil), p. 149
- Cake Board, Fanci-Foil Wrap, p. 132
- Meringue Powder, p. 125
- Buttercream, Royal Icings, p. 93

- Make desired number of Wedded Bliss party favors, following instructions in Bomboniere!™ Party Favor Book. Set aside.
- Using stiffened buttercream or royal icing, make 25 tip 101 white roses with tip 4 bases. Make 30 tip 101S teal apple blossoms with tip 1 white dots. Let dry.
- Ice sides of cake smooth. Outline facial features and body with tip 3. Pipe in eyes, nose, mouth and shoes with tip 3 (flatten with finger dipped in cornstarch).
- Cover face, legs, sleeves and bodice of dress with tip 16 stars. Add tip 127D double ruffle to bottom of dress. Add tip 3 dots on ruffles, tip 3 cornelli lace to shoes.
- Edge base with tip 21 shells. Add roses, tip 349 leaves and apple blossoms to base.
- Position spray of pearls and tulle "veil". Top with a row of 7 roses. Add tip 349 leaves.
- For bridal bouquet, position roses and apple blossoms. Trim with tip 349 leaves.
- Place party favors around cake. Serves 12.

ARBOR LOVE

- 16 in. Round Pan, p. 175, 179
- 9 and 12 in. Hexagon Pans, p. 180
- Tips 2B, 3, 21, 45, 46, p. 134-139
- Hexagon Separator Plates — 13 in. (2 needed), 10 in. (2 needed); p. 172
- Dowel Rods, p. 172
- Cake Boards, Fanci-Foil Wrap, p. 132
- Bomboniere!™ Party Favors Book (Wedding Day Sparkle instructions and materials, p. 14), p. 112
- Filigree Pillars — 3 in. (2 pkgs. needed), 5 in. (2 pkgs. needed); p. 171
- Blossom Tier Top (2 needed), p. 153
- Everlasting Ornament, p. 155
- White Pearl Beading* 4mm (1 pkg. needed), p. 167
- Buttercream Icing, p. 93
- Silk ivy vines

*Remove pearls before cutting and serving.

- Make desired number of favors, following instructions in Bomboniere!™ Party Favors Book. Set aside.
- Prepare 2-layer cakes for pillar construction (see p. 106). Edge separator plates using tip 46.
- On 16 in. tier: With toothpick mark area 2 ½ in. up from base. Following directions on page 103 and with serrated side of tip 46, pipe lattice work in marked area. Edge top of lattice with smooth side of tip 2B, overpipe with serrated side of tip 46. Position pearl beading (see p. 103).
- Pipe tip 46 double e-motion top border. Pipe tip 3 dots on sides. Edge base border with smooth side of tip 2B, overpipe with serrated side of tip 46.
- On 9 in. and 12 in. tiers: With toothpick, dot mark 2 in. up from bottom of cake at each center side for garland area. Pipe lattice with serrated side of tip 46. Edge top of lattice with tip 45, overpipe with serrated side of tip 46. Position pearl beading (see p. 103). Pipe tip 3 dots on cake sides. Pipe tip 45 stripes along corners of cake, overpipe with serrated side of tip 46. Edge top border with tip 46 e-motion. Add tip 21 rosettes for base borders.
- At reception: Position Everlasting ornament, Blossom Tier Tops, silk ivy vines and favors. *Serves 150.*

    NOTE: The top tier is often saved for the first anniversary. Number of servings given does not include top tier.

ADORING HEARTS
- 8, 16 in. Round Pans, p. 175
- 12 in. Petal Pan, p. 180
- Tips 3, 6, 10, 16, 17, 18, 67, 101, 102, 103, 125, p. 134-139
- Flower Nail No. 9, p. 130
- Ivory, Kelly Green*, Sky Blue* Icing Colors, p. 124
- '93 Pattern Book (Garland Pattern for 16 in. Cake), p. 112
- Bomboniere!™ Party Favors Book (Together Forever instructions and materials, p. 4), p. 112
- Nesting Heart Cookie Cutters, p. 120
- Cake Dividing Set, p. 128
- Meringue Powder, p. 125
- Cake Boards, Fanci-Foil Wrap, p. 132
- Tuk 'N Ruffle, p. 133
- 10, 14 in. Crystal-Clear Plates, 7 ½ in. Twist Legs (2 sets needed), p. 170
- Satin Elegance Ornament, p. 163
- Buttercream, Royal Icings, p. 93

*Combine Kelly Green and Sky Blue Icing Color to achieve leaf shade.

- Make desired number of Together Forever favors, following instructions in Bomboniere!™ Party Favors Book. Set aside.
- Using royal icing make the following: 24 tip 101 roses with tip 3 bases; 38 tip 102 roses with tip 6 bases; 25 tip 103 roses with tip 10 bases. Make 9 tip 67 leaves to trim wedding ornament. Let dry.
- Make royal icing hearts: Using 1¼ in. heart cookie cutter, outline pattern on paper and cover with waxed paper. Pipe 16 tip 16 hearts on waxed paper. Let dry. Trace outline of 2 in. heart cookie cutter on waxed paper and pipe 2 tip 16 hearts. Let dry.

- To prepare 2-layer cakes for push-in pillar construction, see p. 106.
- Using cake dividing set, divide 8 in. round cake into 8ths on top and 2 inches from the bottom. Imprint 1¼ in. heart cutter above 2 in. mark on center of cake. Edge base with tip 18 shell border. Add tip 125 ruffle garland and tip 17 zigzag garland. Trim with tip 3 double drop strings and dots. Outline hearts with tip 16. On top border add tip 17 zigzag garland with tip 3 strings and dots.
- For 12 in. cake, divide each petal section in half, mark 1¼ in. down from top edge. Mark each petal indentation 2 inches from bottom for garlands. Edge base with tip 18 shell border. Add tip 125 ruffle garland and tip 17 zigzag garland. Add tip 3 piped hearts on side of cake. Pipe tip 17 zigzag garland to sides of petal, add tip 3 strings and dots. Add tip 17 zigzag garland top border.
  - Divide 16 in. round cake into 8ths at 1¼ in. from top edge. Mark garland pattern with toothpick. Use 1¼ in. heart cutter to imprint design on cake side. Pipe tip 18 shells at base. Add tip 125 ruffle garland, tip 17 zigzag garland and tip 3 strings, dots and piped hearts. Outline hearts with tip 16. Add tip 17 zigzag garland border to top of cake. Pipe tip 3 hearts on top of cake, tip 3 beads around pillars. Position roses and add tip 67 leaves.
- At reception: Add royal icing hearts to cake. Top with Satin Elegance ornament. Position favors around cake. *Serves 137.*

LONGING FOR LACE

- Heart Pan Set (6, 9, 15 ½ in. used), p. 183
- Tips 2, 8, p. 134
- Pink Icing Color, p. 124
- '93 Pattern Book (Lace Pieces Pattern), p. 112
- Heart Separator Plate, 11 in., p. 172
- 7 in. Grecian Spiked Pillars (3 needed), p. 171
- Cake Boards, Fanci-Foil Wrap, Tuk 'N Ruffle, p. 132-133
- Bomboniere!™ Party Favors Book (The Epicure instructions and materials, p. 28), p. 112
- Wired Shaping Ribbon, White (2 pkgs. needed to wrap around cakes), p. 150
- Instant Bow Ribbon, ⁵/₁₆" Pink (3 pkgs. needed to wrap around cakes and make bouquets), p. 150
- Mini Bouquets (1 pkg. needed), p. 153
- Sweet Together Ornament, p. 158
- Glucose, p. 130
- Glycerine, Almond Extract, Meringue Powder p. 125
- Royal, Buttercream Icings, p. 93
- Rolled Fondant (3 recipes needed), p. 94

- Following instructions in Bomboniere!™ Party Favors Book, make desired number of The Epicure napkin holders. Set aside.
- Using Lace Pieces Pattern, royal icing, and directions on page 103, make 170 tip 2 Lace Pieces (make extras to allow for breakage). Let dry.
- Cover 2-layer cakes with fondant following instructions on page 94. Arrange the two 6 in. tiers and the 15 in. tier on foil and Tuk-N-Ruffle covered boards. Position 9 in. tier on Heart Separator Plate. Prepare 15 in. tier for push-in leg construction (see p. 106).
- Remove wire from Wired Shaping Ribbon, and remove the string from 1 package of Instant Bow Ribbon and press with warm iron to eliminate creases. Wrap the ribbon around cakes as shown, secure with icing. Edge bases of all cakes with tip 8 bead borders. Trim edge of ribbon with tip 2 beads and attach royal icing lace pieces.
- Make two Instant Bows using 36 in. Instant Bow Ribbon for each, following package directions. Cut 8 Instant Bow Ribbon lengths, each approximately 12 in. long. Make 2 bouquets using one Mini Bouquet and 4 lengths of ribbon for each.
- On top of 15 in. tier, mark a heart pattern 2 inches in from edge of cake; pipe tip 2 beads around pillars. Outline heart marking with tip 2 beads, add Lace Pieces.
- Attach Instant Bows to points of 9 and 15 in. tiers.
- At Reception: Position tier on pillars. Add Sweet Together ornament and Mini Bouquets as shown. Arrange napkins in holders around cakes. Serves 98.

- Make desired number of Echoes favors, following instructions in Bomboniere!™ Party Favors Book, using Lilac, Peach and Pink Tulle Circles. Set aside.
- Using royal icing and the 1 5/8 in. Lily Nail, make 75 tip 104 and 16 tip 103 Petunias with tip 13 centers (make extras to allow for breakage). Add 3 stamens to each. Let dry.
- Prepare 2-layer cakes for push-in leg construction (see p. 106). Using Cake Dividing Set, divide 12 in. and 8 in. rounds into 8ths. Divide each side of 16 in. square into 3rds.

- On 16 in. Square Tier: At each division, measure 3 in. up from base of cake. Edge base border with tip 18 shells. Between division marks, pipe tip 127 double ruffle garland, edged with tip 16 shells. Add tip 16 rosettes at garland points. Edge top border with tip 16 shells.

- On 12 in. Round Tier: Press pattern at 4 alternating divisions around cake. Outline with tip 16. At the alternating 4 divisions pipe a tip 125 garland 5 in. wide and 1 1/4 in. deep. Edge garland with tip 16 shells. Edge base with tip 18 shell border and top with tip 16 shell border.
- On 8 in. Round Tier: Mark 1 1/4 in. down from top of cake for center of garland. Pipe tip 124 ruffle garland between division marks. Edge garland with tip 16 shells. Add tip 16 rosettes at garland points. Edge base with tip 18 shell border and top with tip 16 shell border.
- Position Petunias as shown with dots of icing. Add tip 352 leaves.
- At Reception: Position tiers on pillars, and Rejoice ornament on top. Arrange Echoes favors around cake. *Serves 184.*

NOTE: The top tier is often saved for the first anniversary. Number of servings does not include top tier.

SOARING SPIRITS

- 10 in. Square Pan, 7, 12, 16 in. Round Pans, p. 174-175
- Tips 1, 2B, 12, 46, 789, p. 134-139
- Arched Tier Set, p. 171
- 4 ½ in. Arched Pillars (1 pkg. needed), p. 171
- Cake Dividing Set, p. 128
- 4 mm. Pearl Beading* (2 pkgs. needed),
  6 mm. Pearl Beading* (2 pkgs. needed), p. 167
- Kolor Flo Fountain, Flower Ring, p. 169
- Plastic Dowel Rods, p. 172
- Cake Boards, Fanci-Foil Wrap, Tuk 'N Ruffle, p. 132-133
- 9 in. Separator Plates (2 needed), p. 173
- Bomboniere!™ Party Favors Book
  (Wired Shaping Ribbon Rose, p. 32), p. 112
- Bombiniere!™ White Wired Shaping Ribbon
  (6 pkgs. needed), p. 150
- Bomboniere!™ Iridescent Leaves (4 pkgs. needed), p. 152
- Bomboniere!™ Pearl Stamens (2 pkgs. needed), p. 152
- Bomboniere!™ Favor Saucers (1 pkg. needed), p. 152
- True Love Ornament, p. 156
- Buttercream Icing, p. 93
- 10 yards Tulle, 6 in. wide
- Fresh greens and baby's breath
- Hot glue gun

*Remove pearls before cutting and serving.

- Make 25 Wired Shaping Ribbon Roses following instructions in Bomboniere!™ Party Favors Book. Trim stamen wires from 10 roses; glue these roses onto favor saucers. Cut six 1 yard lengths from tulle roll; make shoelace-style bow from each 1-yard length; pull bow tight at center and puff out slightly. Tie each bow behind a rose, using wires from stamens. Set all aside.
- To prepare 2-layer cakes for pillar and stacked construction, see p. 106.

- Ice together four 2-layer 10 in. square cakes to form a 20 in. square cake. Using ribbed side of tip 789, ice a band at bottom edge of cake. With smooth side of tip 46, pipe diagonal lines, 2 in. apart, on band. Position 6mm pearls at top and bottom edge of bottom band. Add tip 12 top bead border. Repeat same process on 12 in. round cake.
- Divide 16 in. round cake into 12ths at bottom edge. Divide top edge again into 12ths, beginning at center of divisions at bottom, creating alternating 12ths from top to bottom. This will form diagonal lines. Repeat on 7 in. round cake, dividing into 6ths at top and bottom. Mark diagonal lines with straight side of garland marker (included in Cake Dividing Set). Add tip 2B (smooth side) bands of icing on either side of diagonal line. On 7 in. cake add 1 strand of 4 mm pearls. On 16 in. cake add 2 strands of 4mm pearls. Fill in between diagonal lines with tip 1 sotas. Add tip 2B (serrated side) top and bottom borders to 7 in. and 16 in. cakes. Add tip 12 bead border to tops of each cake. Place 2 strands of 4 mm pearls on either side of bottom borders. Edge separator plates with tip 12.
- At reception: Assemble cakes. Tie six roses with bows onto pillars, using stamen wires. Trim streamers on bows to an even length when all are on pillars. Make swag by gathering 3 yards of tulle and tucking behind roses/bows on pillars; go twice around pillars. Attach 10 roses in favor saucers to sides of 12 in. round cake, pressing lightly into icing. and at corners of 20 in. square cake with dots of icing. Place remaining roses, greens and baby's breath in flower ring. Position ornament. *Serves 270*

NOTE: The top tier is often saved for the first anniversary. The number of servings given does not include the top tier.

74

- 8, 12, 16 in. Round Pans, p. 175, 179
- Tips 3, 10, 101, 103, 124, 125, 349 p. 134-139
- Black Icing Color, p. 124
- 10 in. Round Separator Plates (2 needed); 14 in. Round Separator Plates (4 needed), p. 173
- Grecian Pillars, 5 in. (3 pkgs. needed), p. 171
- Six-Column Tier Set, p. 171
- Kolor-Flo Fountain, p. 169
- Flower Ring, p. 169
- Bomboniere!™ Party Favors Book (Gift of Love, Formal Occasion instructions and materials, p. 20), p. 112
- White Pearl Beading, 4 mm (4 pkgs. needed); 6mm (2 pkgs. needed)*, p. 167
- Pearl Tier Top, p. 153
- Filigree Stairway (2 needed), p. 169
- Timeless Ornament—Black Tux, p. 155
- Designer Bridesmaids—Black Dress (4 needed), p. 160
- Designer Groomsmen—Black Tux (4 needed), p. 160
- Cake Boards, Fanci-Foil Wrap, p. 132
- Plastic Dowel Rods, p. 172
- Flower Nail #9, p. 130
- Meringue Powder, p. 125
- '93 Pattern Book (Oval Scallops Pattern) p. 112
- Buttercream, Royal Icings, p. 93

Make desired number of favors following instructions in Bomboniere!™ Party Favors Book. Set aside.
- Using royal icing, make 114 tip 101 roses with tip 3 bases. Let dry. Note: Ready-to-use Icing Roses — small, white (p. 126) may be used.
- Prepare 2-layer cakes (8 in., 12 and 16 in. for center; 8 and 12 in. for side tiers) for stacked and pillar construction, see p. 106. Using toothpick, mark Oval Scallops Pattern around top edge of all cakes.
- Add tip 10 bead border to bases of all cakes.
- Pipe tip 103 ruffles over markings. Place 4 mm pearl beading inside each ruffle oval (see p. 103). For 16 in. cake pipe tip 125 double ruffle over bead border. Add 6 mm pearls to center of ruffles. For 8 in. and 12 in. cakes pipe tip 124 double ruffle over bead border, add 6 mm pearls to center of ruffles.
- Position roses, add tip 349 leaves.
- At reception: Position tiers on pillars, position Filigree Stairways, Bridesmaids and Grooms-men, Timeless ornament, Pearl Tier Top, Kolor-Flo Fountain with Flower Ring and favors. Serves 318.

*Remove pearls before cutting and serving.

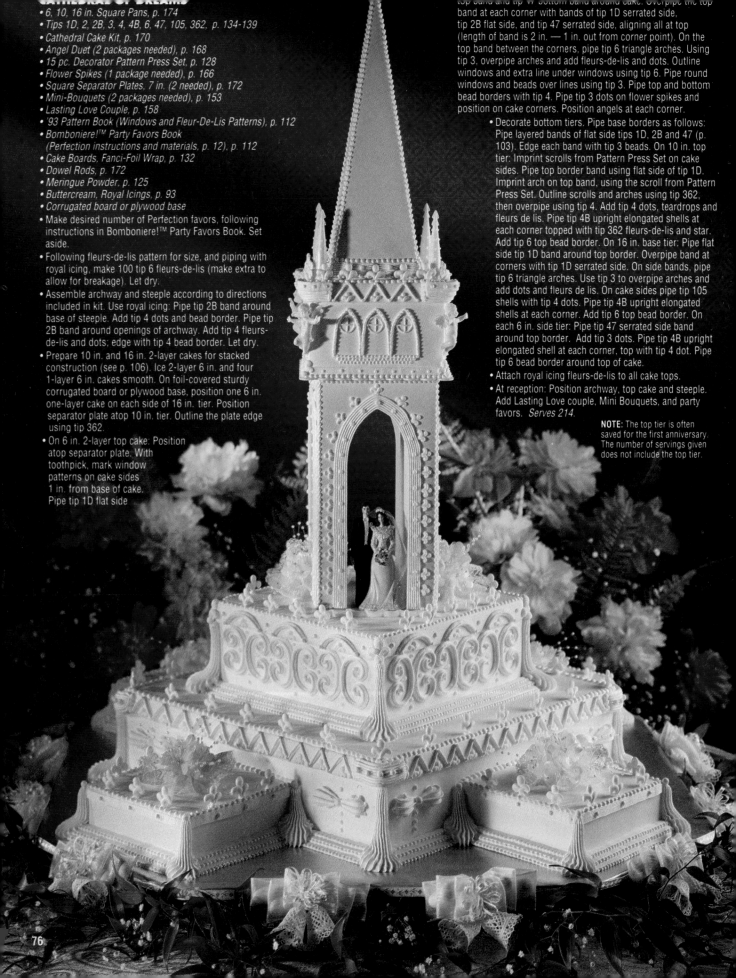

CATHEDRAL OF DREAMS

- 6, 10, 16 in. Square Pans, p. 174
- Tips 1D, 2, 2B, 3, 4, 4B, 6, 47, 105, 362, p. 134-139
- Cathedral Cake Kit, p. 170
- Angel Duet (2 packages needed), p. 168
- 15 pc. Decorator Pattern Press Set, p. 128
- Flower Spikes (1 package needed), p. 166
- Square Separator Plates, 7 in. (2 needed), p. 172
- Mini-Bouquets (2 packages needed), p. 153
- Lasting Love Couple, p. 158
- '93 Pattern Book (Windows and Fleur-De-Lis Patterns), p. 112
- Bomboniere!™ Party Favors Book
  (Perfection instructions and materials, p. 12), p. 112
- Cake Boards, Fanci-Foil Wrap, p. 132
- Dowel Rods, p. 172
- Meringue Powder, p. 125
- Buttercream, Royal Icings, p. 93
- Corrugated board or plywood base
- Make desired number of Perfection favors, following instructions in Bomboniere!™ Party Favors Book. Set aside.
- Following fleurs-de-lis pattern for size, and piping with royal icing, make 100 tip 6 fleurs-de-lis (make extra to allow for breakage). Let dry.
- Assemble archway and steeple according to directions included in kit. Use royal icing: Pipe tip 2B band around base of steeple. Add tip 4 dots and bead border. Pipe tip 2B band around openings of archway. Add tip 4 fleurs-de-lis and dots; edge with tip 4 bead border. Let dry.
- Prepare 10 in. and 16 in. 2-layer cakes for stacked construction (see p. 106). Ice 2-layer 6 in. and four 1-layer 6 in. cakes smooth. On foil-covered sturdy corrugated board or plywood base, position one 6 in. one-layer cake on each side of 16 in. tier. Position separator plate atop 10 in. tier. Outline the plate edge using tip 362.
- On 6 in. 2-layer top cake: Position atop separator plate. With toothpick, mark window patterns on cake sides 1 in. from base of cake. Pipe tip 1D flat side

top band and tip W bottom band around cake. Overpipe the top band at each corner with bands of tip 1D serrated side, tip 2B flat side, and tip 47 serrated side, aligning all at top (length of band is 2 in. — 1 in. out from corner point). On the top band between the corners, pipe tip 6 triangle arches. Using tip 3, overpipe arches and add fleurs-de-lis and dots. Outline windows and extra line under windows using tip 6. Pipe round windows and beads over lines using tip 3. Pipe top and bottom bead borders with tip 4. Pipe tip 3 dots on flower spikes and position on cake corners. Position angels at each corner.

- Decorate bottom tiers. Pipe base borders as follows: Pipe layered bands of flat side tips 1D, 2B and 47 (p. 103). Edge each band with tip 3 beads. On 10 in. top tier: Imprint scrolls from Pattern Press Set on cake sides. Pipe top border band using flat side of tip 1D. Imprint arch on top band, using the scroll from Pattern Press Set. Outline scrolls and arches using tip 362, then overpipe using tip 4. Add tip 4 dots, teardrops and fleurs de lis. Pipe tip 4B upright elongated shells at each corner topped with tip 362 fleurs-de-lis and star. Add tip 6 top bead border. On 16 in. base tier: Pipe flat side tip 1D band around top border. Overpipe band at corners with tip 1D serrated side. On side bands, pipe tip 6 triangle arches. Use tip 3 to overpipe arches and add dots and fleurs de lis. On cake sides pipe tip 105 shells with tip 4 dots. Pipe tip 4B upright elongated shells at each corner. Add tip 6 top bead border. On each 6 in. side tier: Pipe tip 47 serrated side band around top border. Add tip 3 dots. Pipe tip 4B upright elongated shell at each corner, top with tip 4 dot. Pipe tip 6 bead border around top of cake.
- Attach royal icing fleurs-de-lis to all cake tops.
- At reception: Position archway, top cake and steeple. Add Lasting Love couple, Mini Bouquets, and party favors. *Serves 214.*

NOTE: The top tier is often saved for the first anniversary. The number of servings given does not include the top tier.

- 8 in. x 3 in. high Round Pans, p. 175, 179
- 18 in. Half Round Pans, p. 179
- Tips 1, 2, 2B, 3, 5, 7, 14, 48, p. 134-139
- 12 in. Round Plate from Crystal Clear Cake Divider Set, p. 170
- 17 in. Round Crystal-Look Plates (2 needed), p. 171
- 13 3/4 in. Crystal Look Pillars (4 needed), p. 171
- Plastic Dowel Rods, p. 172
- Kolor-Flo Fountain, p. 169
- 15-Pc. Decorator Pattern Press Set, p. 128
- Cake Boards, Fanci-Foil Wrap, p. 132
- Bomboniere!™ Party Favors Book (Pretty Purse instructions and materials, p. 20; Basic Tulle Puff Instructions, p. 30), p. 112
- "I Do" p. 156
- Designer Bridesmaids, Pink (4 needed), Designer Groomsmen, (4 needed), p. 160
- Buttercream Icing, p. 93
- 10 in. x 3 in. high styrofoam round (to hold fountain) Needed for cake ornaments (decorative puffs):
- Pink Tulle Circles (1 pkg. needed), p. 151
- Pearl Sprays (4 pkgs. needed), 1 in. Iridescent Leaves (1 pkg. needed), 4 mm Pearls (1 pkg. needed), p. 152
- Flower Spikes (1 pkg. needed), p. 166
- Florist Wire, p. 130
- Florist or Cellophane Tape
- Note: 18 in. base tier is made with four half rounds. Prepare 18 in. and 14 in. 2-layer cakes for pillar construction (see p. 106). Add extra dowel rods to 14 in. tier, position 12 in. round clear cake divider plate atop 14 in. cake. Cut 7 in. round out of center of styrofoam; cut a wedge in top side to accommodate fountain cord. Ice styrofoam ring smooth and position on 12 in. round plate.
- Make desired number of Pretty Purse favors, following instructions in Bomboniere!™ Party Favors Book. Set aside.
- Ice two 10 in. 2-layer rounds, two 8 in. 1-layer rounds, one 8 in. x 3 in. high one-layer round and half rounds to make one 18 in. 2-layer round smooth.

Pipe over imprints with tip 7, then overpipe with tip 1.
- On 10 in. styrofoam ring and 8 in. x 3 in. 1-layer tier, use tip 2 for the following: Pipe double drop string at end points of scrolls. Pipe a vertical line between scrolls that ends 1 1/4 in. up from base. Trim line and strings with dots.
- On the two 10 in., 14 in., and 18 in. tiers, use tip 2 for the following: Pipe a series of vertical lines alternating in counts of 7 and 9 on sides as shown, with the longest string 1 1/4 in. up from base. Pipe a series of 3 vertical lines with the longest line ending 1 1/4 in. down from top edge. Trim all with tip 2 dots.
  - On the two 8 in. 1-layer tiers, use tip 2 for the following: Pipe a series of 5 vertical lines with the longest line ending 1 in. up from the base. Trim with dots.
  - Edge tier bases: On 8 in. 1-layer tiers pipe tip 48 bands around sides and at base. Trim with tip 3 bead border. On all other tiers pipe tip 2B (serrated edge) bands around sides and at base. Trim with tip 5 bead border.
  - Assemble all four cake top ornaments as follows: Make basic tulle puffs according to directions in Bomboniere!™ Party Favors Book, using 2 tulle circles for each. Cut 12 pieces of florist wire, 4 at 16 in., 4 at 14 in., 4 at 12 in. Wrap pearls around wire, leaving wire bare 2 in. from each side. Twist together to form a loop of pearls. Combine 2 tulle puffs, 12 pearl sprays, 3 graduated-size wired pearl loops and 3 iridescent leaves. Tape together and insert into flower spike.
  - At reception: Position 8 in. x 3 in. layer on 18 in. base tier before adding pillars. Position 14 in. cake and styrofoam iced cake on plate. Position fountain in styrofoam cake, run the cord down the side of pillar and fasten with wire. Add water to fountain. Position bridesmaids, groomsmen, and "I Do" ornament Place favors around cake. *Serves 307.*

77

- 15" Heart Pan, p. 183
- Tips 2B, 32, 301, 362, p. 134-39
- Ivory Icing Color, p. 124
- Cake Boards, Tuk-N-Ruffle, Fanci-Foil Wrap, p. 132
- Golden Jubilee Ornament, p. 164
- 6 mm Pearl Beading* (1 pkg. needed), p. 167
- Bomboniere!™ Wired Shaping Ribbon, White and Gold (1 pkg. each needed), p. 150
- Stamens (1 pkg. needed), p. 130
- Bomboniere!™ Party Favors Book (Sweet Remembrance instructions and materials, p. 6; Wired Shaping Ribbon Rose, p. 32), p. 112
- Buttercream Icing, p. 93
- Assemble desired number of party favors and 5 additional Wired Shaping Ribbon Roses as shown following instructions in Bomboniere!™ Party Favors Book. Set aside.

basketweave (p. 99). Mark where ornament will be positioned; mark 1" from edge, add tip 301 message. Add tip 362 zigzag to cake top. Pipe tip 32 rope for top border. Edge base border with tip 32 rope; add tip 362 zigzags next to rope. Position pearl beading.

- Attach 5 roses onto ornament with stamen wires. Position ornament on cake top. Arrange party favors around cake. *Serves 32.*

*Remove pearls before cutting and serving.

JUBILATION

- 8, 10, 12 in. Round Pans, (3" deep), p. 175, 179
- Tips 2, 4, 6, 10, 12, 104, p. 134, 138
- 10, 12, 14 in. Tall Tier Plates, 7 ³/₄" columns, (2 needed), Top Nut, Base Bolt, p. 170
- 1 ¹/₄" Gold Artificial Leaves, (1 pkg. needed), p. 165
- Decorating Comb, Cake Dividing Set, p. 128
- Cake Corer Tube, p. 170
- Cake Boards, p. 132
- Flower Nail No. 7, p. 130
- Meringue Powder, p. 125
- Bomboniere!™ Party Favors Book (Top Of The World instructions and materials, p. 8), p. 112
- Bomboniere!™ Pouched Gathering Ribbon 2 ³/₈ in. Gold (4 pkgs. needed), p. 150
- 50 Years of Happiness Ornament, p. 164
- Buttercream, Royal icings, p. 93
- Make desired number of Top Of The World favors, following instructions in Bomboniere!™ Party Favors Book.
- Using royal icing, make 30 tip 104 roses with tip 12 bases. Let dry.
- Cut 2 yards of Pouched Gathering Ribbon to make ruffled base. Gather together and place on cake board.
- Ice one-layer cakes smooth. Prepare cakes for tall tier construction (see p. 107). Using Cake Dividing Set, dot mark 8 in. rounds into 8ths, 10 in. rounds into 10ths (Note: eliminate 2 marks from front of 10 in. round as space for message), 12 in. rounds into 12ths. Mark 1 ¹/₂" down from cake top to center of drape design with a dot of icing.
- Using decorating comb, move in a drape motion between dividing dots. Finish off bottom of drapes with tip 4 zigzag. Add tip 6 top bead and tip 10 bottom bead borders. Position roses and leaves. Add tip 2 message.
- For ruffles around columns, cut six 1-yard pieces of Pouched Gathering Ribbon, pull string, wrap 3 around each column and tie. Position ornament, party favors. *Serves 48.*

PICTURE PERFECT ANNIVERSARY

- *10 in. and 14 in. Round Pans, p. 175, 179*
- *Tips 1, 2, 4B, 789, p. 134-139*
- *10, 14, 18 in. Cake Circles, Fanci-Foil Wrap, p. 132*
- *Tuk-N-Ruffle, p. 133*
- *Pearl Tier Tops, p. 153*
- *Bomboniere!™ Party Favors Book (Top Of The World instructions and materials p. 8), p. 112*
- *Floating Tier Stand, p. 170*
- *Make Any Message Letter Press Set, p. 128*
- *Buttercream Icing, p. 93*
- *Picture Frames, Silver Dragees*
- Assemble desired number of party favors following instructions in Bomboniere!™ Party Favors Book. Set aside.
- Position 2 layer cakes on boards, ice smooth. Pipe a band of icing around base of each cake using the smooth side of tip 789. Add Tuk-N-Ruffle. Cover icing band with tip 1 cornelli lace (see p. 97). Note: A 10 in. foil-covered cake board is positioned on the top tier of the stand with the picture frames atop.
- Pipe tip 4B upright shells around base of cakes. Pipe crown border on top of cakes using tip 4B (see p. 103). At the end point of each upright shell and crown pipe tip 2 dots; trim with silver dragees.
- Using letter press set, imprint message on cake sides; pipe tip 2 message.
- Position cakes and frames on stand. Add tier tops on each cake top. Position favors around cake. *Serves 64.*

GOLDEN MOMENTS

- Viennese Swirl Pan, p. 181
- Tips 1D, 2, p. 134, 139
- Lemon Yellow Icing Color, p. 124
- Bomboniere!™ 4 mm. Pearl Beading* (1 pkg. needed), p. 167
- Bomboniere!™ Filigree Heart Boxes (6 needed), p. 152
- Opulence Wedding Ornament, p. 157
- Cake Board, Fanci-Foil Wrap, Tuk 'N Ruffle, p. 132-133
- Poured Fondant, Buttercream Icings, p. 93
- Make fondant according to recipe on p. 93.
- Place cake on a rack over a drip pan; cover with poured fondant icing. Let set.
- Add tip 2 dots at edges of swirls.
- Using smooth side of tip 1D, add an elongated scallop border.
- Place filigree heart boxes on base of cake. Place pearls in each heart box and around cake base. Position ornament in center of cake before serving. *Serves 12.*

*Remove pearls before cutting.

SERENITY OF TIME

- 4 pc. Hexagon Pan Set (9 and 12 in. pans are used), p. 180
- Tips 2, 5, 7, 18, 102, 127, 352, p. 134-139
- Flower Nail No. 9, p. 130
- Violet Icing Color, p. 124
- 13 in. Hexagon Separator Plates (2 needed), p. 172
- Cake Board, p. 132
- Swan Pillars (4 needed), p. 171
- Dowel Rods, p. 172
- Bomboniere!™ Party Favors Book (Gliding Swans favor instructions and materials, p. 8), p. 112
- Buttercream Icing, p. 93
- Make Gliding Swans favors in the amount you desire, following instructions in Bomboniere!™ Party Favors Book. Set aside.
- Make 12 tip 102 roses with tip 7 bases, using stiffened buttercream or royal icing. Let dry.
- Prepare cakes for stacked construction (p. 106).
- Ice two-layer cakes smooth. With toothpick, mark each corner of hexagon 2 1/2" from base and again at 3 1/4" from base. (This determines where ruffles will be placed.)
- Write tip 2 message.
- Add tip 18 bottom shell borders to 9 in. and 12 in. cakes. Add tip 127 ruffles to cakes; 2 rows to 9 in. and 3 rows to 12 in. cakes. Add tip 5 beads on top edges of ruffles and as top borders of cake. Pipe tip 2 dots on ruffles.
- Position roses in corners and trim with tip 352 leaves.
- To serve: Position cakes on pillars and place favors on and around cakes. *Serves 42.*

SEASHELL SALUTE

- Shell Pan, p. 181
- Tips 2, 3, 104, 190, 225, 349, p. 134, 139
- Kelly Green, Teal Icing Colors*, p. 124
- Cake Board, Fanci-Foil Wrap, p. 132
- Meringue Powder, p. 125
- Bomboniere!™ Party Favors Book (Treasured Forever instructions and materials, p. 20; Basic Tulle Puff and Ruffle instructions, p. 30, 31), p.112
- Buttercream, Royal Icings, p. 93
- 1 1/2 Recipes Quick-Pour Fondant, p. 93

Needed for cake ornament (bells):
- 2-2 5/8 In. Filigree Bells, Romantic Heart Base 3 1/4 In., p. 166
- 2 Tulle Circles, Mint, p. 151
- 18 In. Gathering Ribbon 2"" Striped Iridescent White, p. 150
- 1 Favor Saucer, 1 Rubber Band, p. 152

*2 parts Kelly Green, 1 part Teal combined produces the aqua shade shown for cake and flowers—use more color for darker shade.

- Using royal icing, make approximately 32 tip 190 drop flowers (darker shade) and 132 tip 225 drop flowers (38 darker shade, 94 lighter shade). Add tip 3 dot centers to all. Let dry.
- Lightly ice cake with thinned buttercream icing. Cover with poured fondant. Let set.
- Add tip 3 message.
- Using buttercream icing, edge base with tip 104. Position flowers with dots of icing around cake sides and base. Trim with tip 2 dots and tip 349 leaves.
- Assemble cake top ornament as follows: Make a basic tulle puff using tulle circles, favor saucer, rubber band. Glue the 2 bells onto the top portion of the Romantic Heart Base; glue tulle puff behind bells. Ruffle the gathering ribbon into a circle, glue to back of puff. Attach flowers to inside of bells with dots of icing; trim with tip 349 leaves.
- Assemble desired number of party favors, following instructions in Bomboniere!™ Party Favors Book.
- Position ornament on cake top. Arrange party favors around cake. Serves 12.

UNFORGETTABLE DECADE

- Round Tier Set, p. 180
- Tips 3, 57, 362, 363, p. 134-139
- Creamy Peach Icing Color, p. 124
- Cake Dividing Set, p. 128
- Cake Boards, Fanci-Foil Wrap, 12 in. Ruffle Board (1 needed), p. 132-33
- Petite Anniversary Years Ornament, p. 164
- Bomboniere!™ Party Favors Book (Love Story instructions and materials, p. 18), p.112
- Bomboniere!™ Instant Bow Ribbon 5/16 in. White (2 1/2 yards needed), p. 150
- Small Doves (1 pkg. needed), p. 166
- Buttercream Icing, p. 93

- Make desired number of Love Story party favors, following instructions in Bomboniere!™ Party Favors Book. Set aside.
- To color anniversary numeral: Pipe tip 3 icing to cover number and pat smooth with finger dipped in cornstarch.
- Ice 2-layer cakes smooth. Use cake divider to divide each cake into fourths. Pipe tip 57 "ribbons" using "e" motion to create loops.
- Add tip 362 top and tip 363 bottom shell borders.
- Using tip 362, pipe 5 stars on cake sides. Add tip 3 dots around bottom border and stars. Position doves at each "ribbon" end.
- To make bows: Cut one 18" length of ribbon and two 36" lengths of ribbon. Make 3 Instant Bows following package directions. Add the 18" bow to the ornament and place on top tier. Position one 36" bow on each of the bottom two tiers. Position favors around cake. Serves 24.

The Best of Times

HEART TO HEART

- 9 in. Heart Pans, p. 183
- Tips 3, 5, 18, 101, 104, 352, p. 134-139
- Flower Nail No. 9, p. 130
- Pink, Leaf Green Icing Colors, p. 124
- Cake Boards, Fanci-Foil Wrap, Tuk-N-Ruffle, p. 132-33
- Meringue Powder, p. 125
- Seed Pearl Hearts (2 needed), p. 169
- '93 Pattern Book (Heart Pattern), p. 112
- Bomboniere!™ Party Favors Book (Two Hearts As One instructions and materials, p. 12), p.112
- Royal, Buttercream Icings, p. 93
- Make desired number of Two Hearts As One party favors, following instructions in Bomboniere!™ Party Favors Book. Set aside.
- Using royal icing, make 22 tip 101 roses with tip 5 bases. Let dry.
- Ice 2-layer cakes smooth. With toothpick, mark at 2 ½ in. intervals around cake, mark 3 dots of icing at 1 ½ in., 2 ¼ in. and 2 ½ in. from bottom of cake for garland and strings. Using Heart Pattern, mark heart with toothpick at point of each 2 ½ in. string mark. Outline hearts with tip 3 beads. Position Seed Pearl Hearts and write tip 3 message.

- Pipe top border with tip 5 beads.
- Pipe tip 18 shell base border. Using tip 104, add double ruffle garland over shell border. Then add 2 rows of tip 3 drop strings above ruffles.
- Position the two cakes side by side and add roses with tip 352 leaves. Position favors around cakes as desired. Serves 28.

Note: Decorate each cake separately on separate cake boards cut to size. Next, position side-by-side on Tuk-N-Ruffle Board. Decorate as instructed above.

83

SNUGGLY WARM QUILT

- 12 x 18 in. Sheet Pan, p. 174, 179
- Tips 3, 16, 18, 125, p. 134-138
- Peach, Lemon Yellow, Kelly Green Icing Colors, p. 124
- Perimeter Cookie Cutters: hand, butterfly, puppy, locomotive, bear, sailboat, ice cream cone, rocking horse, heart, duck, clown, kitten, bell, p. 120
- Wooden dowel rod, p. 172
- Bomboniere!™ Party Favors Book (Sweet Little One instructions and materials, p. 26), p. 112
- Cake Board, Fanci-Foil Wrap, p.132
- Roll-out Cookie Recipe, p. 105
- Buttercream Icing, p. 93
- Make desired number of favors following instructions

in Bomboniere!™ Party Favors Book. Set aside.
- Cut 5" round and two hand cookies out of cookie dough. Bake and cool. Outline hands with tip 3. Add tip 3 pipe-in dot eyes and dimples (flatten with finger dipped in cornstarch). Pipe tip 16 lock of hair. Pipe tip 3 string mouth.
- Ice cake smooth. Divide cake top into 4 1/8" wide by 4 5/8" long squares. Press cookie cutters into squares.
- Outline imprint with tip 3. Fill in cutter and square area with tip 16 stars. Add tip 125 top ruffle border with tip 16 shell trim. Add tip 18 bottom rosette border.
- Position hands. Attach dowel rod to back of baby's head with buttercream icing. Push into cake. Position party favors near cake. *Serves 30.*

BABE IN THE WOODS

- Stand-up Panda Bear Pan, p. 188
- Tips 4, 8, 352, p. 134-136
- 8 in. Cake Boards (2 needed), Fanci-Foil Wrap, p. 132
- Bomboniere!™ Party Favors Book (Celebrate Baby instructions and materials, p. 26), p. 112
- Bomboniere!™ 5/16" White Instant Bow (2 yds. needed), p. 150
- Buttercream Icing, p. 93
- Make desired number of favors, following instructions in Bomboniere!™ Party Favors Book. Set aside.
- Ice cake with thin layer of icing.
- Ice diaper area smooth, front and back.
- Pipe tip 4 dots for eyes and nose. Outline arms with tip 4.
- Cover entire bear with tip 4 rows of overlapping loops to create a crocheted look.
- Pipe tip 8 knot at ends of diaper. Pipe excess cloth on diaper below knot with tip 352 pull-out leaves.
- Pull Instant Bow string to make bow and position on head. place favors around cake. *Serves 12.*

PIN YOUR HOPES ON BABY

- 2 Pc. Oval Pan Set, p. 180
- Tips 5, 16, 21, p. 134-35
- Royal Blue, Pink Icing Colors, p. 124
- '93 Pattern Book (Safety Pin Pattern), p. 112
- Bomboniere!™ Party Favors Book (Great Expectations instructions and materials, p. 24), p. 112
- Cake Boards, Fanci-Foil Wrap, p. 132
- Buttercream Icing, p. 93
- Make desired number of favors, following instructions in Bomboniere!™ Party Favors Book. Set aside.
- Ice two 2-layer cakes smooth. With tooth-pick, mark Safety Pin Pattern on cake tops.
- Outline safety pin details with tip 5; fill-in with tip 16 stars.
- Edge base border with 2 rows of tip 21 stars. Pipe tip 16 and tip 21 stars randomly on cake sides.
- Position party favors around cakes. *Each Cake Serves 12.*

A Star Is Born

84

ROSES ARE PINK
ROSES ARE BLUE
A HAPPY BABY
IS OUR WISH FOR YOU

MIDNIGHT FEEDING

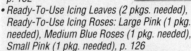

- *Pretty Lady Pan, p. 189*
- *Tips 1A, 3, 8, 12, 13, 16, 48, p. 134-139*
- *Pink, Copper, Royal Blue, Lemon Yellow Icing Colors, p. 124*
- *Cake Board, Fanci-Foil Wrap, p. 132*
- *'93 Pattern Book (Mom and Baby Pattern), p. 112*
- *Bomboniere!™ Party Favors Book (Winning Formula Instructions and Materials, p. 24), p. 112*
- *Baby Things Ready-To-Use Icing Decorations (baby bottle), p. 126*
- *Buttercream Icing, p. 93*

- Assemble desired number of party favors following instructions in Bomboniere!™ Party Favors Book. Set aside.
- Ice top and sides of cake smooth with spatula. Mark Mom and Baby Pattern with toothpick. Outline mom's facial features, robe and blanket with tip 3. Use tip 1A to pipe a mound of icing for baby's head and body under blanket. Smooth with finger dipped in cornstarch. Pipe tip 3 facial features and hair on baby. Cover baby's blanket with rows of tip 13 shells, mom's face, robe and hand with tip 16 stars. Add tip 48 ribbed stripe headband. Pipe tip 16 side-by- side stripe hair. Fill in robe edging and ties with tip 8 piping. Flatten with finger dipped in cornstarch. Position "baby bottle" icing decoration. Pipe tip 3 fingers holding bottle.
- To create baby bracelet border effect: Make a series of four tip 12 white balls, followed by a series of five tip 8 pink balls. Print tip 3 "baby" on each set of white balls.
- Arrange party favors around cake. *Serves 12.*

TO A LONG LIFE

- *Long Loaf Pan, p. 181*
- *Tips 3, 18, p. 134-135*
- *Royal Blue Icing Color, p. 124*
- *Cake Boards, Fanci-Foil Wrap, p. 132*
- *Ready-To-Use Icing Leaves (2 pkgs. needed), Ready-To-Use Icing Roses: Large Pink (1 pkg. needed), Medium Blue Roses (1 pkg. needed), Small Pink (1 pkg. needed), p. 126*
- *Bomboniere!™ Party Favors Book (Baby's 1st Step Instructions and Materials, p. 24), p. 112*
- *Rainbow Jimmy Sprinkle Decorations, p. 127*
- *Buttercream Icing, p. 93*

- Make Baby's 1st Step favors, following instructions in Bomboniere!™ Party Favors Book. Set aside.
- Prepare Long Loaf, adding 6 tablespoons of Rainbow Jimmies to batter. Bake and cool.
- Ice cake smooth with spatula. Pipe tip 3 printed message. With toothpick, mark every ½ in. around top edge of cake. Pipe tip 3 overlapping single drop strings at each point. Add tip 3 "e" motion design to top border. Edge base with tip 18 star border.
- Position roses, leaves, sprinkles and favors. *Serves 12.*

PATTYCAKES

- *Six-Cup Standard Muffin Pan, p. 181*
- *Tip 2D, p. 137*
- *Pink, Royal Blue Icing Colors, p. 124*
- *Teddy Bear Standard Baking Cups, p. 127*
- *"Baby Things" Ready-To-Use Icing Decorations, p. 126*
- *Rainbow Nonpareils Sprinkle Decorations, p. 127*
- *Buttercream Icing, p. 93*

- Pipe tip 2D swirling motion icing on cupcake tops. Add nonpareils. Position icing decorations. *Each serves one.*

BEARLY A BABY

- *Mini Bears Pan, p. 188*
- *Tips 1, 4, 16, 127, p. 134-139*
- *Pink, Royal Blue, Brown Icing Colors, p. 124*
- *Baby Things Ready-To-Use Icing Decorations, p. 126*
- *Bomboniere!™ Party Favors Book (Bundle of Joy Instructions and Materials, p. 26), p. 112*
- *Cake Board, Fanci-Foil Wrap, p. 132*
- *Buttercream Icing, p. 93*

- Assemble desired number of party favors following instructions in Bomboniere!™ Party Favors Book. Set aside.
- Ice sides and diaper area of bears smooth.
- Outline paws, nose and diaper area with tip 4. Pipe in nose and eyes with tip 4. Flatten with finger dipped in cornstarch. Cover body with tip 16 stars.
- On baby girls: add tip 127 ruffled bonnet with tip 4 strings.
- On baby boys: pipe tip 4 pacifiers and tip 4 diaper ties.
- Add tip 1 highlights to eyes. Edge cakes with tip 16 star borders, position decorations and favors. *Each serves 1.*

Time Saver

Baby Shower

87

florist tape and insert into flower spikes; push spikes into cake. Tie Instant Bows on pillars.

- Attach drop flowers to florist wire with tip 4. (See p. 101 for "To Attach Flowers & Leaves to Wire Stems" instructions.) Add tip 349 leaves to flowers. Write tip 3 message.
- Position Lovely Lamb favors around cake. *Serves 64.*

TRAVELLING FIRST CLASS

- *7 x 11" in. Sheet Pan, p. 174*
- *Egg Pan Set, p. 186*
- *6-pc. Nesting Round Cookie Cutter Set (3 1/2 in. size used), p. 120*
- *Tips 2, 17, 20, 32, 47, 127, 225, 349, p. 134-139*
- *Creamy Peach, Teal, Violet Icing Colors, p. 124*
- *5 in. Grecian Pillars (4 needed), p. 171*
- *Cake Boards, Fanci-Foil Wrap, p. 132*
- *Meringue Powder, p. 125*
- *Bomboniere!™ Party Favors Book (Precious Cargo instructions and materials, p. 24), p.112*
- *Bomboniere!™ Instant Bow Ribbon, White, 5/16 in. (4 yards needed), p. 150*
- *White Florist Wire, p. 130*
- *Roll-out Cookie Dough Recipe, p. 105*
- *Rolled Fondant Recipe (1 recipe needed), p. 94*
- *Royal, Buttercream Icings, p. 93*
- *Glue Gun*
- Make desired number of favors, following instructions in Bomboniere Party Favors Book. Set aside.
- Make hood of carriage one to two days ahead of time. To construct hood: lightly grease, with solid vegetable shortening, outside of egg pan 6 inches down from top of pan. With royal icing, ice pan smooth. Cover iced pan with tip 47 basketweave. Let dry 1 to 2 days, then remove. Add tip 127 ruffle to edge.
- For handle: Cut 7 pieces of florist wire to 12 inch length. Twist together to form one thick piece. Fill bag with royal icing and use tip 32 to coat wire (see p. 103). Pull wire out of bag, doing one half at a time. Bend to form handle and let dry. When completely dried, wrap 16 inches of ribbon around handle and add bow (1 yard long).
- With royal icing, make 210 (70 peach, 70 teal, 70 violet) drop flowers with tip 225, add tip 2 white centers. Let dry.
- With 3 1/2 in. round cookie cutter, cut 4 "wheels". Bake and cool. Using buttercream, ice smooth with spatula. Pipe tip 20 elongated shell "spokes" and add drop flowers. Pipe tip 349 leaves. Let set.
- Cut 3 cake boards to 7 x 12 in. Tape together and wrap with Fanci-Foil. Attach pillars to board with glue gun.
- Cut 2 layer cake down to 6 x 11 in. size. Ice cake smooth.
- For pillow, prepare rolled fondant: Roll out white piece of fondant 3 x 2 x 3/4 in. high. Add tip 127 royal icing ruffle and tip 2 bead border.
- For blanket: color rolled fondant peach and roll out a 6 x 6 x 1 in. high piece, place in carriage. Next, roll out a second layer of peach fondant to 6 1/2 x 7 in. size. Lay on top of first piece in carriage and tuck sides under. Fold back top edge on blanket and add tip 2 fringe and dots.
- Cover sides with tip 47 basketweave. Add tip 127 ruffle to base and tip 17 shell border on top of ruffle. Push handle into cake. Position hood of carriage on cake. Cut 2 ribbons, 1 yard long each and pull into bows. Position on sides of carriage hood. Add tip 17 rope border to top edge of carriage. Add drop flowers and tip 349 leaves.
- Add cookie wheels to pillars with icing. Position drop flowers on side of carriage; place favors around cake as desired. *Serves 24.*

LULLABY LAMBS

- *Oval Pan Set (7 3/4 x 5 5/8 in., 10 3/4 x 7 7/8 in. and 13 x 9 7/8 in. pans are used), p. 180*
- *Tips 3, 4, 6, 8, 13, 16, 18, 21, 81, 104, 224, 349, p. 134-139*
- *Pink, Royal Blue, Lemon Yellow, Black, Kelly Green Icing Colors, p. 124*
- *'93 Pattern Book (Garland Pattern), p. 112*
- *8 1/2 x 6 in. Oval Separator Plate, p. 172*
- *7 in. Grecian Spiked Pillars, p. 171*
- *Meringue Powder, p. 125*
- *Flower Spikes (2 needed), p. 166*
- *Cake Boards, Tuk-N-Ruffle, Fanci-Foil Wrap, p. 132, 133*
- *Buttercream, Royal Icings, p. 93*
- *Bomboniere!™ Party Favors Book (for Lovely Lamb favors shown next to cake—instructions and materials, p. 26), p. 112*

For puffs shown on cake:
- *Bomboniere!™ Baby Lambs (5 pkgs. needed), Bomboniere!™ Dotted White Tulle Circles (1 pkg. needed), p. 151*
- *Bomboniere!™ 3/16 in. Instant Bow, 1 pkg. each, pink and blue, p. 150*
- *White Florist Wire, p. 130*
- *White florist tape*
- Make desired number of Lovely Lambs favors (shown around cake), following instructions in Bomboniere!™ Party Favors Book. Set aside.

- Using royal icing, make approximately 200 tip 224 drop flowers (50 each of blue, pink, yellow, green) with tip 3 dot centers. Let dry.
- Prepare 2-layer ovals for pillar and stacked construction, see p. 106.
- Ice all layers smooth. For two-tone effect on top and bottom layers, let white icing set (approximately 15-20 minutes). Make Garland Pattern out of waxed paper and place on coordinating areas. With pink icing, frost exposed areas smooth. Remove waxed paper.
- On top tier add tip 104 ruffle along garland mark. Add tip 3 bead border on ruffle. Pipe tip 3 dots on pink area. Pipe tip 18 shells for base border, tip 16 shells for top border. Pipe tip 104 bows on each side of cake.
- Figure Pipe lambs on middle tier
  Use tip 8 for body, tip 6 for legs, tip 13 reverse shell for hair, tip 81 for ears, tip 3 for eyes.
- On middle tier, pipe tip 104 ruffles at top and edge. Add tip 16 shells between ruffles. Pipe tip 18 shell for base border.
- On bottom tier, pipe tip 104 ruffle along garland mark and add tip 3 beads. Add tip 3 dots to cake sides. Add tip 18 shells to top border. For base border, pipe tip 21 shells, place drop flowers between shells and add tip 349 leaves. Pipe tip 104 bows on sides of cake.
- To make puffs on cakes, assemble gathered tulle circles, Instant Bows, lambs on wire. Secure with

Bundles of Joy

Everyone Can Enjoy Cake Decorating!

Beginners and hobbyists alike will find cake decorating fun, easy and very rewarding. A personally decorated special occasion cake will delight the recipient and prove rewarding for the decorator. The following guide will provide you with the basics of cake decorating as well as more advanced techniques. With just a little practice, you can make specific decorations described in this section that will enable you to create cakes in the "idea" section of this Yearbook. And, if you've already gained some experience with cake decorating, the pages ahead are great for review and new inspirations.

Cake Decorating Equipment

You will need basic cake decorating tools and some of your own kitchen tools and supplies. Here are some basic Wilton tools you will want to make your decorating more fun and rewarding.

Cake Stands, Separator Plates & Cake Circles & Boards
Wilton Cake Stands hold your cake and allow you to rotate the cake while you decorate. Separator plates and cake boards help support your tiered cakes (when you become more advanced!) with the use of pretty pillars. Use dowel rods for tiered cake support.

Cake Tops & Trims
Wilton cake tops are made of fine plastic and molded to fun character, animal and decorative shapes for quick and easy cake decorating. They dress up a cake so special and personalize it for most any celebration. And they become treasured keepsakes after the party.

Coupler
Grooved insert and retainer ring designed to allow tip changes on Wilton Featherweight or disposable decorating bags. This two-piece time-saver eliminates the need for a clean decorating bag every time you wish to use a different tip.

Decorating Bag
A plastic polyester-coated fabric cone, clear plastic cone or parchment paper bag that holds your decorator icing and special tip.

Decorating Tips
Cone-shaped, open-ended metal tips that drop into the decorating bag or attach to a coupler. When icing is squeezed through the tip, the size and shape of the opening determines the types of decorating produced.

Flower Nail
A round, flat metal nailhead used as a turntable for making icing roses and other special flowers.

Icing Colors & Flavors
Wilton Icing Colors are concentrated in a creamy, rich base which will not change your icing consistency. Wilton Flavors are delicious to add to icing or batter for taste appeal.

Cake Decorating Terms to Know

These words are frequently used in cake decorating. Use this as a reference when decorating your cakes.

Attach
To secure royal or buttercream icing flowers or plastic decorations, pipe dots or icing to "attach" the decoration to an iced cake. Royal icing dries hard and is more permanent than buttercream. Use your icing to attach as you would use "glue."

Border
A continuous decoration used around the top, side or base of a cake.

Elongated
When we use the term elongated shells, leaves, etc., it means to taper an icing decoration by relaxing bag pressure and moving before stopping the technique.

Figure Piping
Decorating technique used to form figures out of icing.

Filling
Frosting, preserves or pudding that's spread between cake layers and holds them together.

Leveling
Removing the "crown" of a cake to provide a flat surface for frosting or decorating.

Outline or Strings
When the outlining method is used, the icing that flows out of the tip to follow contours of a shaped cake or to cover pattern design marks are called "strings" or outlines.

Piping
Squeezing icing out of a bag to form decoration. Also see figure piping.

Score
Using your spatula edge to make a mark in icing or marzipan by gently pressing it against the surface.

Decorating Guide

Baking Your Cake

The First Step to Success!
For a beautiful cake, follow these easy instructions. A properly baked cake is the best foundation for your icing and your decorations. NOTE: If you're using one of the Wilton shaped pans, follow the specific instructions included with the pan. For 3-dimensional stand-up cakes, use batters that bake a firm-textured cake such as a pound cake.

GREASE

FLOUR

SHAKE

PLACE RACK

REMOVE

•Preheat oven to temperature specified in recipe or on packaged mix.
•Thoroughly grease the inside of each pan with solid vegetable shortening or use a vegetable cooking spray. Use a pastry brush to spread the shortening evenly. Be sure sides, corners and all indentations are completely covered.
•Sprinkle flour inside of pan and shake back and forth so the flour covers all the greased surfaces. Tap out excess flour and if any shiny spots remain, touch up with more shortening and flour. This tip is essential in preventing your cake from sticking. If you prefer, the bottom of a simple geometric shaped pan (round, square, hexagon, etc.) may be lined with waxed paper after greasing. This eliminates flouring pan. Your cake will unmold easily but with more crumbs on side.
•Bake the cake according to temperature and time specifications in recipe or on package instructions. Remove cake from oven and let cool 10 minutes in pan on a cake rack. Larger cakes over 12-in. diameter may need to cool 15 minutes.
•So cake sits level and to prevent cracking, while in pan, cut away the raised center portion with serrated knife. To unmold cake, place cake rack against cake and turn both rack and pan over. Remove pan carefully. If pan will not release, return it to a warm oven (250⁰) for a few minutes, then repeat procedure. Cool cake completely, at least 1 hour. Brush off loose crumbs and frost.

Baking Hints

•If you like to plan ahead, do so. Your baked cake will stay up to three months wrapped in heavy-duty foil in the freezer. Always thaw cake completely before icing. Your cake will still be fresh and easy to ice because it will be firm.
•Wilton Bake-Even Cake Strips will help prevent crowns from forming on basic shaped cakes as they bake.
•Packaged, two-layer cake mixes usually yield 4 to 6 cups of batter, but formulas change, so always measure. Here's a handy guide: one 2-layer cake mix will make any of the following: two 8-in. round layers, or one 10-in. round layer, or one 9x13x2-in. sheet, or one character cake, or one Wonder Mold cake, or one mini-tier cake.
•If you're in doubt as to how many cups of batter you need to fill a pan, measure the cups of water it will hold first and use this number as a guide. Then, if you want a cake with high sides, fill the pan 2/3 full of batter. For slightly thinner cake layers, fill 1/2 full. Never fill cake pans more than 2/3 full. Even if the batter doesn't overflow, the cake will have a heavy texture.
•For 3-in. deep or 3-D pans, we recommend pound or pudding-added cake batters. Fill pan half full only.
•For 3-D cakes: When using the baking core, it's essential to be exact about baking time, as it's very difficult to test 3-D cakes for doneness. Be sure to preheat the oven. If your 3-D cake is to be given away or sold, after baking you can remove the baking core and insert crumpled aluminum foil into the opening for support.
Hints for cakes-to-go! Use our Cake Pan Cover to protect sheet cakes in our 9x13-in. pan (p.174). The Cake Saver is a great way to take cakes places (p. 174).

Ruffle Boards™

Create a professional presentation for decorated cakes—in an instant! Our ready-to-use Ruffle Boards™ are bleached white cake boards with solid white ruffling already attached. It's a neat look with no brown cardboard peek-thru that's convenient, saves time, and gives the decorator truly beautiful results. Ruffle Boards™ are available in a range of round sizes from 8 in. to 18 in., to accomodate cakes from 6 to 16 in. See page 133 for complete ordering information.

All About Icing

Proper consistency is the key to making decorating icing that will shape the petals of a flower, show the details of a border or cover the surface of a cake. It's important that you use the recommended icing and consistency for any technique. As a general rule, flowers require a stiff icing consistency, borders a medium-stiff consistency and writing or leaves a slightly thinned consistency. Icing that can peak to an inch or more is stiff, less than that is medium consistency. Icing that flows easily from a tip without running is a thin consistency. Every Wilton icing recipe is tested for taste and other important qualities. This chart will tell you each recipe's qualities, so you can determine which is the right one for your cake.

Icing	Recommended Uses	Tinting	Flavor & Consistency	Storing Icing	Special Information
Buttercream (Wilton Mix or Homemade)	• Borders, writing • Roses, drop flowers & sweet peas • Figure piping • Icing cakes smooth	• Deep colors • Most colors deepen upon setting	• Sweet, buttery flavor • Thin-to-stiff consistency	• Refrigerate icing in an airtight container for 2 weeks	• Iced cake can be stored at room temperature for 2-3 days • Flowers remain soft enough to be cut with a knife
Snow-White Buttercream	• Borders, writing • Roses, drop flowers & sweet peas • Figure piping • Icing cakes smooth	• Deep colors • Most colors deepen upon setting • Gives true colors	• Sweet, almond flavor • Thin-to-stiff consistency	• Refrigerate icing in an airtight container for 2 weeks	• Iced cake may be stored for 2-3 days • Air-dried flowers have translucent look • Flowers remain soft to be cut with a knife • Good for wedding cakes • Tints true colors due to pure white color
Deluxe Buttercream (Use Wilton Icing Mix or Ready-To-Use Decorator Icing)	• Borders, writing • Drop flowers & sweet peas • Figure piping • Icing cakes smooth	• Deep colors	• Rich, creamy flavor • Medium-to-stiff consistency	• Refrigerate icing in an airtight container for 2 weeks	• Texture remains soft on decorated cake • Iced cake may be stored at room temperature one day • All-purpose
Cream Cheese	• Basic borders, writing, stars, shells, drop flowers • Icing cake smooth	• Pastels	• Cream cheese • Thin-to-medium consistency	• Refrigerate icing in an airtight container for 2 week	• Iced cake must be refrigerated • Cream cheese flavor is especially good with spice cakes, carrot cakes, etc. • All-purpose
Stabilized Whipped Cream	• Borders, writing • Icing cake smooth	• Pastels only • Paste colors are best to use	• Creamy, delicate sweetness • Light, thin-to-medium consistency	• Use immediately	• Iced cake must be refrigerated • Texture remains soft on decorated cake • Especially good on cakes decorated with fruits
French Buttercream	• Basic borders • Writing • Icing cake smooth	• Pastels only	• Tastes similar to vanilla ice cream • Consistency similar to whipped cream	• Use immediately	• Store iced cake in refrigerator • Texture remains soft on decorated cake • Cooked icing gives a special flavor, similar to vanilla ice cream
Quick-Pour Fondant Icing	• For icing	• Pastels	• Very sweet flavor • Pourable consistency	• Use immediately, excess fondant drippings can be reheated & poured again	• Dries to a shiny, smooth surface to coat cakes, petit fours and cookies • Seals in freshness
Rolled Fondant Icing	• For covering heavy pound or fruit cake • Cutting small decorations and ruffles	• Pastels	• Rich, sweet flavor • Dough-like consistency	• Excess can be refrigerated 3 weeks • Bring to room temperature before kneading	• Gives a perfectly smooth, velvety surface • Seals in freshness and moisture • Always decorate with royal icing • Cake can be stored at room temp. 3-4 days
Royal (made from pasteurized egg whites)	• Flower-making, figure piping, making flowers on wires • Decorating cookies & gingerbread houses	• Deep colors • Some colors may fade upon sitting in bright light	• Very sweet and hard • Thin-to-stiff consistency	• Store in airtight grease-free container at room temperature for 2 weeks	• Dries candy-hard for lasting decorations • Flowers and other decorations will last for months. Air dry. • Bowl & utensils must be grease free • Cover icing with damp cloth to prevent crusting
Boiled Icing 100% Fat-free!	• Borders • Figure piping • Writing stringwork • Icing cakes smooth and fluffy.	• Pastel & deep shades	• Marshmallow-like flavor • Very fluffy consistency	• Use immediately	• Serve within 24 hours • Sets quickly! Ice smooth or fluffy, immediately • Ideal for figure piping

Icing Recipes

Buttercream Icing

1/2 cup solid vegetable shortening
1/2 cup butter or margarine*
1 tsp. Clear Vanilla Extract (p. 125)
4 cups sifted confectioners sugar
 (approx. 1 lb.)
2 Tbsps. milk**
Cream butter and shortening with electric mixer. Add vanilla. Gradually add sugar, one cup at a time, beating well on medium speed. Scrape sides and bottom of bowl often. When all sugar has been mixed in, icing will appear dry. Add milk and beat at medium speed until light and fluffy. Keep icing covered with a damp cloth until ready to use. For best results, keep icing bowl in refrigerator when not in use. Refrigerated in an airtight container, this icing can be stored 2 weeks. Rewhip before using.
YIELD: 3 cups
*Substitute all-vegetable shortening and 1/2 teaspoon Wilton Butter Extract for pure white icing and stiffer consistency.
**Add 3-4 Tbsps. light corn syrup per recipe to thin for icing cake.

Chocolate Buttercream

Add 3/4 cup cocoa or three 1 oz. unsweetened chocolate squares, melted, and an additional 1 to 2 Tbsps. milk to recipe. Mix until well blended.
For a unique change of pace, add Wilton Candy Flavors (p.116), in place of vanilla extract.

Snow-White Buttercream

2/3 cup water
4 Tbsps. Meringue Powder (p. 125)
12 cups sifted confectioners sugar
 (approximately 3 lbs.)
1 1/4 cups solid shortening
3/4 tsp. salt
1/2 tsp. Almond Extract (p. 125)
1/2 tsp. Clear Vanilla Extract (p. 125)
1/4 tsp. Butter Flavor (p. 125)
Combine water and meringue powder; whip at high speed until peaks form. Add 4 cups sugar, one cup at a time, beating after each addition at low speed. Alternately add shortening and remainder of sugar. Add salt and flavorings; beat at low speed until smooth.
YIELD: 7 cups
Note: Recipe may be doubled or cut in half. If cut in half, yield is 2 2/3 cups.

Wilton Creamy White Icing Mix

You'll love its creamy taste, luscious texture and convenience. Ideal for icing smooth and decorating (p.125). Just add butter and milk, the shortening's already in the mix. For chocolate icing: Mix icing according to package directions. Stir in 2-oz. melted, unsweetened baking chocolate. If too stiff, add a few drops of milk. For Deluxe Buttercream: Use 6 Tbsps. butter and 1/4 cup whipping cream.

Ready-To-Serve Decorator White Icing

Easy and tasty! Just stir and use. (p. 125)

French Buttercream

2/3 cup sugar
1/4 cup flour
1/4 tsp. salt
3/4 cup milk
1 cup cold butter; cut in several pieces
1 tsp. Clear Vanilla Extract (p. 125)
Place sugar, flour and salt in sauce pan and mix thoroughly; stir in milk. Cook over medium heat and stir constantly until very thick. Remove from heat and pour into a medium mixing bowl. Cool at room temperature. Add 1/2 cup butter at a time (cut into several pieces) and beat at medium-high speed until smooth. Add vanilla and beat well. Chill icing for a few minutes before decorating. Iced cake must be refrigerated until serving time.
YIELD: 2 cups

Stabilized Whipped Cream Icing

1 tsp. unflavored gelatin
4 tsps. cold water
1 cup heavy whipping cream
1/4 cup confectioners sugar
1/2 tsp. Clear Vanilla Extract (p.125)
Combine gelatin and cold water in small saucepan. Let stand until thick. Place over low heat, stirring constantly, just until gelatin dissolves. Remove from heat and cool, do not let set. Whip cream, sugar, and vanilla until slightly thickened. While beating slowly, gradually add gelatin to whipped cream mixture. Whip at high speed until stiff.
YIELD: 2 cups.
Cakes iced with whipped cream must be stored in the refrigerator.

Cream Cheese Icing

3-8 oz. packages slightly softened cream cheese
3 cups sifted confectioners sugar
Beat cream cheese until smooth. Add confectioners sugar and mix thoroughly. Beat at high speed until smooth. YIELD: 3 1/2 cups

Packaged Topping Mix

Whipped topping mix can be used for decorating similar to stabilized whipped cream. However, use immediately after preparing. Do not allow to stay at room temperature, as topping becomes too soft for well-defined decorations.

Frozen Non-Dairy Whipped Topping

Non-dairy whipped topping must be thawed in the refrigerator before coloring or using for decorating. Can be used for decorating techniques similar to stabilized whipped cream. Do not allow to stay at room temperature, as it becomes too soft for decorating. After decorating, store cake in refrigerator.

Specialty Icing Recipes

Royal Icing

3 level Tbsps. Meringue Powder (p. 125)
4 cups sifted confectioners sugar
 (approx. 1 lb.)
6 Tbsps. water*
Beat all ingredients at low speed for 7 to 10 minutes (10 to 12 minutes at high speed for portable mixer) until icing forms peaks.
YIELD: 3 cups
*When using large counter top mixer or for stiffer icing, use 1 Tbsp. less water.

Boiled Icing Recipe

Meringue:
3 Tbsps. Meringue Powder (p. 125)
1/2 cup cold water
Syrup:
2 cups granulated sugar
1/4 cup corn syrup
1/2 cup water
Beat meringue powder and cold water until stiff, about 4 minutes. In large microwave-safe measuring cup stir sugar, corn syrup and water. In microwave oven, bring syrup mixture to a boil (approximately 5 minutes). Remove when boiling stops. Slowly add syrup to meringue mixture while beating on low. Beat on HIGH for 4 minutes until stiff and glossy.
YIELD: 8 cups
For top of range: Mix sugar, corn syrup and water in 2 quart saucepan. Bring to a boil; cool slightly and follow directions above.

Confectioners Sugar Glaze

Great to drizzle on dessert cakes, muffins and cookies.
1 1/4 cups confectioners sugar
3 Tbsps milk
Stir milk into sugar.
YIELD: 1/2 cup

Quick-Pour Fondant Icing

6 cups confectioners sugar
1/2 cup water
2 Tbsps. light corn syrup
1 tsp. Almond Extract (p. 125)
Wilton Icing Colors (p. 124)
Place sugar in a saucepan. Combine water and corn syrup. Add to sugar and stir until well mixed. Place over low heat. Don't allow temperature of fondant to exceed 100°. Remove from heat, stir in flavor and icing color. Optional: Cakes may be covered with a thin coating of buttercream icing or apricot glaze (See recipe below). Allow to set before covering with fondant. To cover, place cake or cookies on wire rack over a drip pan. Pour fondant into center and work towards edges. Touch up bare spots with a spatula. Let set. Excess fondant can be reheated. Even easier...use Wilton Candy Wafer/ Fondant Center Mix. Fondant Icing Recipe on label. (p. 116) YIELD: 2 1/2 cups
Apricot glaze: Heat 1 cup of apricot preserves to boiling, strain, then brush on cake while still hot. It will dry to a hard finish in 15 minutes or less. This is good to crumb-coat cakes before icing.

Specialty Icing Recipes

Rolled Fondant

This icing is rolled out and used as a covering for a pound or fruit cake, which is traditionally first covered with a layer of marzipan to seal in flavor and moistness of the cake. A light layer of buttercream may also be used. Cakes covered with rolled fondant can be decorated with royal or buttercream icing.

Rolled Fondant Recipe
1 Tbsp. unflavored gelatin
1/4 cup cold water
1/2 cup Glucose (p. 130)
1 Tbsp. Glycerin (P. 125)
2 Tbsps. solid vegetable shortening
2 lbs. confectioners sugar
2-3 drops liquid food color and flavoring, as desired.

Combine gelatin and cold water; let stand until thick. Place gelatin mixture in top of double boiler and heat until dissolved. Add glucose and glycerin, mix well. Stir in shortening and just before completely melted, remove from heat. Mixture should cool until lukewarm.
Next, place 1 lb. confectioners sugar in a bowl and make a well. Pour the lukewarm gelatin mixture into the well and stir with a wooden spoon, mixing in sugar and adding more, a little at a time, until stickiness disappears. Knead in remaining sugar, icing color and flavoring. Knead until the fondant is smooth, pliable and does not stick to your hands. If fondant is too soft, add more sugar; if too stiff, add water (a drop at a time).
Use fondant immediately or store in airtight container in refrigerator. When ready to use, bring to room temperature and knead again until soft. This recipe yields enough to cover a 10 x 3-in. high cake.

To Roll Fondant

Spray work surface and rolling pin with vegetable oil pan spray and dust with a mixture of confectioners sugar and cornstarch. Here are two ways to prepare cake for fondant. Coat with piping gel or apricot glaze, then cover with rolled marzipan. Coat again with piping gel or glaze. Add fondant. Or ice cake with buttercream icing, let dry, then cover with rolled fondant.
Roll out fondant into a circle twice the diameter of the cake you are covering. As you roll, lift and move the fondant to prevent it from sticking to the surface. Gently lift fondant over rolling pin and place over cake.
Smooth and shape fondant on cake, using palm of hand. If large air bubbles are trapped under fondant, prick with a pin and continue to smooth. Trim excess from base. A fondant-covered cake may be kept up to 2 months, when tightly wrapped and frozen.

Coloring Your Icing

Color brings cake decorations to life; therefore it's essential that you learn how to tint icings to achieve different decorating effects. Wilton Icing Color is concentrated color in a creamy, rich base. It gives icing vivid or deep, rich color without changing icing consistency. See page 124 for a complete selection of quality Wilton Icing Colors. Icing Color Kits are also available.

Tinting

•Start with white icing and add the color a little at a time until you achieve the shade you desire. Use a toothpick to add icing color; (use more depending on amount of icing). Hint: Tint a small amount of icing first, then mix in with remainder of white icing. Colors intensify or darken in buttercream icings 1 to 2 hours after mixing, so keep this in mind when you're tinting icing. You can always add extra color to deepen the icing color, but it's difficult to lighten the color once it's tinted. Use White-White Icing Color to make your buttercream icing the purest snow-white!

•To mix deep or dark color icing (such as red for roses), you may need a larger amount of Wilton Icing color. The color should still be added gradually, but use a clean small spatula each time to add the color. Red No-Taste color has no after-taste! It's ideal for decorating large areas. Red-Red or Christmas Red Color is still better to use in royal icing and for accent color, as each offers more color intensity. If you plan to use flavorings, make icing stiff consistency, then use enough flavoring to improve taste.

•Always mix enough of any one color icing. If you're going to decorate a cake with pink flowers and borders, color enough icing for both. It's difficult to duplicate an exact shade of any color. As you gain decorating experience, you will learn just how much of any one color icing you will need.

Important Hints For Coloring

•Royal icing requires more base color than buttercream to achieve the same intensity.

•Use milk , not water, in buttercream icing recipe when using Violet Icing Color, otherwise the icing may turn blue.

•Substitute chocolate icing for dark brown colors. Use 6 Tablespoons unsweetened cocoa powder, or 2 one-ounce squares, of melted unsweetened baking chocolate, 1 Tablespoon milk, and add to 1 1/2 cups white icing.

•Add color to piping gel, color flow, gum paste, cookie dough, marzipan, cream cheese, sugar molds and even cake batter for striking decorating effects!

•To restore the consistency of Wilton Icing Colors that have dried out, add a few drops of Wilton Glycerin. Mix until proper consistency is reached.

•Use a clean toothpick or spatula to add Wilton Icing Colors each time, until you reach desired shade.

Coloring for Special Effects

BRUSH STRIPING

Striping is a method used to give multiple or deep color effects to icing. To do this, one or more colors are applied to the inside of the parchment paper bag with a brush. Then the bag is filled with white or pastel-colored icing and, as the icing is squeezed past the color, out come the striped decorations!

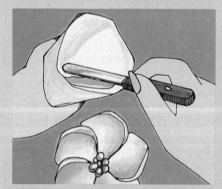

SPATULA STRIPING

Use a spatula to stripe the inside of a decorating bag with pastel-colored icing. Then fill the bag with white icing, or another shade of the same color as the striping, and squeeze out decorations with pastel contrasts. Use the above color techniques when figure piping for exciting results. It's fun to experiment with color! Try to achieve natural-looking flower colors by using the spatula striping method. (Roses look especially beautiful with this effect.)

Icing the Cake

Think of your cake as the canvas on which your beautiful icing decorations will be presented. So it's essential that it be smooth and free of crumbs. By following our 5-easy-steps icing method, we feel you'll get the results you want.

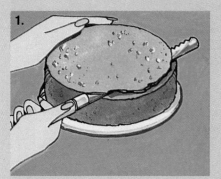

1. Leveling
There are two ways to remove the slight crown your baked cake will have. Cool cake for 10 minutes in the pan. Carefully slice off the raised center with a serrated knife. Or after cake is cooled completely as per directions on p. 91, invert so that its brown top crust is uppermost and trim away the crust for a flat surface (see pic. 1). Our Bake-Even Strips will help prevent crowns from forming on basic shaped cakes (see p. 175 for details).

2. Filling Layers
Place one cake layer on a cake board or circle atop a cake stand or plate, top side up. Hint: To prevent cake from shifting, place a few stripes of icing on base surface before positioning cake. Fit bag with coupler and fill with icing. Make a dam by squeezing out a band of icing about 3/4-in. high around the edge. With your spatula, spread icing, jam, pudding or other filling in center. Position top layer with bottom side up.

3. Icing The Top
Thin your buttercream icing with light corn syrup (approximately 2 teaspoons for each cup). The consistency is correct when your spatula glides over the icing. With large spatula, place mound of icing in center of top and spread across cake pushing excess down onto sides. Always keep spatula on the iced surface. Pulling toward the cake surface will mix in crumbs. Hint: To keep your serving base free of icing, place 3-in. wide strips of waxed paper under each side of cake.

4. Icing The Sides
Cover the sides with excess icing from the top, adding more icing if necessary. Work from top down, forcing any loose crumbs to the cake base. Again, be sure spatula touches only icing. You'll find that an angled spatula is ideal for icing sides. When you're icing a curved side, hold the spatula upright against the side of the cake and, pressing lightly, turn cake stand slowly around with your free hand without lifting the spatula from the side surface. Return excess icing to bowl and repeat procedure until sides are smooth. For angled sides such as on a cross cake, do each straight side individually; hold spatula firmly to smooth.

5. Smooth Top
Place spatula flat on one edge of cake top and sweep it across to center of cake. Lift off, remove excess icing and repeat, starting from a new point on edge of cake top. Repeat procedure until entire top surface is smooth. To smooth center, apply an even pressure to spatula as you turn cake stand around in a full circle. Lift off spatula and any excess icing.

Sheet & Other Flat Surfaced Cakes
Use the same icing procedure as shown here for sheet cakes, heart, oval, square and other shaped cakes with flat surfaces.

Torting

By simply cutting a cake into layers, you can enhance its taste and create impact! Classic and novelty shapes are easy to torte, especially with our Cake Leveler! It cuts perfectly-even layers on cakes up to 10 inches in diameter and adjusts to desired height. Slice the cake horizontally into two or four layers. Make layers the same thickness. Follow package directions for using our Cake Leveler or use a serrated knife. Hold knife level at desired height and with a gentle sawing motion, rotate the cake against blade of knife.
• For easy handling, slide the sliced layer onto a cake board (for each layer follow this procedure).
• Fill bottom layer as shown in number 2 at left. Slide next layer off board onto filled layer.

To Ice Areas on Shaped Cakes
The sides of shaped cakes are usually the only areas iced smooth. Just place icing on side with your spatula and spread. After sides are covered, run spatula lightly over icing in the same direction.
Sometimes small background areas or facial features on top are iced smooth. Use a small spatula or decorating tip (3 or 4) and squeeze icing onto area, then smooth with finger dipped in cornstarch.

The Cake Icer Tip (No.789) Will Save You Time
If you haven't discovered this versatile tip (pg. 139) you should! You'll love how quickly and easily you can cover flat-surfaced cakes with wide bands of icing. Just hold tip flat against cake surface, serrated side up, and squeeze out a ribbed band. Holding the smooth side up gives you a smooth band. To cover side, turn cake stand clockwise as you squeeze out a band of icing, wrapping it around the cake. When your cake is completely iced, use a fork to blend ribbed seams; a spatula to join smooth bands together.

Hints To Make Icing Your Cake Easier
• Thinning buttercream icing with light corn syrup makes consistency best for easy spreading.
• When icing small areas or sides of a shaped cake, be sure to ice a little past the area or edge or top to create a neat surface that can be outlined or covered with stars.
• To smooth the icing surface on 3-dimensional cakes such as the ball, egg, bear, lamb or bunny cakes, let buttercream icing crust slightly. Then place plastic wrap over the icing and smooth over the surface gently with your hands. Carefully remove wrap. For a textured surface, follow the same procedure using a cloth or paper towel.
• To make clean-up easier and quicker when decorating with buttercream icing, use a degreaser liquid soap to dissolve icing from tools. It is especially important to have grease-free utensils when using royal or color flow icings.

Decorating Guidelines

These easy-to-follow guidelines outline the basic steps in decorating. Our steps are very general because each cake you decorate has special needs. We hope these guidelines will inspire you to design original cakes on your own.

• We suggest that flowers, candy, cookies or any special accent be made ahead of time, perhaps while your cake cools. To allow for breakage, make extras of any fragile addition. Heavy trims that protrude out of cake should be attached to a craft stick or coffee stirrer with royal icing. When using cookie trims, easel backs can be cut out of dough and attached with royal icing.

• Before icing or decorating, place each cake to be decorated on a cake circle or board cut to fit. If a small cake is to be set atop a larger cake, we usually recommend that you decorate both cakes first, then put them together. To transfer, let icing set (a slight crust will form and be more workable), then slip a wide spatula under cake and lift. Position cake and slowly pull spatula out (to prevent sticking, lightly dust spatula with cornstarch). If cake is large, support with free hand and redecorate areas that may get damaged.

• Marking design: Use a toothpick, pattern press or cookie cutter. Patterns for more intricate designs are included in the '92 Pattern Book (contains easy pattern transfer instructions). Often geometric shaped cakes are divided into 6ths, 8ths, 12ths, etc. You'll find dividing a round cake is quick 'n easy when you use our Cake Dividing Set (instructions included).

Decorating Hints

• Tips from the same basic group that are close in size may be substituted for one another. The effect will be a slightly smaller or larger decoration.

• Use tip 20, 21 or the super fast Triple-Star Tip, when you're covering a large area with stars. You can also use zigzags or side-by-side stripes to fill in large areas.

• When using parchment bags, you can place a tip with a smaller opening over the tip you're using and tape it in place. This saves time changing bags and tips when you're using the same color icing.

• Stock up on the bags and tips in the sizes you use the most. Your decorating will go faster if several are filled and ready to use. Close tips securely with convenient Tip Covers.

• Overpiping: Outlining a piped decoration with the same technique will add dimension and make it stand out. Overpiping with a different technique in a contrasting color creates an eye-catching effect.

Decorating Step-by-Step

Basic Shapes

• Outline design.
• Pipe in small areas. Fill in areas with stars, zigzags, etc.
• Add top and bottom borders.
• Add message.
• Ruffles and "overpiped" decorations.
• Attach trims such as flowers, cookies, color flow and candy.
Note: If a decoration doesn't seem secure enough, just add a few dots of icing.
• Pipe leaves on flowers.
• Position Wilton cake tops or wedding ornaments.

Novelty Shapes

When decorating a cake that's basically covered with stars, here are the easy steps involved.

1. Ice sides and others areas per instructions smooth.

2. Outline details.

3. Pipe in facial features, small details, windows, doors, etc.

4. Cover areas with stars, stripes, zigzags or hair.

5. Add message.

6. Edge top and base with borders. Attach flowers or trims.

3 Essentials of Bag and Tip Decorating

1. Icing Consistency
Remember, if the consistency of your decorating icing isn't exactly right, your decorations won't be either. Follow the general guidelines on p. 92.

2. Bag Position
To hold the decorating bag correctly, grip the bag near the top with the twisted or folded end locked between your thumb and fingers. Guide the bag with your free hand.

Generally, there are two basic positions for the decorating bag—the 90° angle with the bag straight up, perpendicular to the surface. And the 45° angle with the bag half-way between vertical and horizontal.

Pointing the back end of your decorating bag in the right direction is also important. Sometimes instructions will tell you to hold the back end of bag pointing to the right or towards you.

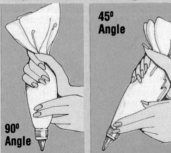

45° Angle

90° Angle

Left-handed decorators do things differently. Hold the decorating bag in your left hand and guide the decorating tip with the fingers of your right hand. If the instructions say to hold the decorating bag over to the right, you should hold your decorating bag over to the left. A right-handed person will always decorate from left to right. A left-handed person

should always decorate from right to left. The only exception to this rule is when you are writing or printing. When decorating a cake on a turntable, rotate the stand counterclockwise. For flower making on a flower nail, turn nail clockwise in right hand as you pipe petals using left hand.

HEAVY   MEDIUM   LIGHT

3. Pressure Control
The size and uniformity of your icing design are directly affected by the amount of pressure you apply to the decorating bag and the steadiness of the pressure— how you squeeze and relax your grip on the decorating bag. Strive to apply pressure so consistently that you can move the bag in a free and easy glide while just the right amount of icing flows from the tip. Practice to achieve this control.

The Techniques

PLAIN OR ROUND TIPS

Use to outline details, filling and piping in areas, printing and writing messages, figure piping, stringwork, beads, dots, balls, stems, vines, flower centers, lattice, cornelli lace. These tips are smooth and round—small plain tips include numbers 1,2,3,4; medium, 5,6,7,8,9,10,11,12; large, 1A, 2A. For fine stringwork, use 1S, 1L, 2L, 0L, 00L,000. For Philippine method flower making, oval tips 55 and 57. Writing tip 301 pipes fine, flat lines.

Printing & Writing

Use a small round tip and thin icing consistency. **Hint:** With a toothpick or Message Pattern Presses draw guidelines to follow. With practice, you'll achieve control and soon be piping out messages free-handed.

To Print: Hold bag at 45° angle with tip resting lightly on surface with back of to the right for horizontal lines, toward you for vertical. With a steady, even pressure, squeeze out a straight line, lifting tip off surface to let icing string drop. Be sure to stop squeezing before you lift the tip to end the line so a tail doesn't form.

To Write: You must move your whole arm to write effectively with icing. Hold bag at a 45° angle with back of bag to the right. The tip should lightly touch the cake as you write.

To Outline:
Use thin icing consistency and bag at a 45° angle and touch tip (usually 3 or 4) to surface. Now raise the tip slightly and continue to squeeze. The icing will flow out of the tip while you direct it along the surface. To end an outline, stop squeezing, touch tip to surface and pull away.

To Pipe In: After area is outlined, squeeze out tip 3 or 4 zigzag motion strings to fill area. Immediately smooth over strings with finger tip or spatula dipped in cornstarch.

To Fill In: Follow same procedure as Pipe In, but thin icing before piping.

Dots

Use medium icing consistency. Hold bag at a 90° angle with tip slightly above surface. Squeeze and keep point of the tip in icing until dot is the size you want. Stop pressure, pull away; use tip to clean point away or smooth with finger dipped in cornstarch. To make large dots or balls, lift tip as you squeeze to allow greater icing build-up.

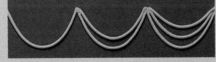

Beads

Use medium icing consistency. Hold bag at 45° angle with tip slightly above surface and end of bag pointing to the right. Squeeze and lift tip slightly so icing fans out into base. Relax pressure as you draw tip down and bring bead to point. Ideal for borders or piped in side-by-side rows to cover large areas.

For Hearts: Pipe two beads side by side and smooth together with finger dipped in cornstarch.

For Shamrocks: Pipe 3 bead hearts so points meet. Add tip 3 outline stem.

Cornelli Lace

With thin icing, use a 90 angle with tip slightly above surface. Pipe a continuous string of icing, curve it up, down and around until area is covered. Stop pressure; pull tip away. Make sure strings never touch or cross.

Drop Strings

Use stiff consistency icing that has been thinned with corn syrup. Icing is the right consistency if you can drop a loop of icing from your finger. With toothpick, mark horizontal intervals in desired widths. Hold bag at 45° angle to surface so that end of bag points slightly to the right. Touch tip to first marks and squeeze, holding bag in place momentarily so that icing sticks to surface.

Then pull tip straight out away from surface, allowing icing to drop into an arc. Stop pressure as you touch tip to second mark to end string.

Repeat procedure, attaching string to third mark and so on, forming row of drop strings. It's very important to let the string, not your hand, drop to form an arc. Try to keep your drop strings uniform in length and width.

For Double Drop Strings: Start at first mark again, squeeze bag. Let icing drop into a slightly shorter arc than arc in first row. Join end of string to end of corresponding string in first row and repeat procedure.

Always pipe longest drop strings first and add shorter ones. This technique is ideal for cake sides. Practice is important in making drop strings uniform.

Dropped Lattice Garlands: With stiff royal icing, connect garland marks with drop string guidelines. Cover strings with three rows of tip 16 zigzags (overpipe rows). Ease pressure at ends so icing doesn't build up too high. Drop a string guideline directly on top of zigzags. From cake to edge of zigzags, pipe tip 3 diagonal lines across area. From the opposite side, work strings in the other direction. Cover edges of lattice with tip 3 strings.

STAR TIPS

The star-shaped openings create the most popular decorations… stars, zigzags, shells, rosettes and more. The most often used star tips are numbers 13 through 22. Star tips range in size from small to extra large. For deep ribbed decorations, try tips 23-31, 132, 133 and 195. Large star tips include numbers 32, 96, 4B, 6B and 8B. Fine cut star tips are numbers 362, 363, 364, 172 and 199. For these techniques use medium icing consistency.

Stars

Hold bag at 90° angle with tip slightly above surface. Squeeze bag to form a star, then stop pressure and pull tip away. Increase or decrease pressure to change star size. An entire cake or just one area can be covered with stars made very close together so that no cake shows between stars. Use the triple-star or use large star tips to save time.

For Pull-Out Stars: Hold bag at 45° angle to surface. As you squeeze out icing, pull tip up and away from cake. When strand is long enough, stop pressure and pull tip away. Work from bottom to top of area to be covered with pull-out stars.

For Star Puffs: Use a large tip and hold tip in place to allow icing to build up.

For Star Flowers: Squeeze and keep tip in icing until star petals are formed. Stop pressure and pull tip away. Add tip 2 or 3 dot centers.

Ropes

Hold bag at 45° angle to surface with end of bag pointing over right shoulder. Touch tip to surface and squeezing bag, move tip down, up and around to the right forming a slight "s" curve. Stop pressure, pull tip away. Tuck tip under bottom arch of first "s" and repeat procedure. Continue joining "s" curves to form rope.

The Techniques

The size and shape of the opening on a decorative tip identifies the basic group to which the tip belongs and determines the type of decorations the tip will produce.

Zigzags
Hold bag at 45° angle to surface, so that end of bag points out to the right and fingers on the bag are facing you. Allow the tip to touch the surface lightly. Steadily squeeze and move hand in a tight side-to-side motion. To end, stop pressure and pull tip away. **Elongated Zigzags:** Follow procedure but keep an even pressure as you move hand in the desired length. Very large areas can be covered in this manner. **Relaxed Zigzags:** Simply relax pressure as you move bag along.

Zigzag Garlands
Hold bag as for basic zigzag procedure. Allow tip to touch the surface lightly and use light-to-heavy-to-light pressure to form curves of garland. To end, stop pressure, pull tip away. Practice for rhythmic pressure control so garlands are uniform.

Puffs
Hold bag at 45° angle to surface, finger tips on bag facing you. Touch tip to surface and use a light-to-heavy-to-light pressure and zigzag motion to form puff. Repeat procedure again and again as you move tip in a straight line to form row of puffs. To end row, stop pressure, pull tip away.

C, E & S-Motion (only "E" motion shown)
Hold bag at 45° angle to surface, finger tips on bag facing you. As you squeeze out icing, move tip down, up to the right and around as if writing the letter "c, e or s." Use a steady, even pressure as you repeat procedure. To end, stop pressure, pull tip away.

Shells
Hold bag at 45° angle with tip slightly above surface and end of bag pointing to the right. Squeeze with heavy pressure and slightly lift tip as icing builds and fans out into a full base. Relax pressure as you pull bag down to the right as you make the tail. Stop pressure completely, pull tip away. When you make the shells, always work to the right; starting each new shell slightly behind tail of previous shell. **For Elongated Shells:** Extend tail while relaxing pressure, until desired length is achieved. **For Upright Shells:** Hold bag at 90° angle to cake sides. Follow same procedure as elongated shells.

Note: Once you've mastered the motion of shell making, you can create unique borders with other tip groups such as leaf and ruffle.

Reverse Shells
Hold bag at 45° angle with tip slightly above surface. Squeeze to let icing fan out as if you were making a typical shell, then swing tip around to the left in a semi-circular motion as you relax pressure to form a tail of a shell. Stop pressure, pull tip away. Repeat procedure, only this time, swing tip around to the right as you form tail of shell. Continue procedure alternating directions for a series of reverse shells.

Fleur-De-Lis
Make a shell. Keep bag at 45° angle and starting at the left of this shell, squeeze bag to fan icing into shell base. Then as you relax pressure to form tail, move tip up slightly around to the right, relaxing pressure, forming tail similar to reverse shells. Join to tail of the first shell. Repeat procedure to right side of first shell.

Scrolls
Hold bag at 45° angle to surface so that end of bag points to the right. Use tip 3 to draw an inverted "C" center and use circular motion to cover inverted "C." You may overpipe (go over lines) with tip 13 or any small star tip. Use a heavy pressure to feather the scroll, relaxing pressure as you taper end. Add side petals like reverse shells.

Reverse Scrolls
With tip 3 squeeze out an inverted "C" scroll. Then, starting at the top of this "C," squeeze and move tip down, up and around for a backward "C." Cover outlines with tip 13. Add reverse shell side petals.

Hint: Use our Scroll Pattern Presses to imprint an easy-to-follow guide on cake top or sides.

Rosettes
Hold bag at 90° angle with tip slightly above surface. Squeeze and move hand to the left, up and around in a circular motion to starting point. Stop pressure and pull tip away. For a fancy effect, trim center with a star.

Spirals
Follow rosettes technique. Starting at outer edge, move tip in a clockwise direction in a continuous circular motion decreasing size of circles until center is reached. Stop pressure and pull tip away.

DROP FLOWER TIPS
These are the easiest flowers for a beginning decorator to do. The number of openings on the end of the tip determines the number of petals the flower will have. Each drop flower tip can produce two different flower varieties—plain or swirled. Swirled drop flowers cannot be made directly on cake. Some form center holes. Small tips include numbers 107, 108, 129, 217, 220, 224, 225; medium tips are 109, 131, 135, 140, 177, 190, 191, 193, 194, 195; for large flowers, tips 1B, 1C, 1E, 1G, 2C, 2D, 2E and 2F.

Drop Flowers
Icing consistency should be slightly stiffer. Hold bag at a 90° angle with tip touching surface and pipe as you would a star. For swirled flowers: Curve wrist around to the left and as you squeeze out icing, bring hand back to the right. Stop pressure, pull tip away. Add tip 2 or 3 dot centers.

LEAF TIPS
The v-shaped openings of these tips give leaves pointed ends. With any leaf tip you can make plain, ruffle or stand-up leaves. Make leaves with center veins from small 65s, 65-70, to large, 112-115 and 355. Other popular numbers are 71-76, 326, 349, 352.

Basic Leaf
Use thin icing consistency and hold bag at 45° angle to surface, back of bag facing you. Squeeze and hold tip in place to let icing fan out into base, then relax and stop pressure as you pull tip towards you and draw leaf to a point.

Stand Up Leaf
Hold bag at a 90° angle. Touch tip lightly to surface and squeeze, holding tip in place as icing fans out to form base. Relax and stop pressure as you pull tip straight up and away, creating stand-up leaf effect.

Holly Leaf: With tip 68, follow basic leaf method and use medium consistency royal icing to pipe desired size leaf. While icing is wet, pull out tiny points around edge with a dampened Decorator's Brush. Let dry on flower formers for a curved look. Do not make directly on cake.

The Techniques

PETAL TIPS

These tips have an opening that is wide at one end, narrow at the other. This teardrop-like shaped opening yields a variety of petals that form flowers like the rose, carnation, daisy, pansy and more (see pages 101-103). Petal tips can also make ribbons, drapes and swags; bows and streamers. Plain rose tips include numbers 101s, 101, 102, 103, 104, 124, 125, 126, 127 and giant roses, tip 127D. Swirled rose tips that make instant-curled petals are 97, 116, 118 and 119. Others include 59s, 59, 60, 61, 121, 122, 123, 62, 63, 64 and 150.

Ruffle

Use medium icing consistency. Hold bag at a 45° angle to surface, finger tips on bag facing you. Touch wide end of tip to surface, angle narrow end out about ¼-in. away from surface. As you squeeze, move hand up and down slightly to ruffle the icing. **For Stand-Up Ruffle** just turn tip so wide end is at the top.

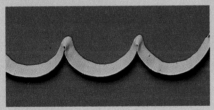

Swag/Drape

Use same procedure as for ruffle. As you squeeze, swing tip down and up to the right forming ribbon drape.

Bows

Creating bows with a petal tip is different from a round or star tip because of the shape of tip but otherwise the technique is the same. With tip 104 and medium icing consistency, hold bag at a 45° angle to surface. The wide end of the tip should touch the surface and the narrow end should point straight up. While squeezing, move the tip up and around to the starting point and continue around, making a second loop on the left. The two loops should form a figure 8. Still holding bag in the same position return to the center and squeeze out two streamers.

STRIPE/BASKETWEAVE TIPS

These are decorating tips with a smooth side for making smooth, wide icing stripes and/or one serrated side for making ribbed, wide icing stripes. When short ribbed horizontal stripes are interwoven in vertical rows the effect is that of a basketweave. Tips are 46 and 47. For smooth stripes, 44 and 45. For ribbed stripes, 48 and 327. Large ribbon tips include 1D, 2B and 789 (Cake Icer).

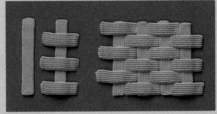

Basketweave

Use star or basketweave tips and medium consistency icing. For an interesting effect, use a round tip to make vertical lines.

• Hold bag at 45° angle to cake with serrated side of tip facing up (or use round tip). Touch tip lightly to surface and squeeze out a vertical line of icing.

• Next, hold bag at 45° angle to surface, finger tips gripping bag facing you. Touch tip, serrated side facing up, to top left side of vertical line and squeeze out a horizontal bar. Add two more horizontal bars, each about a tip width apart, to cover vertical line.

• With bag and tip at 45° angle, make another vertical line of icing to right of first one, overlapping ends of horizontal bars. Use same procedure as step two to cover this line with horizontal bars, working them in spaces of bars in first row.

• Repeat entire procedure, alternating vertical lines and horizontal bars, to create a basketweave effect. Other tips may be used for basketweave, but serrated tips 46-48 give icing a ribbed basket effect.

Violet Leaf

• With tip 102 (petal tip), begin at center of the flower nail. Move out towards edge of nail and begin jiggling out ruffles. Gradually move hand upwards as you turn nail. After curve is formed, move hand back down to starting place. Paint veins and stems with icing color. For curved effect, place in flower former to dry.

Stripes

• This versatile technique can be made with star and ribbon tips. They can be piped straight, curved or side-by-side to fill in an area. Hold decorating bag at 45° angle to surface. As you squeeze out icing with steady, even pressure, move tip in vertical direction laying out a ribbed stripe of icing. Stop pressure and pull tip up and away. When covering an area, stripes can be slightly overlapped for added dimension.

Ribbon Stripe Bow

• To make a bow with a basketweave tip as shown, hold bag at a 45° angle with the ribbed side of tip up. Start in center and move bag up and to the right. As you bring bag down to form loop, turn tip so that the ribbed side is now down. Repeat procedure for left loop. Pipe streamers with smooth or ribbed side up.

Flutes

• A pretty effect to add between rows of shells. Hold tip 104 (petal tip) at 45° angle so that wide end of tip is between two shells. Squeeze and move tip up slightly as icing fills in between shell. Stop pressure, lower tip, pull away.

Making a Rose

The flower nail (p. 130) is a decorating tool used to make the most popular flower of all, the rose. It is also used to make pretty flowers, like the violet, apple blossom and daisy. Flower nails come in a variety of sizes. No. 7 and 9 are the popular choices for small and average size blooms. Large flowers would use a 2 or 3-in. flower nail.

The key to making any flower on the nail is to coordinate the turning of the nail with the formulation of a petal. The stem of the nail is held between your left thumb and forefinger, so you can turn the flat nailhead surface at the same time you're piping a flower with your right hand. Using the flower nail takes practice, but the beautiful results are well worth the effort!

Note: Left-handed decorators should use the nail opposite of above instructions.

Make all flowers on the nail with royal or stiffened buttercream icing (see p. 93), and the tips specified for each flower. Air dry flowers made in royal icing, and freeze buttercream flowers (buttercream roses can also be placed directly on iced cake) until firm at least 2 hours. Then, when you're ready to decorate, remove the frozen flowers, a few at a time, and position them on the cake. (Snow White Buttercream Icing flowers can be air dried).

For each flower you make, attach a 2-in. square of waxed paper to the nailhead with a dot of icing. Make a flower; remove waxed paper and flower together. For more about rose making, order the **Wilton Celebrates The Rose, p. 112.**

 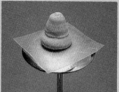   

Make The Rose Base
• Use tip 10 or 12. Hold the bag perpendicular at a 90° angle to nail with tip slightly above center of nailhead.
• Squeeze with a heavy pressure, keeping bottom of tip in icing until you've made a full, round base.
• Ease pressure as you raise tip up and away from nailhead, narrowing base to a dome head. The base is very important for successful rose-making. Be sure that it is secure to nail and can support all the petals. Practice until you feel comfortable with the technique.

The Center Bud
• Use tip 104. Hold bag at a 45° angle to nail with wide end of tip just below top of dome, and narrow end pointed in slightly. Back of bag should be pointed over your shoulder.
• Now you must do three things simultaneously...squeeze, pull tip up and out away from top of dome stretching icing into a ribbon band, as you turn the nail counterclockwise.
• Relax pressure as you bring band of icing down around dome, overlapping the point at which you started.

 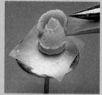   

1st Row of 3 Petals
• Hold bag at 45° angle with end of bag pointed over your shoulder. Touch wide end of tip 104 to midpoint of bud base. Turn nail counterclockwise and move tip up and back down to midpoint of bud base forming first petal of rose.
• Start slightly behind end of 1st petal and squeeze out 2nd petal same as first.
• Start slightly behind end of 2nd petal and add a 3rd petal, ending this petal overlapping starting point of 1st petal. Now you have a full rosebud made on a nail to use just as you would a rosebud made on a flat surface

2nd Row of 5 Petals
• Touch wide end of tip 104 slightly below center of a petal in 1st row, angle narrow end of tip out slightly more than you did for 1st row of petals. Squeeze and turn nail counterclockwise, moving tip up, then down to form 1st petal in second row.
• Start slightly behind this last petal and make a 2nd petal. Repeat this procedure for a total of 5 petals, ending last petal overlapping the 1st petal's starting point.

3rd Row of 7 Petals
• Touch wide end of tip 104 below center of petal in 2nd row, again angling narrow end of tip out a little more. Squeeze and turn nail counterclockwise and move tip up and down forming 1st petal. Repeat for a total of 7 petals.
• Slip waxed paper and completed rose off nail. Attach another square of waxed paper and start again. Have several squares of waxed paper cut

ahead of time so you can continue rose making without stopping. HINT: An easy way to place a buttercream icing rose directly on your cake is to slide open scissors under base of rose and gently lift flower off waxed paper square and flower nail. Position flower on cake by slowly closing scissors and pushing base of flower with stem end of flower nail. Practice & watch your talent grow!

Two-Tone Roses
Create a dramatic effect by making the center petals of your rose contrast with the outer petals. You'll need to pipe the base, center bud and 1st row of petals with one color. Then in your contrasting shade, add remaining petals.

Flowers
Flat Surface Flowers:
Rosebuds, Half Roses & Sweet Peas

These are flowers you can make right on a cake, or any other flat surface. To make all these, use tip 104 and royal or stiffened buttercream icing. Attach a sheet of waxed paper to the back of a cookie sheet with dots of icing or use Wilton Practice Board.

Make your practice flowers in horizontal rows and when you've filled the entire sheet, loosen the waxed paper with a spatula to remove it and start again.

When you're decorating a cake with lots of flat-surface flowers, make all the ones you need ahead of time using the same cookie sheet method. Air dry flowers made with Royal or Snow-White Buttercream. Freeze flowers made with buttercream until hard (at least 2 hours). Remove buttercream flowers with your spatula, a few at a time as you decorate, so they stay firm. Note: When you make flowers directly on a cake, use buttercream, not royal icing.

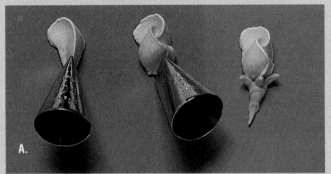

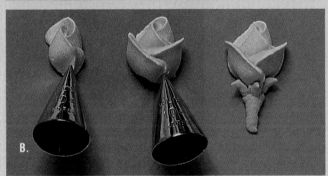

A. Rosebud
• Make base petal. Hold bag at a 45° angle so that the end of bag points over your right shoulder, finger tips gripping bag facing you. Touch wide end of tip 104 to surface, point narrow end to the right. Squeeze, move forward ¼-in.; hesitate so icing fans out, then move back as you stop pressure.
• Make overlapping center petal. Hold bag in same position as above with wide end of tip touching inside right edge of base petal, narrow end of tip pointing slightly up above base petal. Squeeze as icing catches inside edge of base petal and rolls into interlocking center bud, Stop pressure; touch large end back to surface and pull tip away.
• Make sepals and calyx directly on cake with tip 3 and thinned icing. Hold bag at a 45° angle to base of bud with end of bag pointing towards you. Touch tip to bud. Squeeze and pull tip up and away from flower, relaxing pressure as you draw calyx to a point. Add three tip 3 sepals.

B. Half Rose
• Make a rosebud without sepals and calyx. To make left petal: Hold bag at a 45° angle so the end of bag points to the right, finger tips gripping the bag should face you. Touch wide end of tip 104 to bottom left side of bud. Squeeze, move it up, around to the right and down, relaxing pressure.
• To make right petal: Hold bag in opposite position as for left petal. Touch wide end of tip to bottom right side of bud base. Squeeze, move up, around to the left and down to center of bud base. Stop pressure, pull tip away.
• Make sepals and calyxes with tip 3 and thinned icing. Follow same procedure as for step 3 of rosebud, starting at bottom center of half rose.

C. Sweet Pea
• Make center petal. Hold bag at a 45° angle to surface so that back end of bag points towards you. Touch wide end of the tip to surface with narrow end of tip straight up. Squeeze, raise tip slightly and let icing roll into center petal. Stop pressure, lower tip, pull away.
• Make side petals. Touch wide end of tip to bottom left edge of center rolled petal, point narrow end up and out to the left. Squeeze, lift tip slightly, stop pressure, lower tip, pull away. Repeat procedure for right petal, starting at bottom edge of center petal.
• Add calyx to flower base with tip 3 and thinned icing. Hold bag at 45° angle to surface so that end of bag points towards you. Insert tip into flower base and hold in place as you squeeze to build up pressure as you draw tip down, narrowing calyx to a point.

D. To Attach Flowers & Leaves To Wire Stems.
• **For flowers:** On waxed paper square, using royal icing, pipe a dot base with tip 4. Make 1/8-in. hook on one end of 4-in. florist wire and insert hook into base. With slightly moistened decorator's brush, smooth and taper icing on the wire. Push other end of wire into a piece of styrofoam to dry base. Remove waxed paper and attach flower with dots of icing. **For Leaves:** Pipe tip 3 royal icing dot on a waxed paper square and immediately push in hooked end of wire. Use tip 352 and royal icing to pipe a leaf directly on top of wire. Again, push into styrofoam to dry. Then remove waxed paper square. Entwine stems together. Note: Use only royal icing for attaching flowers to stems.

Flower Nail Flowers

For best results, use royal icing to pipe these impressive blooms. To curve petals, dry on convexed or concaved flower formers. Instructions will indicate the number of flowers needed, so make extras to allow for breakage.

Daisy (and Brown-Eyed Susans) (p. 35)
• Use royal icing and tip 103. Dot center of nail with icing as guide for flower center. Hold bag at a 45° angle with tip almost parallel to nail surface, wide end of tip pointing to nail center, narrow end pointing out. Now, starting at any point near outer edge of nail, squeeze and move tip towards center icing dot. Stop pressure, pull tip away. Repeat procedure for a total of twelve or more petals.
• Add tip 4 yellow flower center and press to flatten. For pollen-like effect, dampen your finger, press in edible glitter, then flatten center.
• For Brown-Eyed Susans: Make yellow petals, brown centers, and use granulated brown sugar for pollen at centers.

Chrysanthemum
• Hold bag at 90° angle to nail and pipe tip 6 mound of icing on nail center. Use tip 79 and very stiff royal icing for short petal effect. Hold bag at a 45° angle to outer base edge of mound, with half-moon opening of tip 79 pointing up. Squeeze row of ½-in. long cupped base petals using pull-out star technique.
• Add second row of shorter petals atop and in between those in first row. Repeat procedure making each additional row of petals shorter than the previous row. When entire mound is covered, add a few stand-up petals to top and tip 1 center dots.

Bachelor Button.
• Like the chrysanthemum, start with a tip 7 dot base. Pipe a cluster of short pull-out dots in the center with tip 1. With tip 14, cover the rest of the mound with pull-out stars.

Daffodil And Jonquil
• Use tip 104 for daffodil or tip 103 for jonquil. Hold bag at a 45° angle to nail, with large end of tip touching nail, narrow end pointed out and almost parallel to nail surface. Squeeze and as you turn nail, move tip out about ½-in. and back to center of nail to form petal. Repeat procedure for five more petals. Dip fingers in cornstarch and pinch ends of petals to form points. Pipe row-upon-row of tip 2 string circles and top with tip 1 zigzag for center.

Narcissus
• Use tip 102 and same procedure as for daffodil to make six ¾-in. long petals. Add tip 1 coil center and tip 1 zigzag.

Apple Blossom
• Use tip 101 or 101s and hold bag at a 45° angle to flower nail with wide end of tip touching nail center, narrow end pointed out 1/8-in. away from nail surface.
• Squeeze bag and turn nail as you move tip 1/8-in. out from nail center and back, relaxing pressure as you return to starting point.
• Repeat procedure to make four more petals. Add five tip 1 dots for center.

Forget-Me Nots
• Very similar to the apple blossom. Use tip 101 and move tip out just 3/8-in. from center, curve around and return, letting the turn of the nail form petals. Dot center with tip 1. Use large flower nail No. 7 and pipe several at once!

Violet
• Use tip 59s and same procedure as for apple blossom to make three ¾-in. long petals and two ¼-in. base petals. Add two tip 1 center dots.

Pansy
• Fit two decorating bags with tip 104. Fill one with yellow icing, the other with violet. Hold bag with yellow icing at a 45° angle to nail center, squeeze and move tip out to edge of nail. Turn nail as you squeeze, relax pressure as you return to nail center. Repeat to form second yellow petal. Use same procedure to add two shorter yellow petals atop the first two.
• Now with bag of violet icing, squeeze out a base petal that equals the width of the yellow petals, using a back and forth hand motion for a ruffled effect.
• Use a decorator's brush to add veins of violet icing color after flower has air dried. Add tip 1 string loop center.

Wild Rose
• Use tip 103 and hold bag at a 45° angle. Touch nail with wide end of tip with narrow end just slightly above nail surface. Begin at center of nail and press out first petal, turning nail as you move tip out toward edge of nail, and return to center of nail as you stop squeezing. Repeat 4 more times. Pull out tiny stamens with tip 1.

Lilacs (p. 32)
• Make many four-petalled blossoms with tube 101s, each petal less than ¼ in. long. Dry. Pipe elongated shells on cake using tip 21. Attach blossoms to shells with dots of icing, covering completely. Add tip 1 buds and tip 4 branch. Pipe tip 352 leaves and tip 2 stems.

Lily Nail Flowers

The Wilton Lily Nail Set lets you make natural-looking flowers with bell-like shapes and cupped, turned-up petals. Different lily nail sizes relate to the size of flowers you can make. The larger the nail, the larger the flowers. Always use royal icing for flowers made on the lily nail since softer icing will not hold their deeply-cupped shapes. To make any flower on the lily nail, place an aluminum foil square in bottom half of nail. Press in top half to form a foil cup. Remove the top half. Lightly spray foil with vegetable oil spray. This makes it easier to remove from foil after icing has dried and reduces breakages. Pipe a flower on the foil cup and lift out flower and foil to dry.

Petunia
• Prepare 1 ⅝ in. lily nail. Then with wide end of tip 102 held down, narrow end up, start piping icing deep inside nail.
• Move up to outer edge as you turn nail, jiggling hand slightly all the while to form ruffled petal edge, then go back to starting point.
• Pipe 5 separate petals in all. Add tip 14 green star center. Push in artificial stamens.

Bluebell
• Use 1 ¼ in. lily nail. With tip 66, pipe three ¾ in. long petals, pulling only to top of nail. Between these petals, add three more.
• Push in three short artificial stamens.

California Poppy (p. 35)
• Press foil halfway into 1 ⅝ in. lily nail, use stiff royal icing and tip 103. Touch center, pull icing over edge, straight across, back to center for square, cupped petals. Smooth with damp brush, then fill centers with tip 8 dot. Add artificial stamens (tops cut and brushed with orange icing).

Borders & More

Trees (p. 16, 47)
Use tip recommended with instructions. Wrap waxed paper around tree formers. Secure by tucking paper under base or use tape. Pipe a guideline around base. Cover line with a row of leaves, turning former counterclockwise as you decorate. Repeat procedure, overlapping each successive row of leaves until former is covered. Pipe tip 13 "pine cones" randomly on tree, if desired. Let dry. Carefully loosen waxed paper from former and lift off icing tree.

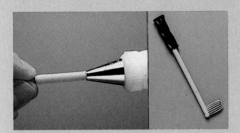

Golf Club Handles (p. 28), Nails (p. 35), Carriage Handle (p. 88)
Break pieces of uncooked spaghetti into desired lengths. Fill decorating bag, fitted with tip 7, with royal icing. Insert a piece of spaghetti into open end of tip, then as you squeeze bag, pull spaghetti out of tip, coating "handle" with icing. Push end into craft block to dry.

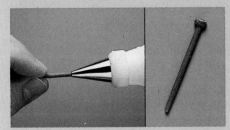

For Nails: Using tip 4, coat uncooked spaghetti as above. Pipe dot of icing at end, flatten with finger dipped in cornstarch to resemble nail head. Use the same technique to coat florist wire handle on Baby Carriage, with tip 32.

Multi-Overlapping Drop Strings (p. 69)
Divide sides into thirds. Drop tip 2 string 1 1/4 in. down and half the width of the marked side section. Continue dropping strings 1/4 in. apart until 6 are completed to fill each section.

Upright Shells (p. 32)
Pipe out a tip 32 standing shell directly on base of cake. Let build up slightly, so bottom of shell flattens out a bit. Then, keeping an even pressure, pull smoothly upward so shell flows into pillar shape.

Crown Border with Overlapping Drop Strings (p.42)
Use tip 32 to make a row of side-by-side upright shells. Add overlapping drop strings with tip 4 following procedure above.

Overlapping Drop Strings
With toothpick, dot mark specified intervals on sides of your cake. Touch tip 3 to a mark, allow your string to skip the next mark and attach to the following one. Return to the mark that was skipped and drop string to connect the next mark. Be sure to keep depth of strings even.

Lace Pieces (p. 72)
Trace Lace Pieces pattern from '93 Pattern Book, page 46, onto waxed paper. Tape onto a cake board or circle, tightly cover with waxed paper or plastic wrap. Hint: If sprayed very lightly with vegetable oil, decorations are easier to remove. Following pattern outline, pipe-in lace pieces using royal icing and tip 2. Allow to dry on board, remove carefully. These lace pieces are extremely delicate, so make extras to allow for breakage. Position lace pieces on cake with dots of icing.

Cathedral Steps Border (p. 76)
Use the flat edge of tips 1D, 2B, and 47 for this border. Pipe tip 1D band of icing flat around base of cake. Top with tip 2B band followed by a tip 47 band, aligning each at cake edge to create a "step" effect. Trim each band edge with tip 3 beads.

Crochet-Look (p. 84)
Starting at the top and using tip 4, pipe a row of ovals approximately 1/2 in. high. Overlap the next row, positioning ovals between those on the previous row. Repeat for each successive row until area is completely covered.

Pull-out Grass, Fur or Hair
Use tip 233 or 234 and medium icing consistency. Hold bag at a 90° angle. As you squeeze out icing, pull tip up and away from surface. When icing strand is long enough (about 1/2 in.), stop pressure and pull tip away.

Lace, Ribbons, Tulle, Flower Puffs & Fabric
Leaves are easy to work with and look quite stunning. Here are a few hints to remember: Nylon lace will not absorb grease so it is the best choice. Be sure to use waterproof, satiny ribbon for the same reason. Before attaching real trims, let icing crust a bit, then anchor in place with dots of icing.

Lattice
Lattice is piped from the center of the design, outward. Use thinned icing and a tip 2 or 3, hold bag at a 45° angle at the top of design with tip slightly above cake. Squeeze out a diagonal line to the right, all the way to the edge of your design. On both sides of the first line, fill in more lines, evenly spaced and going in the same direction. Return to starting point in center and pipe diagonal lines to left.

Sotas
This cornelli-like lacework is a Philippine technique. Randomly pipe tip 2 curls, V's and C's so that they touch.

Tinted Coconut or Sugar
Place shredded coconut or sugar in a plastic sandwich bag. Add a few drops of paste icing color (diluted slightly with water) or use liquid icing color. Shake bag until color is evenly distributed.

Pearl Beading
In the idea section several cakes were dripping with pearls and the effects. . .spectacular. To work with pearl beading, we suggest that the complete length (5 yds.) be used. Cut strand after wrapping around cake to insure that strand won't be too short. For safety, it is advisable to decorate only with long strands of pearl beading. Remove pearls before cutting.

Figure Piping

Cat (p. 14)
Use tip 7, hold bag at 90⁰ angle to cake top; pipe a line of icing for body. Pipe a ball of icing for head, add tail. Pipe tip 3 ears, add tip 1 facial features and stripes.

Campers in sleeping bags, Dog (p. 17)
Pipe campers with royal icing. Use tip 403, hold tube with open side down, pipe length of sleeping bag back. Turn tip over and pipe top of sleeping bag. Pipe a total of 4 layers to fill. When icing sets, press edges together at seams. Pipe tip 6 pillows, tip 12 ball heads with tip 1 facial features and hair. Add tip 6 arms with tip 2 hands. Pipe dog with royal icing. Use tip 6, hold bag at 90⁰ angle, pipe a line of icing for body and a ball of icing for head. Pipe tip 4 legs, tail, snout and ears. Add tip 1 facial features.

Raccoons & Squirrels (p. 40)
Use royal icing.

For Raccoons: Using tip 6, pipe a ball of icing for body and head; add a line of icing for arms. Pipe tip 3 snout, ears, and whites of eyes; trim with tip 3 facial features and fingers. Finish with tip 5 line of icing for hat, trim with tip 13 star for tassle and hat trim.

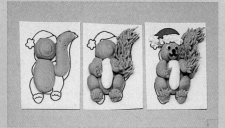

For Squirrel: Using tip 6, pipe line of icing for tail; ball of icing for head and body. Cover tail with tip 233 pull-out fur. Add tip 6 arms; tip 3 white belly area. Pipe tip 3 dot snout, add tip 2 facial features. Pipe tip 5 hat with tip 13 zigzag trim.

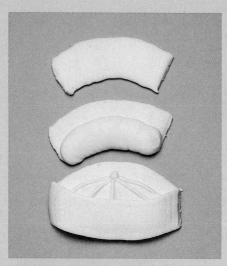

Sailor's Cap (p. 29)
Pipe back brim using tip 1D; pipe center of hat with tip 8 in one line just below back brim; pipe front brim with tip 1D. Add tip 3 lines and dot on center of hat.

30 year old scandal sheet (p. 36)
Use medium consistency buttercream and tip 10, hold bag at a 90⁰ angle and squeeze out a body using zigzag motion. Smooth with spatula. Squeeze out a line of icing for each arm and leg using tip 10. Use tip 7 to pipe shoes. Add tip 2 dots and zigzag trim on dress, and lines for fingers.

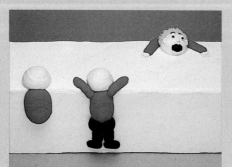

40 year old slipping away (p. 36)
Use medium consistency buttercream and tip 1A, hold bag at a 90⁰ angle and squeeze out a line of icing for body and a ball of icing for head. Pipe tip 10 arms and legs in a line. Add tip 2 fingers, hair, and facial features. Trim with tip 233 pull-out hair.

Bride of Frankenstein (p.57)
Apply piping gel to doll pick hair. Fold hair back to be half the original length. Place on waxed paper and let dry. Paint face and arms with thinned royal icing. Let dry and apply second coat. When hair is dry, ice smooth with royal icing. Cover hair with tip 134 zigzags. Add tip 1 facial features.

Mr. Frankenstein (p.57)
Cut hair off doll pick. With royal icing, pipe tip 6 zigzag for top of forehead (pat smooth with finger dipped in cornstarch) to create built-up look. With tip 6, overpipe nose and chin for square-jawed effect; add ears. Continuing with tip 6 and royal icing, complete piping zigzag formation down to neck. (Smooth with finger dipped in cornstarch).) When head is dry, paint with same color thinned royal icing. Let dry, paint another coat. Pipe tip 2 lines for hair, then pat down (do not smooth) with finger. Add tip 1 facial features.

Ghosts (p. 58)
With tip 12, pipe a ball shape for head and pull out a body, tapering off the end as you gradually decrease pressure. Tuck tip into body and pull out arms. Add tip 1 facial features.

Lambs (p. 64)
Using medium consistency buttercream and tip 12, hold bag at a 90⁰ angle and, using heavy pressure, pipe a line of icing for body; add head. Cover body and top and sides of head with tip 16 reverse shells. Add tip 79 ears and tip 3 feet. Add tip 3 dot eyes.

Color Flow

Color Flow Technique

• Tape pattern and waxed paper overlay to your work surface. (The back of a cookie pan makes a great work surface.) For curved decorations, use flower formers. Use full-strength Color Flow icing and tip 2 or 3 to outline the pattern with desired colors. If you're going to use the same color icing to fill in the outlines, let the icing outlines dry a few minutes until they "crust." If you're going to fill in with icing that differ in colors from the outlines, then let outlines dry thoroughly (1-2 hours) before filling in.

• Soften icing for filling in pattern outlines as specified in recipe. Don't use a tip for filling in outlines; instead, cut a very small opening in end of parchment bag. Begin filling in along the edges of the outline first, squeezing gently and letting the icing flow up to the outline almost by itself. Work quickly; filling in design from the

Color Flow Icing Recipe

(Full-Strength for Outlining)
1/4 cup water + 1 teaspoon
1 lb. sifted confectioners sugar (4 cups)
2 Tablespoons Wilton Color Flow Icing Mix

In an electric mixer, using grease-free utensils, blend all ingredients on low speed for 5 minutes. If using hand mixer, use high speed. Color Flow icing "crusts" quickly, so keep it covered with a damp cloth while using. Stir in desired icing color. In order to fill an outlined area, this recipe must be thinned with 1/2 teaspoon of water per 1/4 cup of icing (just a few drops at a time as you near proper consistency.) Color Flow is ready for filling in outlines when a small amount dropped into the mixture takes a full count of ten to disapppear. Use grease-free spoon or spatula to stir slowly.
Note: Color Flow designs take a long time to dry, so plan to do your Color Flow piece at least 2-3 days in advance.

Cookie Recipes

Grandma's Gingerbread Recipe

5 to 5 1/2 cups all-purpose flour
1 tsp. baking soda
1 tsp. salt
2 tsps. ginger
2 tsps. cinnamon
1 tsp. nutmeg
1 tsp. cloves
1 cup shortening
1 cup sugar
1 1/4 cups unsulphured molasses
2 eggs, beaten

Preheat oven to 375⁰.

Thoroughly mix flour, soda, salt and spices.

Melt shortening in large saucepan. Cool slightly. Add sugar, molasses and eggs; mix well. Add four cups dry ingredients and mix well.

Turn mixture onto lightly floured surface. Knead in remaining dry ingredients by hand. Add a little more flour, if necessary, to make a firm dough. Roll out on a lightly floured surface to 1/4 in. thickness for cut-out cookies.

If you're not going to use your gingerbread dough right away, wrap dough in plastic and refrigerate. Refrigerated dough will keep for a week, but be sure to remove it 3 hours prior to rolling so it softens and is workable. 1 recipe of this gingerbread dough will yield 40 average-size cookies.

outside edges in and from top to bottom. If you have several outlined sections, fill in one at a time.

If you're filling in a large area, have two half-full parchment bags ready, otherwise icing could "crust" before you finish filling in the patttern.

Hint: Since buttercream icing will break down color flow, either position color flow decoration on cake shortly before serving or place a piece of plastic wrap cut to fit on area first set atop sugar cubes.

To Pipe with Piping Gel

Pour off any liquid, then tint desired color with paste icing color. Add a small amount of color at a time. (it takes color very fast). Use a cut bag to flow piping gel into desired area.

Roll-Out Cookies

1 cup butter
1 cup sugar
1 large egg
2 tsps. baking powder
1 tsp. vanilla
3 cups flour

Preheat oven to 400⁰. In a large bowl, cream butter and sugar with an electric mixer. Beat in egg and vanilla. Add baking powder and flour, one cup at a time, mixing after each addition. The dough will be very stiff; blend last flour in by hand. Do not chill dough. **Note:** Dough can be tinted with Icing Color.

Add small amounts until desired color is reached. **For chocolate cookies**: Stir in 3 ounces melted, unsweetened chocolate (if dough becomes too stiff, add water, a teaspoon at a time).

Divide dough into 2 balls. On a floured surface, roll each ball into a circle approximately 12 inches in diameter and 1/8 in. thick. Dip cutters in flour before each use. Bake cookies on an ungreased cookie sheet on top rack of oven for 6-7 minutes, or until cookies are lightly browned.

Cookie Icing Recipe

This icing dries to a shiny, hard finish and tastes good, too. Great to use for icing or to outline and fill in with tip 2 or 3.

1 cup sifted confectioners sugar
2 teaspoons milk
2 teaspoons light corn syrup

Place sugar and milk in bowl. Stir until mixed thoroughly. Add corn syrup and mix well. For filling in areas, use thinned icing (add small amounts of light corn syrup until desired consistency is reached.)

All About Tier Cakes

There are many methods of constructing tiered cakes. Here are some of the most popular.

To Prepare Cake For Assembly

Place base tier on a sturdy base plate or 3 or more thicknesses of corrugated cardboard. For heavy cakes, use masonite or plywood. Base can be covered with Fanci-Foil Wrap and trimmed with Tuk-N-Ruffle or use the Wilton Ruffle Boards™. Each tier in your cake must be on a cake circle or board cut to fit. Smear a few strokes of icing on boards to secure cake. Fill and ice layers before assembly.

To Dowel Rod Cakes For Pillar & Stacked Construction

Center a cake circle or plate one size smaller than the next tier on base tier and press it gently into icing to imprint an outline. Remove circle. Measure one dowel rod at the cake's lowest point within this circle. Using this dowel rod for measure, cut dowel rods (to fit this tier) the same size using pruning shears. If the next tier is 10-in. or less, push seven ¼-in. dowel rods into cake down to base within circle guide. Generally the larger and more numerous the upper tiers, the more dowels needed. Very large cakes need ½-in. dowels in base tier.

Stacked Construction

This method is often combined with pillar construction. Dowel rod bottom tier. Center a corrugated cake circle, one size smaller than the tier to be added, on top of the base tier. Position the following tier. Repeat procedure for each additional tier. To keep stacked tiers stable, sharpen one end of a dowel rod and push through all tiers and cardboard circles to base of bottom tier. To decorate, start at top and work down.

Pillar Construction

Dowel rod tiers. Optional: Snap pegs into separator plates to prevent slipping (never substitute pegs for dowel rods). Position separator plates on supporting tiers, making sure that pillar projections on each tier will line up with pillars below. Mark center backs of cakes. Decorate cakes. At reception, align pillar projections and assemble cakes on pillars.

Fast & Easy Push-In Leg Construction

Dowel rods are not needed because legs attached to separator plates push right through the tiers down to the plate below.

Ice cakes on cake circles. To mark where legs will go, simply center separator plate for tier above (projections down) and gently press onto the tier. Lift plate off. Repeat this procedure for each tier (except top). Position upper tiers on separator plates. Decorate cakes.

To assemble: Insert legs into cake at marks. Push straight down until legs touch cake board. Add plate with cake to legs. Be sure plates are securely fastened to legs. Continue adding tiers in this way until cake is assembled.

Dowel Rod

Stacked

Mark Center Back

Pillar

Mark Where Legs Go

Push-In Leg

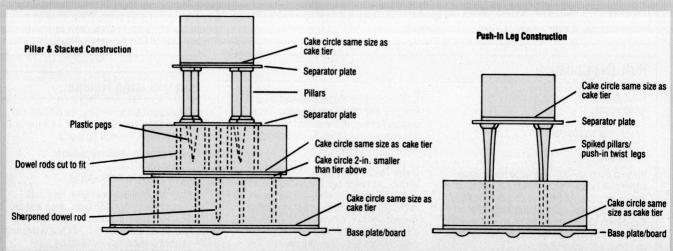

Pillar & Stacked Construction

Cake circle same size as cake tier
Separator plate
Pillars
Separator plate
Plastic pegs
Cake circle same size as cake tier
Dowel rods cut to fit
Cake circle 2-in. smaller than tier above
Sharpened dowel rod
Cake circle same size as cake tier
Base plate/board

Push-In Leg Construction

Cake circle same size as cake tier
Separator plate
Spiked pillars/ push-in twist legs
Cake circle same size as cake tier
Base plate/board

Hints for Assembling & Transporting Tiered Cakes

• Before placing separator plate or cake circle atop another tier, sprinkle a little confectioners sugar or coconut flakes to prevent plate or circle from sticking. Letting icing crust a bit before positioning plate on cake will also prevent sticking.
• You will have less crumbs when icing if cakes are baked a day in advance.
• When filling or torting large layers, use less than you usually would. Your dam of icing should also be far enough from edge so filling doesn't form a buble.
• The cake icer tip (789) is an invaluable timesaver in icing wedding tiers.
• The 16-in. bevel pan takes 1 ½ cakes mixes. So your beveled sides bake properly, pull batter out from center to add depth to the sides.
• When transporting tiers, place cakes on damp towels or carpet foam and drive carefully.
• To keep balance, cut cakes on the Tall Tier Stand from top tier down.
• To divide tiers, use the Cake Dividing Set. The Wheel Chart makes it easy to mark 2-in. intervals on 6 to 18-in. diam. cakes. The triangle marker gives precise spacing for stringwork and garlands. The raised lines on separator plates can also be followed for each dividing.
• When using Spiked Pillars and stacked construction, double cake boards or use separator plates between layers to prevent the weight of tiers from causing the pillars to pierce thrugh cake.

Wedding Cake Data

One cake mix yields 4 to 6 cups of batter. Pans are usually filled ½ to ⅔ full; 3-in. deep pans should be filled only ½ full. Batter amounts on this chart are for pans two-thirds full of batter. Icing amounts are very general and will vary with consistency, thickness applied and tips used. These amounts allow for top and base borders and a side ruffled border. For large cakes, always check for doneness after they have baked for one hour.

The charts to the right show how to cut popular shaped wedding tiers into pieces approximately 1-in. x 2-in. by two layers high (about 4-in.). Even if you prefer a larger serving size, the order of cutting is still the same.

Number of servings are intended as a guide only.

Pan Shape	Size	# Servings 2 Layer	Cups Batter/ 1 Layers 2"	Baking Temps	Baking Time	Approx. Cups Icing to Frost and Decorate
Oval	7¾ x 5¾"	13	2½	350°	25	3
	10¾ x 7⅞"	30	5½	350°	30	4
	13 x 9¾"	44	8	350°	30	5½
	16 x 12¾"	70	11	325°	30	7½
Round	6"	14	2	350°	25-30	3
	8"	25	3	350°	30-35	4
	10"	39	6	350°	35-40	5
	12"	56	7½	350°	35-40	6
	14"	77	10	325°	50-55	7¼
	16"	100	15	325°	55-60	8¾
Round 3" Deep (# Servings for 1 layer)	8"	15	5	325°	60-65	2¾
	10"	24	8	325°	75-80	4¾
	12"	33	11	325°	75-80	5¾
	14"	45	15	325°	75-80	7
Half Round 18"						
2" layer		127†	9*	325°	60-65	10½
3" layer		92††	12*	325°	60-65	10½
Petal	6"	8	1½	350°	25-30	3½
	9"	20	3½	350°	35-40	6
	12"	38	7	350°	35-40	7¾
	15"	62	12	325°	50-55	11
Hexagon	6"	12	1¾	350°	30-35	2¾
	9"	22	3½	350°	35-40	4¾
	12"	50	6	350°	40-45	5¾
	15"	72	11	325°	40-45	8¾
Heart	6"	11	1½	350°	25	2½
	9"	24	3½	350°	30	4½
	12"	48	8	350°	30	5¾
	15"	76	11½	325°	40	8¾
Square	6"	18	2	350°	25-30	3½
	8"	32	4	350°	35-40	4½
	10"	50	6	350°	35-40	6
	12"	72	10	350°	40-45	7½
	14"	98	13½	350°	45-50	9½
	16"	128	15½	350°	45-50	11
	18"	162	18	350°	50-55	13

*Batter for each half round pan.   †Four half rounds.   ††Two half rounds.

Center Column Construction with the Tall Tier Stand

• Each cake involved in this type of construction should be placed on a cake circle or board (cut to fit) with a pre-cut center hole. To do this, trace pan shape on waxed paper. Note: To make positioning easier, place top tier on a board slightly larger than cake. Fold pattern into quarters to determine the exact center of each tier. Snip away the point to make a center hole (use cake corer as a guide to size). Trace hole pattern onto boards and cut out.
• Place all tiers on prepared cake boards, attaching with a few strokes of icing. Ice tiers smooth. Core out cake centers by pushing the cake corer down to the cake base. Pull out and press cake out of corer.
• Screw a column to prepared base plate, attaching with the bottom column bolt from underneaththe plate. Slip bottom tier over the column to rest on plate.
• The bottom of the plates will not sit level, so to decorate, set plates on the Flower Holder Ring, a pan or bowl.
• Since the column cap nut attaches under the top tier, this cake must be positioned after assembling the Tall Tier Stand. Add base borders after assembling the top tier. Or you may place the top tier on a foil-covered cake circle so decorating can be done ahead.
• To assemble at reception, position plate onto base column section and screw column tight. Continue adding tiers with columns. At top plate, secure columns with cap nut bolt. Position top tier and decorate base.

Wedding Cake Cutting Guide

The first step in cutting is to remove the top tier, and then begin the cutting with the 2nd tier followed by 3rd, 4th and so on. The top tier is usually saved for the first anniversary so it is not figured into the serving amount.
Cutting guides for shapes not shown can be found in other Wilton publications.
The diagrams below show how to cut popular shaped wedding tiers into pieces approximately 1-in. x 2-in. by two layers high (about 4-in.). Even if you prefer a larger serving size, the order of cutting is still the same.

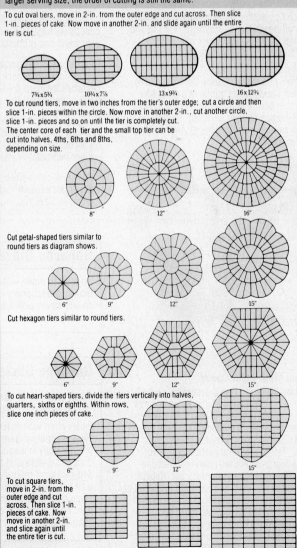

To cut oval tiers, move in 2-in. from the outer edge and cut across. Then slice 1-in. pieces of cake. Now move in another 2-in. and slide again until the entire tier is cut.

7¾ x 5¾   10¾ x 7⅞   13 x 9¾   16 x 12¾

To cut round tiers, move in two inches from the tier's outer edge; cut a circle and then slice 1-in. pieces within the circle. Now move in another 2-in., cut another circle, slice 1-in. pieces and so on until the tier is completely cut. The center core of each tier and the small top tier can be cut into halves, 4ths, 6ths and 8ths, depending on size.

8"   12"   16"

Cut petal-shaped tiers similar to round tiers as diagram shows.

6"   9"   12"   15"

Cut hexagon tiers similar to round tiers.

6"   9"   12"   15"

To cut heart-shaped tiers, divide the tiers vertically into halves, quarters, sixths or eighths. Within rows, slice one inch pieces of cake.

6"   9"   12"   15"

To cut square tiers, move in 2-in. from the outer edge and cut across. Then slice 1-in. pieces of cake. Now move in another 2-in. and slice again until the entire tier is cut.

8"   12"   16"

Candy Making

Wilton Candy Melts™ brand confectionery coating take the guesswork out of making candy at home. They melt easily, right to the ideal consistency for molding and dipping, and have a creamy, rich flavor. For a change of taste, they can be flavored with Wilton Candy Flowers. See our complete collection of candy making products (p. 114-116).

Candy Melts Are So Easy To Use

For melting, molding and dipping directions, simply refer to the back of the Candy Melts package. Remember that constant stirring is very important to insure even heating, when using the double boiler method. Here's a no-mess way of melting in the microwave: Fill an uncut disposable decorating bag half-full of Candy Melts. Microwave 1 minute at half power; knead candy. Repeat at 30-second intervals until candy is completely melted. Then cut the tip and squeeze melted coating out into candy molds.

To Flavor: The creamy, rich taste can be enhanced by adding approximately $1/4$ teaspoon Wilton oil-based Candy Flavor (p. 116) to 1 lb. of melted Candy Melts. Never use alcohol based flavorings; they will cause coatings to harden.

To Color: Add Wilton Candy Colors (p. 116) to melted Candy Melts a little at a time. Mix thoroughly before adding more color. Colors tend to deepen as they're mixed. Pastel colored candies are most appetizing, so keep this in mind when tinting.

To Mold Multi-Color Candy

"Painting Method: Use a decorator's brush dipped in melted Candy Melts. Paint features or details desired. Let set. Fill mold. Refrigerate until set. Unmold. **"Layering" Method:** Pour melted coating into dry molds to desired height. Refrigerate until partially set. Pour contrasting color melted coating to desired height. Refrigerate until partially set. Repeat until desired numbers of layers are formed. Let candy harden in refrigerator. Unmold. Wilton Classic Candy Molds are available in a wonderful variety of unique and traditional shapes. Their generous depth makes painting and layering fun and easy. See page 114-115 for our outstanding Classic Candy Molds selection.

To Mold Candy Plaques

Molding a section or the entire pan out of Candy Melts is easy and impressive.

• Pour melted coating into center of pan. Tap pan gently on counter to break up bubbles and spread coating evenly over bottom (approximately $1/4$ in. thick). For control, use a decorating bag fitted with tip 2 or snip off a very small end off disposable bag.

• Place pan in refrigerator for approximately 5 to 10 minutes (check occasionally, if coating becomes too hard it will crack). Unmold onto hand or soft towel (tap pan gently, if necessary).

• Cookie cutters work great, too. Place cutter on waxed paper; pour in candy. Unmold when set per instructions above.

• For multi-color effect: Paint desired area with a decorator's brush. Let set. Pour in melted coating to fill remaining area.

Ganache Glaze

So easy to make with our Candy Melts™ brand confectionery coating. Elegantly covers cakes with a luscious, satiny-smooth finish.

Ganache Glaze Recipe

14 oz. package of Candy Melts
$1/2$ cup whipping cream

Finely chop wafers (use food processor). Heat whipping cream just to boiling point (do not boil) in a sauce pan. Add chopped wafers and stir until smooth and glossy. If mixture is too thin to pour, wait a few minutes until cool. To cover, place cake on a wire rack over a drip pan. Pour glaze into center and work toward edges.

Piping Decorations with Candy

• Use any appropriate pattern and place on a heavy board or piece of glass, cover with waxed paper and tape securely.

• Cut bag method: Fill a parchment or disposable bag with melted Candy Melts. Cut a very small opening in end of bag (approximately the size of a tip 3). If candy thickens, bag can be reheated in microwave. For thicker decorations such as panels, pipe candy using a round tip. Outline edges of pattern design and let set 5 to 10 minutes. Flow in candy (to smooth surface, skim area with end of bag immediately) and let set. Allow piece to set completely 10 to 15 minutes.

It's easy to make a 3-dimensional tree to grace your holiday table.

• Use melted Wilton Candy Melts in the color you desire and pipe over your tree pattern. Use a cut bag or tip 2. You'll need 1 full tree and 2 half tree pieces for each 3-D tree.

• When set, attach a half in center of full tree with melted candy. Let set 10 to 15 minutes. Set tree upright and attach remaining half to opposite side following the same procedure. Since these are very delicate, you may want to make extras, in case of breakage.

Modeling Candy "Clay"
- 14 oz. bag of Candy Melts
- 1/3 cup light corn syrup
- Candy or Icing Color (optional)

Melt candy as directed on package. Stir in corn syrup and mix only until blended.

Shape mixture into a 6 in. square on waxed paper and let set at room temperature until dry.

Wrap well and store at room temperature until needed. Modeling candy handles best if hardened overnight.

To use: If you wish to tint candy, add candy or icing color. Knead a small portion at a time. If it gets too soft, set aside at room temperature or refrigerate briefly. Lasts for several weeks in a well-sealed container at room temperature.

When rolling out candy, sprinkle surface with cornstarch to prevent sticking. Thickness of rolled-out candy should be approximately 1/8 in. Hint: Secure pieces together with dots of buttercream icing, if necessary.

Modeling a Rose
Start with the base and mold a cone that's approximately 1 1/2 in. high from a 3/4 in. diameter ball of modeling candy. Next, make petals. Flatten 3/8 in. ball of modeling candy into a circle that's about 1/4 in. thick on one side and about the diameter of a dime. Make several petals this size.

- Wrap first petal around the point of the cone to form a bud. Now press three more petals around the base of the bud.

- Gently pinch edges of petals. Make five more petals using slightly larger balls of modeling candy. Flatten, then thin edge with finger and cup petals. Press petals under first rows of petals. Continue adding petals, placing them in between and slightly lower than previous row. For a fuller flower, continue adding petals in this manner.

To Make Flowers
Use tools and instructions included in our Gum Paste Flowers Kit for making daffodil, violet and leaves.

Make 1 recipe of Modeling Candy with white Candy Melts. Tint 1/2 of recipe yellow. Divide remainder into 3rds. One remains white, tint rest green and violet with icing colors.

For Daffodil: Do steps 1 through 3 (in gum paste kit instruction book), except use cornstarch instead of grease. Let petals dry on flower

formers. For trumpet or cup, roll out white modeling candy. Cut out trumpet with small carnation cutter. With a knife, cut away a triangular 4th. Dip modeling stick (included in kit) in cornstarch and form trumpet around it. Let dry. Attach trumpet to petals with royal icing. Edge top with tip 2 royal icing zigzags.

For Leaves: Roll out green modeling candy. Cut out leaves with large leaf cutter. Dip leaf mold into cornstarch, then press candy into mold. Remove leaf from mold and allow it to dry on flower former.

For Violets: Follow steps 1 thru 3 in gum paste kit instruction book. Let flowers dry on flower formers. For centers, make tiny balls from yellow modeling candy. Attach with dots of royal icing.

To Make Rolled Fondant Roses
Follow modeling a rose instructions (at left), using rolled fondant (recipe, p. 93) instead of modeling candy clay. To color fondant, add color a few drops at a time to ball of fondant and knead in with hands.

Sugar Mold Recipe

4 1/2 cups granulated sugar
3 Tablespoons water

Place sugar in large mixing bowl. Mix sugar so there are no lumps in it. Make a well in sugar, then add water. Rub mixture between your hands and knead for about 1 minute or unitl well-blended and mixture packs like wet sand. Be sure there are no lumps in mixture. NOTE: Keep sugar mixture covered with a damp cloth when not in use.

SUGAR MOLDS
Carriage (p. 10)

- Mix 2 batches of sugar according to recipe above. Dust each half of the Sports Ball with cornstarch to prevent sticking. Pack sugar mixture into each half, pressing firmly with heel of hand. Scrape a metal spatula at a 45⁰ angle over pan halves to remove excess sugar. Unmold at once by placing cardboard circle over pans and turning upside down. To loosen, tap top of pan with spatula and carefully lift mold off. Use a thread, string, or metal spatula to saw 1 in. off front and back

of each half. Later, when you join halves, if they do not match exactly you can use sandpaper to make edges even. Let halves dry for approximately 1 to 1 1/2 hours. Turn right side up and carefully hold in palm of hand. Do not squeeze or move sugar mold while it's in your hand or it will crack. Use a spoon to mark 1/4 in. thick shell on inside rim of ball.

Start at center of ball and gently scoop out soft sugar (if ball cracks in two, wet and fill in crack with sugar mold mixture, then carefully press together). After sugar is scooped out, smooth inside and opening of ball with your fingers. Place ball halves right side up on cardboard circle to finish drying for about 24 hours, or place on cookie sheet in 200⁰ F oven for 20 minutes. Allow to cool to room temperature before touching.

The Wilton School
of Cake Decorating
and Confectionery Art

Learn how to decorate from the experts! Since 1929, when Dewey McKinley Wilton first opened the Wilton School, hundreds of thousands of students have learned the fundamentals of decorating the Wilton Way. The Wilton Method of Cake Decorating stresses classic decorating – beginning with a thorough understanding of the fundamentals. Students are then encouraged to express themselves creatively.

The Wilton School has a Certificate of Approval to operate issued by the Illinois State Superintendent of Schools. Students receive instruction, supervision and guidance by expert instructors/decorators.

World renowned, the Wilton School has greatly expanded its curriculum since the Wilton Method was first introduced 60 years ago. Today the basic Master Course is supplemented by courses in foreign methods, Lambeth, chocolate artistry, gum paste, pulled sugar, cakes for catering and more. The following is a summary of courses we offer:

MASTER COURSE – 2 weeks, 70 hours. Focuses on the fundamentals of cake decorating. Designed for the cake decorating shop owner, baker, caterer, chef or enthusiast.
TUITION: $525   **Registration Fee $75.00***

INTRODUCTION TO GUM PASTE COURSE – 12 hours–four afternoons during the Master Course. This mini-course teaches the art of making lovely gum paste flowers, bouquets and more.
TUITION: $100   **Registration Fee $25.00***

ADVANCED GUM PASTE/FOREIGN METHODS COURSE – 2 weeks, 80 hours. Designed for the more serious decorator. Covers: Nirvana, the English method of cake decorating that uses color flow panels; South African and Australian Methods, which use delicate royal icing wings and are done on rolled fondant-covered cakes; gum paste flowers and arrangements. A gum paste doll is constructed. Previous decorating experience is required.
TUITION: $525   **Registration Fee $75.00***

LAMBETH CONTINENTAL COURSE – 1 week, 40 hours. Teaches intricate overpiping of borders on royal icing and rolled fondant-covered cakes. All students decorate cakes using a combination of overpiped borders. Previous decorating experience is required.
TUITION: $275   **Registration Fee $50.00***

PULLED SUGAR COURSE – 9 hours, 3 afternoons during Master Course. Learn how to use pulled sugar to cover a cake, make flowers, candy dishes, ribbons, bows and more.
TUITION: $150   **Registration Fee $25.00***

CHOCOLATE ARTISTRY WITH ELAINE GONZALEZ – 5 days, 30 hours. Well-known chocolatier and author of *Chocolate Artistry* presents an in-depth course devoted exclusively to making and decorating candy. Professional techniques for creating fabulous candies from molded treats to delicious truffles are taught.
TUITION: $300   **Registration Fee $50.00***

CAKES FOR CATERING – A 5 day, 40-hour course where students learn to ice and decorate cakes to serve large or small groups. The class covers wedding and other tiered cakes, sheet cakes, large rounds and squares and petit fours. Learn to design theme party cakes and get special tips for quick and easy, but spectacular designs. Decorating experience required.
TUITION: $275   **Registration Fee $50.00***

The Wilton School is located in Woodridge, Illinois (a suburb of Chicago). Course enrollment is limited. Apply early.

*****When registering for multiple classes the TOTAL Registration Fee is only $100.**

Wilton Home Study Course in Cake Decorating

Even if you've never tried cake decorating before, the Wilton Home Study Course will show you how to decorate beautiful cakes for every occasion. Easy-to-follow 5-lesson course includes the specialty tools you need plus the step-by-step instructions, illustrations and photographs that make it easy!

Enroll in the Wilton Home Study Course in Cake Decorating now. The cost is only $17.99 plus $3.50 postage and handling per lesson. See details on page 128.

LESSON 1
Discover the easy way to pipe buttercream icing stars, zigzag borders and more! Learn how to prepare and color icing for your decorating bag, the correct angle to use, and how to control the pressure for expert results. Make a "Happy Birthday" cake.

Lesson 1 includes:
- Notebook Easel and Lesson Pages
- Decorating Tips 4, 16 and 18
- Quick-Change Plastic Coupler
- Two Jars of Paste Icing Color
- Shaped "Happy Birthday" Cake Pan
- 12" Featherweight Decorating Bag
- Pattern Sheets and Practice Board
- Cardboard Cake Circle
- *Cake Decorating Easy As 1-2-3 Book*

LESSON 2
Make royal icing drop flowers, star flowers and leaves. Mold a sugar basket. Create a blooming basket cake. Learn how to achieve special effects with color and floral sprays plus how to print or write personalized messages!

Lesson 2 includes:
- Lesson Pages
- Flower Basket Sugar Mold
- Large Stainless Steel Angled Spatula
- Decorating Tips 3, 20, 67 and 131
- 2 Jars of Paste Icing Color
- Meringue Powder (4 oz. canister)
- Pack of 50 Parchment Paper Triangles
- Cardboard Cake Circle
- 6 Pattern Sheets

LESSON 3
Learn the proper techniques for making shells, rosebuds, sweet peas, ruffles, bows, and more! Learn to make bouquets on a heart-shaped cake ideal for anniversaries, birthdays, Valentine's Day, weddings, showers.

Lesson 3 includes:
- Lesson Pages
- Two 9" Heart-Shaped Aluminum Pans
- Decorating Tips 22, 103 and 104
- 12" Featherweight Decorating Bag
- Quick-Change Plastic Coupler
- Cardboard Cake Circle
- Jar of Paste Icing Color
- 4 Pattern Sheets

LESSON 4
Pipe daisies and chrysanthemums using a flower nail. Weave basketweave stripes. Create symmetrical cake designs, pipe rope borders and more. Use your new cake turntable to decorate a round cake.

Lesson 4 includes:
- Lesson Pages
- Trim 'N Turn Cake Stand
- Decorating Tips 48 and 81
- Cardboard Cake Circle
- Flower Nails 7 and 9
- Jar of Paste Icing Color
- Wilton Cake Marker
- 6 Pattern Sheets

LESSON 5
Shape a magnificent icing rose! Pipe stringwork and create a mini-tiered cake using the pans and separator set we'll send. After this lesson you'll qualify for your Wilton Certificate of Completion!

Lesson 5 includes:
- Lesson Pages
- Round Mini-Tier Kit (includes 3 cake pans, separator plates and columns)
- Decorating Tips 2, 12, 87 and 102
- Cardboard Cake Circle
- 4 Pattern Sheets

You can do it!

We'll show you how. Even if you don't know a decorating bag from a coupler, by the end of this course, you'll be a pro.

Learn creative techniques on which you will constantly rely. Piping, drop flowers, shells, daisies, chrysanthemums and magnificent roses. The ideas and options are endless. You will quickly realize, with confidence, that "you can do it."

Publications

NEW! CHRISTMAS BOOK
The ideal place to begin new holiday traditions, filled with dozens of recipes and ideas to make the season brighter. Create festive main dishes, appetizers, cakes, cookies, crafts, gingerbread designs and more, using our easy-to-follow instructions and timely hints. A great source for your holiday party or to add imagination to the family Christmas dinner. Soft cover, 96 color pages. 8 1/4 x 10 3/4 in.
902-Z-250 $6.99 each

HOLIDAY
A complete collection of cakes, cookies, centerpieces and candy for holiday baking and making. Dozens of unusual festive ideas you'll love to make from gingerbread, cookie dough, cakes, candy and other confections, plus unique cookie baskets. Holiday characters, trimmed ornaments-even create your own heirlooms. Festive designs you'll use again and again. Soft cover; 80 color pages; 8 1/2 x 11 in.
902-Z-1225 $6.99 each

A TREASURY OF WILTON WEDDING CAKES
The newest and most exquisite collection of wedding cakes and ornaments anywhere. This book reflects more than half a century of experience Wilton has in designing wedding cakes. From Victorian to contemporary cakes and designer series porcelain ornaments. Soft cover; 96 color pages; 8 1/2 x 10 3/4 in.
908-Z-105 $6.99 each

WEDDING CAKES- A WILTON ALBUM
Mark those cherished occasions with a culinary masterpiece. Create wedding, shower and anniversary cakes-from classic to contemporary. Complete, easy-to-follow instructions, patterns, recipes and wedding cake data and cutting guide are also included. Soft cover; 82 color pages; 8 1/4 x 10 3/4 in.
908-Z-100 $6.99 each

NEW! 1993 YEARBOOK OF CAKE DECORATING
Over 150 new cake decorating ideas in addition to cookie, candy and wedding cake creations. Step-by-step decorating instructions and helpful hints included. Soft cover; 192 pages. 8 1/4 x 10 3/4 in.
1701-Z-930 $5.99 each

NEW! 1993 PATTERN BOOK
Just the helping hand you need to duplicate many cake ideas from the 1993 Yearbook. Many innovative designs. 8 1/4 x 10 3/4 in.
408-Z-930 $4.99 each

CELEBRATE! WEDDING CAKES BY WILTON
From intricate cakes that serve hundreds to dainty creations for the most intimate gathering, this book has everything for that special bride. Scores of designs using innovative techniques including foreign methods, stairways and fountains. Instructions and patterns included. Hard cover; 192 color pages; 8 3/4 x 11 in.
916-Z-847 $12.99 each

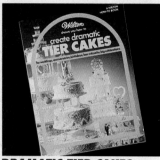

DRAMATIC TIER CAKES
With this complete Wilton guide learn the fundamentals of constructing and decorating lavish tier cakes, from the basics of building a cake to the safest way to transport wedding tiers to the reception. Includes uses of stairways and fountains, plus tested recipes, decorating descriptions and a complete selection of products needed to make the cakes shown. A must-have for any decorator. Soft cover; 80 color pages; 8 1/2 x 11 in.
902-Z-1725 $6.99 each

WILTON CELEBRATES THE ROSE
Learn all about this most popular icing flower. Includes easy-to-follow classic rose-making directions plus a quick, impressive method. Also learn how to create petal-perfect candy flowers, how to model marzipan and gum paste roses, and how to stencil cakes. Recipes and patterns included. Soft cover; 66 color pages; 8 1/2 x 11 in.
916-Z-1218 $6.99 each

NEW! BOMBONIERE! PARTY FAVOR BOOK
Learn step-by-step how to make over 100 easy, beautiful favors—there are styles for weddings, anniversaries, showers, baby showers, rehearsal dinners and more! Complete instructions for each favor plus sections on basic techniques and flowers and bows make favor-making easy and fun. Soft cover; 48 color pages. See complete product selection p. 148-151. 8 1/4 x 10 3/4 in.
916-Z-825 $4.99 each

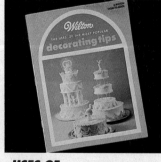

USES OF DECORATING TIPS
Extremely valuable quick reference/idea book. Shows the versatility and range of many tips by depicting design variations. Soft cover; 48 color pages; 8 1/2 x 11 in.
902-Z-1375 $6.99 each

CAKE DECORATING- EASY AS 1-2-3
Shows and explains the basics of cake decorating in simple terms. Perfect for beginners! Soft cover; 36 color pages; 5 1/2 x 8 1/2 in.
902-Z-1792 $1.99 each
902-Z-1790 Italian version $1.99 each

ADVENTURES IN COOKIE LAND
This fun cookie cutter activity book contains a variety of games, puzzles, coloring activities and craft ideas for children. Soft cover; 32 pages. 8 1/2 x 11 in.
900-Z-1990 $1.49 each

Publications

Our Three Part Encyclopedia:
THE WILTON WAY OF CAKE DECORATING

The comprehensive cake decorating reference book for professionals and amateurs alike! Explore this must-have trilogy of techniques, tools, ideas, instructions and hints. All found in three invaluable volumes you'll be constantly consulting.

VOLUME ONE- BEGIN WITH THE BASICS!

More than 600 full-color photos portray the Wilton method of decorating. Specialty techniques, such as Color Flow, Figure Piping, Sugar Molding and Marzipan Modeling are easy to master. Includes recipes. Hard cover; 328 color pages; 8 1/2 x 11 in.
904-Z-100 $29.99 each

VOLUME TWO- ADVANCED TECHNIQUES

Our 328-page encyclopedia is brimming with Wilton-American and foreign techniques: English (Nirvana and over-piped), Australian, Continental, Mexican, Philippine and South African. Includes gum paste flowers and figures and the art of pulled sugar taught and demonstrated by Norman Wilton. Soft cover; 328 color pages; 8 1/2 x 11 in.
904-Z-119 $29.99 each

VOLUME THREE- USING DECORATING TIPS

More than 400 color photos highlight over 40 beautiful borders, plus dozens of flowers and other decorative motifs. Exciting figure piped and gum paste creations are demonstrated and explained. Hard cover; 328 color pages; 8 1/2 x 11 in.

ENGLISH VERSION
904-Y-348 $29.99 each

SPANISH VERSION
Features a full chapter of quinceanos cakes and easy-to-follow "pictorial dictionary."
904-Z-1348 $34.99 each

THE COMPLETE WILTON BOOK OF CANDY

Treat family and friends to luscious molded and dipped chocolates, dessert shells, fudge, truffles, confectionery coated candies, marzipan, hard candies. It's easy with our recipes and hints. Soft cover; 176 color pages; 7 1/2 x 10 1/2 in.
902-Z-1243 $10.99 each

LET'S MAKE CANDY

A step-by-step guide for beginning and experienced candy makers. Basic techniques such as molding and dipping, plus specialty ideas, such as candy clay and candi-pan are clearly explained. Soft cover; 44 color pages, 5 1/2 x 8 1/2 in.
902-Z-2100 $1.99 each

Video Home Study

IT'S CONVENIENT...see actual decorating techniques demonstrated right in your own home. Learn step-by-step, how to create these wonderful icing techniques yourself ...then practice them on your practice board right in front of your TV.

IT'S A TREAT...learn from our experts. Now you can gather all the secrets of experienced cake decorators. See and hear all the hints and tips that make decorating easy.

ENROLL IN THE WILTON VIDEO HOME STUDY COURSE NOW.

The cost is only **$29.99** plus $3.50 shipping and handling per lesson...and the videos and all the pans and tools are yours to keep. Don't delay. Return the card on page 128 with your first payment to Wilton and we'll send you Lesson I. If you are not completely satisfied, you can return the materials within 30 days for a full refund or credit.

Lesson 1
Learn the fundamentals of baking and frosting shaped cakes, about icing, how to use decorating tools and more! Learn how to decorate **2 fun, shaped cakes.**
Includes
Lesson I 30 minute VHS video, Lesson Plan/Guide, Huggable Bear shaped pan, 10 in. Soft Touch decorating bag, 3 disposable decorating bags, 4 metal decorating tips, 2 quick-change couplers, practice board with practice sheets, 2 jars of icing color, heavy duty cake board, Trim 'N Turn cake stand, 1993 Wilton Yearbook of Cake Decorating.

Lesson 2
Learn how to torte, how to ice a cake smooth, how to make shells, drop flowers, leaves, figure pipe. Learn how to decorate **2 cakes and a clown cupcake,** using figure piping and drop flowers.
Includes
Lesson II 30 minute VHS video, Lesson Plan/Guide, 9" Round Pan Set, 3 metal decorating tips, large angled spatula, 2 jars of icing color, 3 disposable decorating bags, 30 parchment sheets, 2 cake circles, Clown Heads cake tops.

Lesson 3
Learn how to make the rose and other icing flowers, how to make bows, and how to position flower sprays on cakes. Learn how to decorate **2 heart-shaped cakes** with basketweave and flowers.
Includes
Lesson III 30 minute VHS video, Lesson Plan/Guide, 9" Happiness Heart Pan Set, 3 metal decorating tips, #7 flower nail, 2 jars icing color, a container of meringue powder, 2 cake circles, a decorating comb and a Certificate of Completion.

How To Videos

HOW TO MAKE WEDDING CAKES

Receive invaluable lessons on how to design and assemble dramatic tier cakes for weddings, showers, anniversaries and other special occasions. Hints for transporting and serving also included in this 60 min. video.
VHS. 901-Z-128 $19.99

HOW TO MAKE ICING FLOWERS

Learn how to make roses, Easter lilies, violets, pansies, daisies, poinsettias and more! Five cake designs incorporate all the flowers included in this 60 min. video.
VHS. 901-Z-119 $19.99

CAKE DECORATING - EASY AS 1,2,3!

Zella Junkin, Director of the Wilton School, takes you through the basics. See how to level and frost a cake perfectly, make simple borders, flowers, leaves and more. 60 min.
VHS. 901-Z-115 $19.99

CANDY MAKING - EASY AS 1, 2, 3!

Learn how to make truffles, candy novelties, dipped fruit, molded and filled candy. Melting candy in the microwave included. 80 min.
VHS. 901-Z-125 $19.99

Candy Molds

1. CLOWNS
8 molds; 8 designs
2114-Z-92824 **$1.99 each**

2. 2 PC. CREATE A FACE SET
18 molds; 15 designs
2114-Z-97535 **$3.49 set**

3. DINOSAURS
9 molds; 4 designs per sheet.
2114-Z-98888 **$1.99 each**

4. TEDDY BEARS
8 molds; 8 designs
2114-Z-92826 **$1.99 each**

5. BEARS
4 cute designs.
2114-Z-94055 **$1.99 each**

6. ALUMINUM PANDA MOLD
Ideal for baking or molding a great treat. Sides clip together, base opens for easy filling. 5 x 5 in. Instructions, base and clips included.
518-Z-489 **$5.99 each**

7. MUSICAL NOTES
13 molds; 6 designs.
2114-Z-92832 **$1.99 each**

8. TEDDY BEARS & GUMBALL MACHINES
8 molds; 2 designs.
2114-Z-94232 **$1.99 each**

9. BALLERINA LOLLIPOPS
8 molds; 4 designs.
2114-Z-92834 **$1.99 each**

10. LOLLIPOPS I
5 molds; 5 designs.
2114-Z-90882 **$1.99 each**

11. LOLLIPOPS II
5 molds; 5 designs on sheet.
2114-Z-90861 **$1.99 each**

12. FLOWERS
10 molds; 7 designs
2114-Z-92830 **$1.99 each**

13. ROSES 'N BUDS
10 molds on sheet; 2 designs; 2 lollipops.
2114-Z-91101 **$1.99 each**

14. ROSES
10 molds; 3 designs on sheet.
2114-Z-91511 **$1.99 each**

15. BABY SHOWER
4 designs, 10 molds per sheet.
2114-Z-92816 **$1.99 each**

16. MINT DISCS
12 molds; 1 design on sheet.
1/4 in. deep.
2114-Z-91226 **$1.99 each**

17. ACCORDIAN RUFFLES
10 molds; 1 design on sheet.
2114-Z-91013 **$1.99 each**

18. NEW BABY ARRIVAL
8 molds; 7 designs
2114-Z-92822 **$1.99 each**

19. BON BONS
12 molds; 1 design on sheet.
2114-Z-91072 **$1.99 each**

20. LARGE BON BONS
8 molds; 1 design on sheet.
2114-Z-92656 **$1.99 each**

21. BRIDAL TREATS
8 molds; 5 designs.
2114-Z-92820 **$1.99 each**

22. WEDDING SHOWER
3 designs for bridal showers and weddings; 12 molds, including 2 lollipops.
2114-Z-91104 **$1.99 each**

23. ROUNDS
8 molds; 2 designs on sheet.
2114-Z-90466 **$1.99 each**

24. FANCY CHOCOLATES I
12 molds; 2 designs.
2114-Z-91269 **$1.99 each**

25. LEAVES
10 molds; 2 designs on sheet.
2114-Z-90629 **$1.99 each**

26. TEENAGE MUTANT NINJA TURTLES ®
7 molds; 7 designs
2114-Z-90110 **$1.99 each**
© &® 1990 Mirage Studios, U.S.A.
Exclusively licensed by Surge Licensing, Inc.

27. NEW! BARBIE ®
8 molds; 8 designs
2114-Z-9050 **$1.99 each**
Barbie and associated trademarks are owned by and used under license from Mattel, Inc.
©1992 Mattel, Inc. All Rights Reserved.

28. GARFIELD HALLOWEEN
8 molds; 7 designs
2114-Z-92828 **$1.99 each**
GARFIELD Characters: ©1978 United Feature Syndicate, Inc.

29. GARFIELD
7 molds; 6 designs
2114-Z-90100 **$1.99 each**
GARFIELD Characters: ©1978 United Feature Syndicate, Inc

30. THE SIMPSONS
8 molds; 8 designs
2114-Z-91910 **$1.99 each**
© MATT GROENING
TM & © 1990 Twentieth Century Fox Film Corporation. All rights reserved.

31. BATMAN ™
7 molds; 6 designs
2114-Z-90105 **$1.99 each**
TM & © 1989 DC Comics Inc., All Rights Reserved.

1. CHRISTMAS I
8 festive molds, 7 designs.
2114-Z-94136 $1.99 each

2. CHRISTMAS II
10 molds, 9 joyful designs
per sheet.
2114-Z-94152 $1.99 each

**3. CHRISTMAS
LOLLIPOP**
8 molds; 8 designs
2114-Z-97536 $1.99 each

4. SNOWFLAKES
8 molds. 2 designs on sheet.
2114-Z-90661 $1.99 each

**5. 2-PC. CHRISTMAS
CLASSICS SET**
Santas, Sleigh, Reindeer and
Toys. 6 designs, 18 molds.
2114-Z-1224 $3.99 set

**6. 2-PC. CHRISTMAS
CLASSICS II SET**
Trees, trims & holiday friends.
6 designs. 18 molds.
2114-Z-1225 $3.99 set

7. CHRISTMAS TREES
14 molds on sheet.
2114-Z-91099 $1.99 each

8. HEARTS
15 classic molds on sheet.
2114-Z-90214 $1.99 each

**9. I LOVE YOU
LOLLIPOP**
8 molds; 8 designs
2114-Z-91911 $1.99 each

10. HEARTS I
11 molds, 3 designs on sheet.
2114-Z-91030 $1.99 each

11. HEARTS II
8 molds; 2 designs on sheet.
2114-Z-90645 $1.99 each

12. _NEW!_ TRUE LOVE
8 molds on sheet; 6 designs.
2114-Z-9324 $1.99 each

**13. GREAT EGGS!™
KIT**
Includes 2 egg molds, tips,
coupler, brush, 2 candy mold
sheets, recipes, instructions.
2104-Z-3615 $9.99 kit

14. EGG MOLD SET
2-pc. plastic molds. Includes
one each; 5 x 4 in.; 4 1/2 x 3 in.;
3 x 2 in.
1404-Z-1040 $3.99 set

15. EASTER LOLLIPOP
8 molds; 8 designs
2114-Z-91912 $1.99 each

16. EASTER RABBITS
12 cottontails per sheet.
2114-Z-91200 $1.99 each

17. EASTER TREATS
8 designs. 8 molds.
2114-Z-91000 $1.99 each

**18. _NEW!_ WHOLE
EGGS EASTER MOLD**
4 designs. 1 1/2 x 1 3/4 in. long.
2114-Z-9313 $2.99 each

19. EGG CLASSIC
Each 1 x 1 1/2 in. long; 12 molds
per sheet.
2114-Z-90998 $1.99 each

20. PLAYFUL BUNNIES
8 designs. 8 molds.
2114-Z-90999 $1.99 each

21. THANKSGIVING
3 traditional designs, including
turkey lollipops. 9 molds.
2 lollipops.
2114-Z-91128 $1.99 each

**22. 2-PC. HALLOWEEN
VARIETY SET**
2 sheets of molds. 11 designs.
18 molds.
2114-Z-1031 $3.99 set

23. JACK-O-LANTERNS
2 1/2 in. wide. 3 jolly-faced
molds on sheet.
2114-Z-91056 $1.99 each

24. PUMPKINS
12 identical smiling molds.
2114-Z-90740 $1.99 each

25. NUMBERS
18 molds per sheet.
2114-Z-92912 $1.99 each

26. SCRIPT WORDS
Best, Wishes, Congratulations.
2114-Z-92914 $1.99 each

27. SCRIPT WORDS II
Happy, Birthday, Anniversary.
2114-Z-92915 $1.99 each

**28. 2-PC. ALPHABET
SET**
Capital letters; two of each
vowel; plus two t's and s's
2114-Z-92910 $3.49 set

Candy Tools

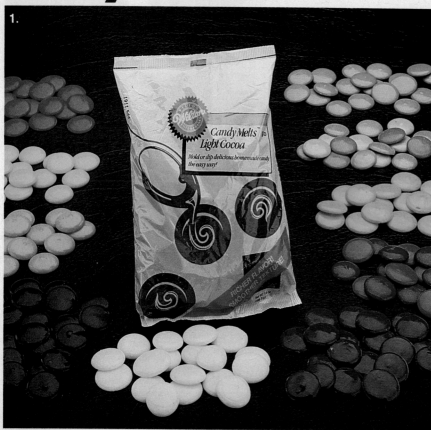

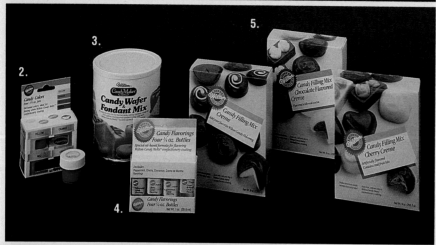

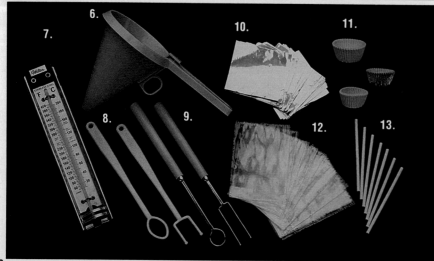

1. CANDY MELTS ™
The multi-talented brand confectionery coating. Creamy, easy-to-melt wafers are ideal for all your candy making—molding, dipping and coating. Delicious taste that can be varied with our Candy Flavors. 14 oz. bag. Certified Kosher. **$2.50 each**

White	1911-Z-498
Light Cocoa (All natural, cocoa flavor)	1911-Z-544
Dark Cocoa (All natural, cocoa flavor)	1911-Z-358
Pink	1911-Z-447
Yellow	1911-Z-463
Green	1911-Z-404
Christmas Mix (Red, Green)	1911-Z-1624
(Available 9/4-12/15)	
Pastel Mix (Pink, Lavender, Blue)	1911-Z-1637
(Available 12/1-5/31)	
Orange (Available 7/16-10/31)	1911-Z-1631
Red (Available 9/4-1/31)	1911-Z-499

All colors are vanilla flavored
*brand confectionery coating

2. CANDY COLORS KIT
Rich, concentrated oil-based color that blends beautifully into Wilton Candy Melts. Contains red, green, yellow and orange; 1/4 oz. jars. Convenient and economical.
1913-Z-1299 $3.99 kit

3. CANDY WAFER AND FONDANT MIX
Great for satiny smooth candies or icing cakes creatively. 16 oz.
1911-Z-1427 $3.99 each

4. 4-PC. CANDY FLAVOR SET
It's easy to add your favorite flavor. Cinnamon, Cherry, Creme De Menthe and Peppermint. 1/4 oz. bottles.
1913-Z-1029 $4.99 set

5. CANDY CENTER MIX
Create creamy centers that can be dipped or molded for candy favorites. 9 oz.

Creme Center Mix	1911-Z-1901	$2.49 each
Chocolate Flavored	1911-Z-1903	$2.49 each
Cherry	1911-Z-1905	$2.49 each

6. EASY-POUR FUNNEL
Push button controls the flow. 5 x 4 in. wide; nylon.
1904-Z-552 $3.99 each

7. CANDY THERMOMETER
Necessary accessory for hard candy, nougat, more.
1904-Z-1168 $19.99 each

8. 2-PC. CANDY DIPPING SET
White plastic spoon and fork, each 7 3/4 in. long.
1904-Z-800 $2.99 set

9. 2-PC. DIPPING SET
Sturdy metal with wooden handles; 9 in. long.
1904-Z-925 $8.99 set

10. FANCY CANDY WRAPPERS
Gold foil to protect and add a professional finish to your candy. 125 sheets, each 3 x 3 in.
1912-Z-2290 $3.49 pack of 125

11. CANDY CUPS
Crisply pleated cups, just like professionals use. Gold foil or white glassine-coated paper.

White-1 1/4 in. diam.	1912-Z-1245	$1.29 pack of 75
Gold Foil-1 in. diam.	415-Z-306	$1.49 pack of 75
White-1 in. diam.	1912-Z-1243	$1.19 pack of 100

Cups below shown on page 127.

Red & Green		
1 1/4 in. diam.	1912-Z-1247	$1.19 pack of 72
White Pattie Cup		
1 3/4 in. diam.	1912-Z-1241	$1.29 pack of 75

12. LOLLIPOP BAGS
Plastic bags for lollipops and other candies.
3 x 4 in. 50 bags in a pack.
1912-Z-2347 $2.69 pack of 50

13. LOLLIPOP STICKS
Sturdy paper sticks are easy to add to candy molds.
4 1/2 in. long. 50 sticks per pack.
1912-Z-1006 $1.69 pack of 50

1. COOKIE PRESS
Spritz cookie press from Italy. Complete with 12 cookie-forming discs and 8 decorating nozzles.
0000-Z-231 $38.99 set

2. SPRITZ COOKIE PRESS SET
Easy-squeeze trigger action. Includes 13 plastic disks in classic holiday shapes.
2104-Z-4000 $10.99 set

3. 5-PC. ROSETTE SET
Create light and delicate rosettes in five beautiful shapes.
0000-Z-1744 $7.79 set

4. ROLL ALONG COOKIE CUTTER SET
18 interchangeable holiday designs. Cuts 6 different designs at once.
2104-Z-2404 $6.99 set

5. MADELAINE MOLD
Sophisticated baking made easy in this fine quality tinned steel mold. Recipe ideas included.
0000-Z-1289 $11.69 each

6. SEA SHELL MOLD
Make beautiful tea cakes of light sponge cake in this high quality tinned steel pan. Tasty topped with jam or whipped cream.
0000-Z-2318 $8.19 each

7. MINI MADELAINE MOLD
Bake bite-sized delicacies in an instant. Extra heavy-gauge tinned steel.
0000-Z-1317 $23.39 each

ICE CREAM SCOOPS
Small and average size, for ice cream, mashed potatoes, cookie dough, more!

8. SMALL SIZE ICE CREAM SCOOP
18/8 stainless steel. Smaller size creates 100 scoops from one quart of ice cream.
0000-Z-632 $10.69 each

9. ICE CREAM SCOOP
18/8 stainless steel. Average size creates 50 scoops from one quart of ice cream. Also use for cookie dough, mashed potatoes, more!
0000-Z-630 $11.19 each

10. COOLING GRIDS
Even the smallest shapes won't fall through. Chrome-plated steel.
10 x 16 in.   2305-Z-128 $4.99 each
14 1/2 x 20 in. 2305-Z-129 $7.99 each

11. NON-STICK COOLING GRIDS
Even moist cakes, cookies, and baked goods won't stick! Easy to clean.
10 x 16 in.   2305-Z-228 $7.99 each
14 1/2 x 20 in. 2305-Z-229 $11.99 each

12. MULTI-LEVEL COOLING GRID
Great counter space-saver cools dozens of cookies within a small area! Unstack and use side-by-side for larger breads and cakes.
10 x 16 in.   2305-Z-151 $9.99 each

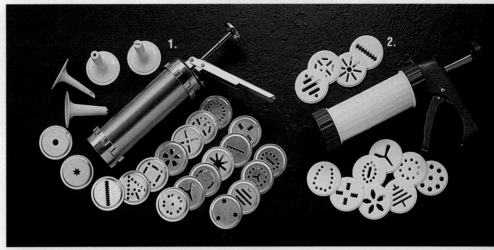

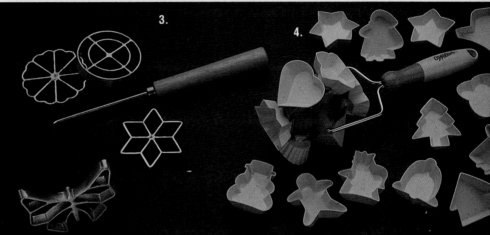

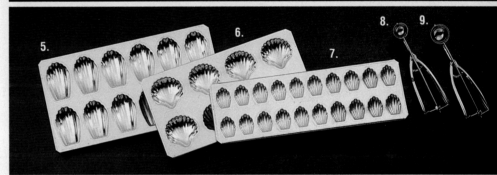

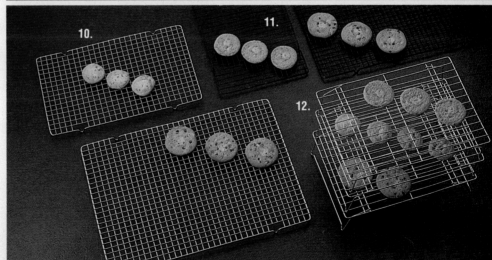

Cookie Cutters

Be sure to order the children's activity book, *Adventures in Cookieland.*
900-Z-1990 $1.49

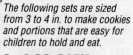

 **1.**

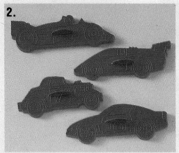 **2.**

 **3.**

 **4.**

 **5.**

 **6.**

 **7.**

 **8.**

 **9.**

 **10.**

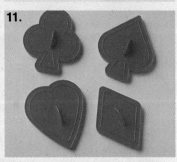 **11.**

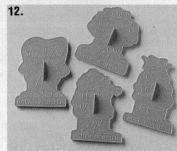 **12.**

 **13.**

 **14.**

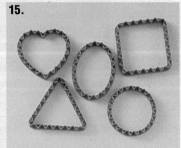 **15.**

The following sets are sized from 3 to 4 in. to make cookies and portions that are easy for children to hold and eat.

1. 4-PC. BABY THINGS SET
2304-Z-1522 $2.99 set

2. 4-PC. RACE/ SPORTS CAR SET
2304-Z-112 $2.99 set

3. 4-PC. CIRCUS TRAIN SET
2304-Z-1513 $2.99 set

4. 4-PC. COMICAL CLOWNS SET
2304-Z-1516 $2.99 set

5. 4-PC. PUPPY PALS SET
2304-Z-1505 $2.99 set

6. 4-PC. PLAYFUL DRAGONS SET
2304-Z-1507 $2.99 set

7. 5-PC. SPORTS SET
2304-Z-2101 $2.99 set

8. 4-PC. CUTE KITTENS SET
2304-Z-1509 $2.99 set

9. 4-PC. CUDDLY TEDDY BEARS SET
2304-Z-1504 $2.99 set

10. 4-PC. DINOSAURS SET
2304-Z-1990 $2.99 set

11. 4-PC. PLAYING CARDS SET
2304-Z-1512 $2.99 set

12. 4-PC. MONSTERS! SET
2304-Z-1503 $2.99 set

13. 5-PC. FARMYARD FRIENDS SET
2304-Z-432 $2.99 set

14. 4-PC. NESTING TEDDY BEARS SET
Open nesting cutters. 1 3/4 to 6 3/8 in. tall; 1 3/8 to 4 7/8 wide.
2304-Z-1520 $2.99 set

15. 5-PC. CRINKLE CUTTERS SET
Great for canapes and hors d'oeuvres as well as cookies.
2304-Z-109 $2.99 set

16. *NEW!* GIANT HEART & BEAR CUTTERS
For cookie lovers. Great for crafts, too!
Heart 7 x 7 1/2 in.
2303-Z-95 $1.50 each
Bear 9 x 7 in.
2303-Z-98 $1.50 each

16. *NEW!*

118

Cookie Cutters

1. NEW! 4-PC. WORLD WRESTLING FEDERATION® SET
Wrestling shapes are winners!
2304-Z-9051 **$2.99 set**
©1992 Titan Sports, Inc. Hulk Hogan is a trademark of the Marvel Entertainment Group Inc. All Rights Reserved.
(Available Sept. 1, 1992)

2. NEW! 4-PC. BARBIE® SET
Make fun cookies with pretty pink Barbie® cutters.
2304-Z-9050 **$2.99 set**
BARBIE and associated trademarks are owned by and used under license from Mattel, Inc.
© 1992 Mattel, Inc. All Rights Reserved.
(Available Sept. 1, 1992)

3. 4-PC. TEENAGE MUTANT NINJA TURTLES® SET*
Raphael, Michelangelo, Leonardo, Donatello.
2304-Z-1500 **$2.99 set**
© & ® 1990 Mirage Studios, U.S.A. Exclusively licensed by Surge Licensing, Inc.

4. 4-PC. SUPER MARIO BROTHERS® SET*
2304-Z-1502 **$2.99 set**
1989 Nintendo of America Inc.

5. 4-PC. GARFIELD SET*
Trouble-making duo; Garfield and Odie.
2304-Z-1501 **$2.99 set**
GARFIELD Characters:
©1978 United Feature Syndicate, Inc.

6. 4-PC. BATMAN™ SET*
Caped-crusader and his arch rival, Joker.
2304-Z-1506 **$2.99 set**
TM & © 1989 DC Comics Inc.

7. 4-PC. LOONEY TUNES SET*
Bugs Bunny, Porky Pig, Sylvester, Tweety.
2304-Z-404 **$2.99 set**
TM & © Warner Bros. Inc. 1988. All Rights Reserved.

8. 4-PC. SESAME STREET SET*
Big Bird, Cookie Monster, Ernie, Bert.
2304-Z-129 **$2.99 set**
Sesame Street Characters
© Jim Henson Productions, Inc. All Rights Reserved.

9. 5-PC. SIMPSONS FAMILY SET
2304-Z-1517 **$2.99 set**
© Matt Groening
TM & ©1990 Twentieth Century Fox Film Corporation All Rights Reserved

10. 8-PC. "GOING PLACES" SESAME STREET CANISTER SET*
2304-Z-118 **$5.99 set**
Sesame Street Characters
© Jim Henson Productions, Inc. All Rights Reserved.

11. 13-PC. NUMBERS CANISTER SET
Addition, subtraction, multiplication and equal signs included in this 13-piece set. Sturdy, reusable plastic storage container.
2304-Z-92 **$5.99 set**

12. 26-PC. CHILDREN'S A TO Z CANISTER SET*
Spell out F-U-N so many ways with this educational 26-piece set. Sturdy, reusable plastic storage container.
2304-Z-91 **$5.99 set**

13. 26-PC. ALPHABET SET
26-piece set. 2 x 1 ⅛ in. each.
2304-Z-1521 **$8.99 set**

*Cookie recipes included.

1. NEW!

2. NEW!

3.

4.

5.

6.

7.

8.

9.

10.

11.

12.

13.

Cookie Cutters

NEW! PERIMETER CUTTERS.
A shape for every occasion!
3 in. wide x 4 in. long. **All are 69¢ each**

NEW! ANIMALS

Rocking Horse	2303-Z-127
Butterfly	2303-Z-116
Pig	2303-Z-103
Fish	2303-Z-128
Teddy Bear	2303-Z-133
Kitten	2303-Z-118
Elephant	2303-Z-145
Unicorn	2303-Z-108
Dog Bone	2303-Z-123
Puppy	2303-Z-137
Cow	2303-Z-126
Duck	2303-Z-148
Dinosaur	2303-Z-112

NEW! PLAYING CARDS & CHILDREN'S FUN SHAPES

Ice Cream Cone	2303-Z-111
Hand	2303-Z-147
Club	2303-Z-138
Heart	2303-Z-100
Diamond	2303-Z-144
Spade	2303-Z-130
Finger Cookie	2303-Z-136
One	2303-Z-142
Foot	2303-Z-113
Boy	2303-Z-124
Girl	2303-Z-120

NEW! TRANSPORTATION & SEASONAL

Airplane	2303-Z-101
Christmas Tree	2303-Z-132
Cross	2303-Z-141
6 Pt. Star	2303-Z-122
18-Wheeler	2303-Z-115
Sailboat	2303-Z-129
Egg	2303-Z-119
Race Car	2303-Z-102
Bell	2303-Z-125
Star	2303-Z-135
Roller Skate	2303-Z-114
Snowman	2303-Z-105
Locomotive Engine	2303-Z-139

NEW! FANCY DESIGNS

Clown	2303-Z-109
Crinkle Round	2303-Z-143
4 Leaf Clover	2303-Z-134
Crinkle Square	2303-Z-110
Maple Leaf	2303-Z-107
Umbrella	2303-Z-131
Sea Shell	2303-Z-146
Apple	2303-Z-104
Flower	2303-Z-117
Musical Note	2303-Z-140
House	2303-Z-106

6-PC. NESTING OVAL SET
3 1/4 - 7 in. long. 2 1/8 - 4 3/4 in. wide.
2304-Z-388 **$2.99 set**

6-PC. NESTING STAR SET
From 1 5/8 to 4 5/8 in.
2304-Z-111 **$2.99 set**

6-PC. NESTING HEART SET
1 1/2 to 4 1/8 in.
2304-Z-115 **$2.99 set**

6-PC. NESTING ROUND SET
1 1/2 to 4 in.
2304-Z-113 **$2.99 set**

MINI GINGERBREAD HOUSE KIT
Kit includes patterns, disposable bags, tips and instruction booklet.
2104-Z-1528 **$3.99 kit**

NO-BAKE GINGERBREAD HOUSE KIT
Just assemble and decorate house pieces provided in kit. Candy and all necessary tools are included.
2104-Z-2990 **$9.99 kit**

GINGERBREAD HOUSE KIT
Kit includes patterns, 3 plastic gingerbread people cutters, disposable bags, tips, instruction booklet.
2104-Z-1525 **$7.49 kit**

SANTA SLEIGH AND REINDEER COOKIE KIT
Two-sided cookie cutters make flat or stand up Santas and reindeer. Kit is complete with 4 plastic cutters, disposable bags, tips and easy-to-follow instruction book.
2104-Z-1500 **$7.99 kit**

Christmas Cookie Kits

Christmas Cookie Cutters

All these fun cutters include a cookie recipe on the label.

1. NEW! 10-PC. CHRISTMAS COOKIE COLLECTION
Yuletide cutters make holiday baking a breeze! Each cutter 3 x 4 in.
2304-Z-802 $3.99 set

2. NEW! 4-PC. CHRISTMAS FAVORITES SET
Cookies make the season jolly! Each cutter 3 x 4 in.
2304-Z-801 $2.99 set

3. NEW! GIANT CHRISTMAS TREE & GINGERBREAD BOY
It's Christmas fun in grand proportions! Each cutter approximately 9 x 7 $\frac{1}{2}$ in. high.
TREE   2303-Z-96 $1.50 each
BOY   2303-Z-97 $1.50 each

4. NEW! SANTA'S COOKIE WHEEL
Rolls out six 2 in. holiday-shaped cookies quick and easy; tree, bell, snowman, bear, gingerbread boy and star.
2304-Z-803 $5.99 each

5. 4-PC. NESTING GINGER-BREAD BOY SET
Fun plain or decorated. Recipe and decorating instructions. 1 $\frac{3}{4}$ to 6 $\frac{3}{8}$ in. tall; 1 $\frac{3}{8}$ to 4 $\frac{3}{4}$ in. wide.
2304-Z-1530 $2.99 set

6. 4-PC. NESTING CHRISTMAS TREE SET
Festive fun; easy to decorate. Recipe and decorating instructions. 2 $\frac{5}{8}$ to 6 $\frac{3}{8}$ in. tall; 1 $\frac{3}{8}$ to 4 $\frac{3}{4}$ in. wide.
2304-Z-1531 $2.99 set

7. 4-PC. NESTING TEDDY BEAR SET
Poppa, Mama and Baby Bear join in the holiday festivities. Recipe and decorating instructions.
1 $\frac{3}{4}$ to 6 $\frac{3}{8}$ in. tall; 1 $\frac{3}{8}$ to 4 $\frac{7}{8}$ in. wide.
2304-Z-1532 $2.99 set

8. 4-PC. GINGERBREAD FAMILY SET
Set includes two 5 $\frac{1}{2}$ x 4 in. adults and two 2 $\frac{1}{2}$ x 1 $\frac{1}{2}$ in. children. Recipe on label.
2304-Z-121 $2.99 set

9. 4-PC. CHRISTMAS SET
Favorite holiday shapes. Angel, Santa, Wreath, Tree. Recipe on label. 4 $\frac{1}{4}$ to 5 in.
2304-Z-995 $2.99 set

10. 4-PC. CHRISTMAS TREATS SET
Fun-loving Yuletide favorites. Cottage, holly, reindeer, snowman. 4 $\frac{3}{4}$ to 5 $\frac{1}{2}$ in.
2304-Z-1290 $2.99 set

11. 10-PC. CHRISTMAS CANISTER SET
10 festive holiday shapes. 2 $\frac{1}{2}$ to 3 $\frac{1}{2}$ in. Reusable sturdy plastic container.
509-Z-1225 $3.99 set

12. 4-PC. GARFIELD CHRISTMAS SET
He's festive and fun in his holiday finery. Recipe included. 3 to 3 $\frac{7}{8}$ in. tall; 2 $\frac{1}{4}$ to 4 in. wide.
2304-Z-114 $2.99 set

Garfield: © 1978 United Feature Syndicate, Inc.

1. NEW!

2. NEW!

3. NEW!

4. NEW!

5.   6.   7.   8.

9.   10.

11.   12.

Holiday Cookie Cutters

1. NEW!

2.

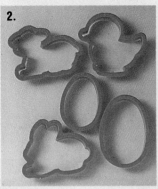

3.

4.

5.

6. NEW!

7.

8.

9. NEW!

10.

11. NEW!

12.

13.

All these fun cutters include a cookie recipe on the label.

1. NEW! 4-PC. EASTERTIME FAVORITES SET
Shapes that herald the beginning of spring! Each cutter approximately 3 x 4 in.
2304-Z-807 **$2.99 set**

2. 5-PC. EASTER FAVORITES SET
Open cutters for the family to decorate. 3 1/4 to 4 3/8 in. tall; 2 1/2 to 4 1/2 in. wide.
2304-Z-1519 **$2.99 set**

3. 4-PC. HAPPY EASTER SET
The season's most popular quartet. Bunny, lamb, chick and egg. 3 1/4 to 3 3/4 in.
2304-Z-110 **$2.99 set**

4. 10-PC. EASTER CANISTER SET
10 Easter and spring shapes all ready for munching. 2 to 3 5/8 in. tall; 2 1/8 to 4 in. wide.
2304-Z-1106 **$4.99 set**

5. 10-PC. I LOVE YOU COOKIE CANISTER SET
10 novelty cutters in a reusable container. 1 5/8 to 3 7/8 in. tall; 2 3/8 to 4 in. wide.
2304-Z-1105 **$4.99 set**

6. NEW! 4-PC. VALENTINE FAVORITES SET
Lovely symbols of the February holiday! Each cutter approximately 3 x 4 in.
2304-Z-808 **$2.99 set**

7. 4-PC. SWEETHEART COOKIE CUTTER SET
Four romantic shapes and messages. 4 to 4 1/2 in.
2304-Z-1214 **$2.99 set**

8. 4-PC. HEART TO HEART SET
Four ways to say "I love you." 2 1/2 to 3 1/2 in. tall; 3 3/8 to 4 in. wide.
2304-Z-1518 **$2.99 set**

9. NEW! GIANT HEART
Show your love in a big way! 7 1/2 x 7 in.
2303-Z-95 **$1.50 each**

10. 6-PC. NESTING HEARTS SET
An invaluable collection of 6 different sized nesting hearts. 1 1/4 to 4 1/8 in.
2304-Z-115 **$2.99 set**

11. NEW! HALLOWEEN FAVORITES SET
Make trick-or-treat cookies for all your goblins! Each cutter approximately 3 x 4 in.
2304-Z-800 **$2.99 set**

12. 10-PC. HALLOWEEN CANISTER SET
Ten not-so-spooky characters in a handy reusable container. 3 to 4 1/4 in.
2304-Z-1031 **$3.99 set**

13. 4-PC. JACK-O-LANTERN CUTTER SET
This silly jack-o-lantern goes through four funny moods. 3 to 3 1/4 in.
2304-Z-90 **$2.99 set**

14. HAUNTED HOUSE KIT
Kit includes patterns, sturdy plastic cookie cutters, 4 disposable bags, 1 round tip, liquid colors, easy-to-follow instructions, and cookie recipe.
2104-Z-1031 **$7.49 kit**

14.

122

1. ROLLING PINS
Many great pastries begin with a great rolling pin. This collection offers many styles and options. All made of rock maple with nylon bearings. The perfect weight for home or professional use.

15 x 3 in.	0000-Z-561	$29.29 each
12 1/2 x 2 in.	0000-Z-564	$14.89 each
10 1/2 x 2 in.	0000-Z-560	$12.59 each

2. MARBLE ROLLING PIN/CRADLE
Stay-cool surface provides for easy rolling.
10 in. 0000-Z-580 $13.19 set

3. ROLLING PIN COVERS
Handy cover prevents dough from sticking to pin. Stretches to fit any size rolling pin. Each package contains two covers.

20 inches long	0000-Z-194	$1.99 each
14 inches long	0000-Z-193	$1.89 each

4. PASTRY CLOTH AND ROLLING PIN COVER
Contains one heavyweight pastry cloth, 20 x 24 in., and one 14 in. stretch rolling pin cover.
0000-Z-196 $4.99 each

5. SPATULAS
Four handy kitchen pleasers that go to all lengths to help.

0000-Z-810	9 3/4 in. jar spatula	$2.69 each
0000-Z-811	12 3/4 in. spatula	$2.89 each
0000-Z-812	15 in. spatula	$5.39 each
0000-Z-160	Spatch-It spatula	$1.29 each

6. WOODEN SPOONS
Many sizes provide many uses in the kitchen. You'll reach for these over and over again.

0000-Z-486	10 in. spoon	$1.79 each
0000-Z-487	12 in. spoon	$1.99 each
0000-Z-488	14 in. spoon	$2.19 each
0000-Z-489	16 in. spoon	$2.89 each

7. MIXING BOWLS
A handy trio to have. High quality stainless with easy-to-grip thumb ring.

0000-Z-702	1 1/2 Quart	$3.79 each
0000-Z-703	3 Quart	$5.39 each
0000-Z-704	5 Quart	$6.99 each

8. 3-CUP SIFTER
Easy-turn crank for uniform sifting. Stainless steel.
0000-Z-736 $17.39 each

9. MEASURING SPOONS
Stainless steel set of 4 includes 1/4, 1/2 and 1 teaspoons and 1 tablespoon.
0000-Z-363 $4.19 set

STAINLESS STEEL WHISKS
Two versatile 10 in. versions.

10. Ridged wires make it sturdy enough to mix batters, sauces and cream. 0000-Z-814 $5.39 ea.

11. Delicate wires ideal for whipping egg white and light liquids. 0000-Z-796 $3.19 each

12. PASTRY BLENDER
Sturdy wooden handle with sleek metal blades.
0000-Z-349 $6.69 each

13. BLENDING/MASHING FORK
Back bladed tines make it easy to mash, cut, blend.
0000-Z-176 $2.89 each

14. 1 IN. PASTRY AND PAINTING BRUSH
100% natural bristles. Ideal for pastry buttering, basting sauces and glazing breads.
0000-Z-1190 $2.19 each

15. FEATHER PASTRY BRUSH
A natural for brushing egg whites, butter and more. Leaves no marks and doesn't shred.
0000-Z-110 $1.69 each

16. CAKE TESTER
Cake is done when it comes out clean! Neat and money-saving. Great shower favors.
0000-Z-387 $1.89 each

17. DUAL PASTRY WHEEL
Metal wheels cut exact plain or scalloped edges.
0000-Z-139 $4.49 each

18. PASTRY CRIMPER
Crimps, seals and cuts.
0000-Z-1205 $3.79 each

19. MRS. T's TART TAMPER
Makes two sizes of tarts.
0000-Z-837 $4.49 each

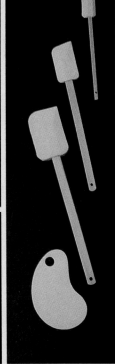
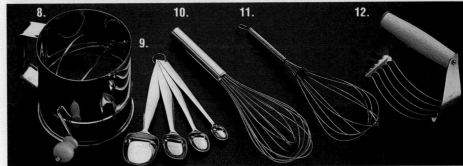

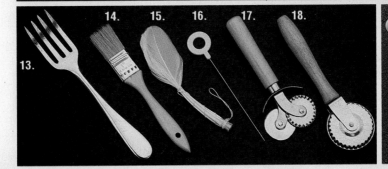

Icing Colors

Color is vital to your decorating. With color you can add realism and vitality to all your character cakes, personalize special events cakes, highlight holiday cakes and add beauty and vibrancy to all your cakes.

Wilton Icing Colors are concentrated in a rich, creamy base, are fast-mixing and easy to use, and will not change your icing consistency. Our extensive range of icing colors makes it convenient for you to achieve the colors you need and want.

DAFFODIL YELLOW*	LEMON YELLOW	GOLDEN YELLOW	ORANGE	PINK	CHRISTMAS RED	RED-RED	RED (no taste)
IVORY	TEAL	TERRA COTTA	ROSE	COPPER	BROWN	ROSE PETAL PINK	CREAMY PEACH
VIOLET	BURGUNDY	ROYAL BLUE	CORNFLOWER BLUE	SKY BLUE	WILLOW GREEN	KELLY GREEN	LEAF GREEN
MOSS GREEN							
BLACK							

ICING COLORS	CONCENTRATED * PASTE 1 oz.		AIR * BRUSH 8 oz.		ICING COLORS	CONCENTRATED * PASTE 1 oz.		AIR * BRUSH 8 oz.	
Daffodil Yellow	610-Z-175	1.99	N/A		Copper	610-Z-450	1.49	609-Z-6	4.20
Lemon Yellow	610-Z-108	1.49	609-Z-12	3.80	Brown	610-Z-507	1.69	609-Z-14	3.80
Golden Yellow	610-Z-159	1.49	N/A		**Rose Petal Pink	610-Z-410	1.49	N/A	
Orange	610-Z-205	1.49	609-Z-11	3.80	**Creamy Peach	610-Z-210	1.49	609-Z-5	4.40
Pink	610-Z-256	1.49	609-Z-16	4.20	Violet	610-Z-604	1.49	609-Z-13	4.40
Christmas Red	610-Z-302	1.49	609-Z-10	4.40	Burgundy	610-Z-698	1.99	N/A	
Red-Red	610-Z-906	1.99	609-Z-9	4.40	Royal Blue	610-Z-655	1.49	609-Z-4	4.40
Red (no taste)	610-Z-998	1.99	N/A		**Cornflower Blue	610-Z-710	1.49	609-Z-3	4.20
**Ivory	610-Z-208	1.49	N/A		Sky Blue	610-Z-700	1.49	609-Z-17	3.80
**Teal	610-Z-207	1.49	609-Z-2	4.20	**Willow Green	610-Z-855	1.49	N/A	
**Terra Cotta	610-Z-206	1.49	609-Z-1	4.40	Kelly Green	610-Z-752	1.49	609-Z-7	3.80
Rose	610-Z-401	1.49	N/A		Leaf Green	610-Z-809	1.49	609-Z-8	3.80
Moss Green	610-Z-851	1.49	N/A		Black	610-Z-981	1.69	609-Z-15	4.40

**Special Blend Color

Air Brush

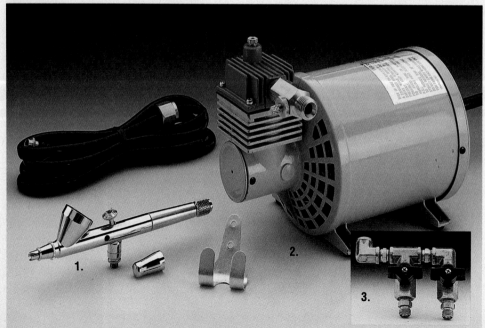

1. AIR BRUSH AND HOSE
Create colorful special effects on your cakes with this superior quality single action air brush. Perfect way to add beautiful color backgrounds, highlight your borders and tint your flowers. Nickel-plated solid brass. Generous capacity angled color-holder cup. Includes 6-ft. PVC hose and airbrush holder.
415-Z-4000 $117.99 air brush with hose and holder

2. AIR BRUSH COMPRESSOR
Professional quality, piston-type compressor for maximum dependability. $1/12$ horsepower provides maximum pressure of 40 lbs. per square inch. Easy to control; on/off switch.
415-Z-4001 $199.99 each

3. TWO-BRUSH MANIFOLD ADAPTER
Allows two air brushes to be used with just one compressor.
415-Z-4100 $59.99 each

* Certified Kosher

Color Kits, Fillings Icings & Flavorings

1. 10-ICING COLORS KIT *
1 oz. jars of icing colors. Violet, Leaf Green, Royal Blue, Brown, Black, Pink, Watermelon, Moss Green, Orange, and Lemon Yellow.
601-Z-5569 $12.99 kit

2. 8-ICING COLORS KIT *
1/2 oz. jars of colors. Christmas Red, Lemon Yellow, Leaf Green, Sky Blue, Brown, Orange, Pink, and Violet.
601-Z-5577 $8.99 kit

3. 4-ICING COLORS KIT *
(SOFT PASTEL COLORS) 1/2 oz jars of paste colors. Petal Pink, Creamy Peach, Willow Green, Cornflower Blue.
601-Z-25588 $3.49 kit

4. WHITE-WHITE ICING COLOR *
Just stir into icing to make icing made with butter or margarine white. Perfect for wedding cakes. 2 oz. plastic bottle.
603-Z-1236 $2.99 each

5. CAKE AND PASTRY FILLING *
Luscious, chunky real fruit filling ready to use from the 10 oz. resealable glass jar. Perfect to fill and torte up to 10" round cake, a real treat in tarts, pies and fancy pastries! 10 oz.

Filling	Stock No.	Price
Cherry	709-Z-3	$1.99 each
Strawberry	709-Z-1	$1.99 each
Raspberry	709-Z-2	$1.99 each

6. READY-TO-USE DECORATOR ICING
Perfect for decorating and frosting. Use for borders, flowers, writing, etc. Just stir and use! Delicious homemade taste! 16 oz.
710-Z-117 $1.99 each

7. CREAMY WHITE ICING MIX
Convenient mix that provides rich, home-made taste. Just add butter and milk. Ideal for frosting as well as decorating. Yields 2 cups.
710-Z-112 $2.39 each

8. PIPING GEL *
Clear gel. Can be tinted with paste color. Use for glazing, writing, more. 10 oz.
704-Z-105 $3.29 each

9. GLYCERIN *
A few drops stirred into dried-out icing color restores consistency. 2 oz.
708-Z-14 $1.99 each

10. BUTTER FLAVOR *
Gives a rich, buttery taste to icing, cakes, cookies. Adds no color! 2 oz.
604-Z-2040 $1.79 each

11. CLEAR VANILLA EXTRACT *
Perfect for decorating because it won't change the color of your icing. 2 oz. Great for baking, too!
604-Z-2237 $1.79 each

12. ALMOND EXTRACT *
Delicious almond flavor for icing, cookies, cakes. 2 oz.
604-Z-2126 $1.79 each

13. COLOR FLOW MIX *
Add water and confectioners sugar for smooth icing for color flow designs. 4 oz. can yields about ten 1 1/2 cup batches.
701-Z-47 $7.49 each

14. MERINGUE POWDER MIX *
For Royal icing, meringue, boiled icing.
4 oz. Can 702-Z-6007 $4.49 each
8 oz. Can 702-Z-6015 $6.99 each

* Certified Kosher

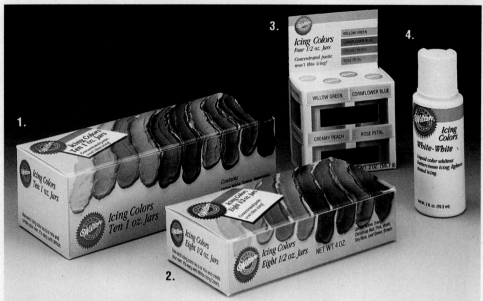

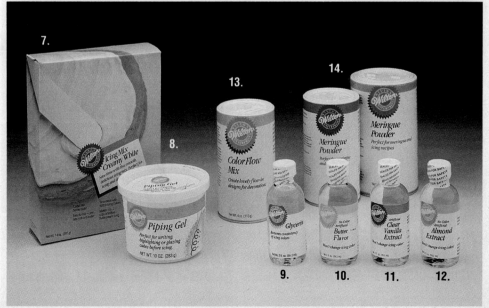

Icing Decorations

1. READY-TO-USE ICING ROSES

Instant beauty, in a variety of colors and sizes to finish your cake perfectly. A lovely touch on cupcakes, too! Made of edible hard icing, with decorating ideas on the package.

Large (1 ¼ in.) $3.99 Package of 9
Medium (1 ⅛ in.) $3.99 Package of 12
Small (¾ in.) $3.99 Package of 15

White	Large	710-Z-411
	Medium	710-Z-311
	Small	710-Z-706
Yellow	Large	710-Z-414
	Medium	710-Z-314
	Small	710-Z-709
Red	Large	710-Z-412
	Medium	710-Z-312
	Small	710-Z-707
Pink	Large	710-Z-413
	Medium	710-Z-313
	Small	710-Z-708
Peach	Large	710-Z-415
	Medium	710-Z-315
	Small	710-Z-710
NEW! Ivory	Medium	710-Z-723
NEW! "Chocolate" Brown	Medium	710-Z-722
NEW! Blue	Medium	710-Z-721

NEW! FLORAL ACCENTS

Save time with these elegant, edible decorations. Create a beautiful floral arrangement atop your next cake, using the decorating ideas on the package. Medium size.

2. NEW! FLORAL SPRAY SET

Includes 6 roses, 5 rosebuds, 8 leaves.

Pink	710-Z-718	$3.99 pkg.
Red	710-Z-717	$3.99 pkg.
White	710-Z-720	$3.99 pkg.
Yellow	710-Z-719	$3.99 pkg.

3. NEW! ROSE BUDS

Contains 25 buds.

Peach	710-Z-716	$3.99 pkg.
Pink	710-Z-715	$3.99 pkg.
Red	710-Z-712	$3.99 pkg.
White	710-Z-713	$3.99 pkg.
Yellow	710-Z-714	$3.99 pkg.

4. NEW! LEAVES

Make all flowers more realistic in no time. Contains 24 green leaves. 710-Z-711 $3.99 pkg.

NEW! PARTY AND HOLIDAY DESIGNS

Add these fun edible shapes to cakes or cupcakes for an instant celebration! A real treat for kids (Nos. 5 thru 12 are mint-flavored). Sized to fit any cupcake, jumbo to mini. All priced at $1.99.

5. NEW! ALPHABET/NUMERALS   Pkg. of 68
    710-Z-494

6. NEW! BABY THINGS   Pkg. of 9
    710-Z-495

7. NEW! CLOWNS   Pkg. of 9   710-Z-496

8. NEW! CRAYONS   Pkg. of 8   710-Z-493

9. NEW! DINOSAURS   Pkg. of 9   710-Z-497

10. NEW! HEARTS   Pkg. of 9   710-Z-501

11. NEW! LITTLE PEOPLE   Pkg. of 9
    710-Z-498

12. NEW! TEDDY BEARS   Pkg. of 9
    710-Z-499

13. NEW! CATS AND BATS   Pkg. of 9
    710-Z-1032

14. PUMPKINS   Pkg. of 20   710-Z-1031

15. EASTER BUNNIES   Pkg. of 16   710-Z-500

16. CHRISTMAS TREES   Pkg. of 12
    710-Z-1226

17. SANTA CLAUS   Pkg. of 9   710-Z-1225

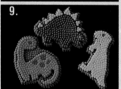

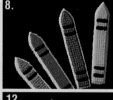

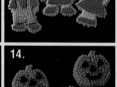

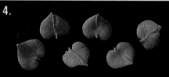

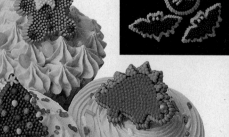

Wilton cups are more fun! Exclusive designs, holiday themes and favorite patterns that add to the enjoyment of whatever you're serving. Cups are made of grease-resistant, microwave-safe paper. They're great for baking or using to hold candy and nuts. Unless noted, prices and quantities are as shown here.
JUMBO - $1.49 pack of 40   STANDARD - $1.49 pack of 50   MINI - $1.49 pack of 75

Baking Papers

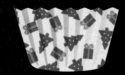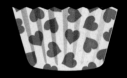

NEW! EASTER		**NEW! HALLOWEEN**		**SANTA CLAUS**		**CHRISTMAS TREES**		**HEARTS**	
Standard	415-Z-219	Standard	415-Z-213	Standard	415-Z-208	Standard	415-Z-209	Standard	415-Z-210
Mini	415-Z-319	Mini	415-Z-340	Mini	415-Z-308	Mini	415-Z-309	Mini	415-Z-310

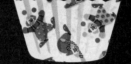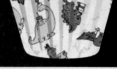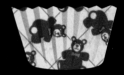

NEW! BARBIE [1]		**NEW! GARFIELD** [2]		**CLOWNS**		**DINOSAURS**		**TEDDY BEARS**	
Jumbo	415-Z-100	Jumbo	415-Z-118	Jumbo	415-Z-104	Jumbo	415-Z-112	Jumbo	415-Z-102
Standard	415-Z-200	Standard	415-Z-218	Standard	415-Z-204	Standard	415-Z-212	Standard	415-Z-202
Mini	415-Z-300	Mini	415-Z-318	Mini	415-Z-304	Mini	415-Z-312	Mini	415-Z-302

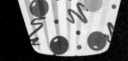

PARTY! PARTY!		**BALLOONS**		**BELLS & RIBBONS**	
Jumbo	415-Z-103	Jumbo	415-Z-101	Standard	415-Z-205
Standard	415-Z-203	Standard	415-Z-201	Mini	415-Z-305
Mini	415-Z-303	Mini	415-Z-301		

SILVER FOIL
Standard	415-Z-207
(24 pure aluminum/24 paper)
| Bon Bon | 415-Z-307 |
(36 pure aluminum/36 paper)

GOLD FOIL
Wax-laminated paper on foil.
Standard	415-Z-206
(24/pkg.)
| Bon Bon | 415-Z-306 |
(75/pkg.)

WHITE
Jumbo	415-Z-2503
Standard	415-Z-2505
Mini	415-Z-2507

NEW! BLUE
Standard	415-Z-214

NEW! PINK
Standard	415-Z-215

NEW! YELLOW
Standard	415-Z-216
RED
| Standard | 415-Z-211 |

1. PETIT FOURS
Multicolors; 200 per box
| 0000-Z-1038 | $2.69 pkg. |

2. GLASSINE CUPS
Candy and Party Cups fit large and small Wilton candy mold shapes.
White Bon Bon (1 in.)
| 100/pkg. | 1912-Z-1243 | $1.19 pkg. |
White Mini (1 1/4 in.)
| 75/pkg. | 1912-Z-1245 | $1.29 pkg. |
White Pattie (1 3/4 in.)
| 75/pkg. | 1912-Z-1241 | $1.29 pkg. |
Red & Green Mini (1 1/4 in.)
72 count (36 ea. color per pkg.)
| | 1912-Z-1247 | $1.19 pkg. |

3. NUT AND PARTY CUPS
White Standard
| (24/pkg.) | 415-Z-400 | $1.49 pkg. |
White Mini
| (36/pkg.) | 415-Z-500 | $1.49 pkg. |

[1] Barbie and associated trademarks are owned by and used under license from Mattel, Inc. © 1992 Mattel, Inc. All Rights Reserved.

[2] GARFIELD: ©1978 United Feature Syndicate, Inc.

Sprinkle Decorations

NEW! Shake up your cakes, cookies and cupcakes with delicious Wilton Sprinkles! Sprinkle control box has two openings for fine line, detailed pouring or shaking the amount you need. 4 - 5 1/4 oz. Certified Kosher. **$1.99 pkg.**

Rainbow Nonpareils	710-Z-800
Chocolate-Flavored Jimmies	710-Z-801
Rainbow Jimmies	710-Z-802
Cinnamon	710-Z-814
Red Crystal	710-Z-813
Green Crystal	710-Z-812
Pumpkin Mix	710-Z-810
Holly Mix	710-Z-811
Baby Jellies	710-Z-803

Decorating Tools

Stainless Steel Spatulas with flexible, non-rust blades and durable rosewood handles.

1. MAKE ANY MESSAGE LETTER PRESS SET
Now you can customize that perfect message, right down to the letter. 56 piece interchangeable set.
2104-Z-0010 **$7.99 set**

2. ALL-OCCASION SCRIPT PATTERN PRESS SET
Press and pipe messages easily with all-occasion and seasonal words and phrases: Merry Christmas, Happy New Year, Easter, Thanksgiving, God Bless You, I Love You and Good Luck.
2104-Z-2090 **$3.99 set**

3. 15-PC. DECORATOR PATTERN PRESS SET
Traditional designs ready to solo or use in combination. Many can also be reversed for symmetrical designs.
2104-Z-2172 **$4.99 set**

4. 9-PC. PATTERN PRESS SET
Discover fancy florals; classic curves make any occasion so special.
2104-Z-3101 **$4.49 set**

5. SCRIPT PATTERN PRESS MESSAGE SET
Lets you put it into words so beautifully. Combine the words Happy, Birthday, Best, Wishes, Anniversary, Congratulations and make a lasting impression.
2104-Z-2061 **$3.69 set**

6. MESSAGE BLOCK LETTER PATTERN PRESS SET
Have just the right words at your fingertips. Includes the same six words as the Script Set. 2 x 6 3/4 x 3/4 in. high.
2104-Z-2077 **$3.69 set**

7. CAKE DIVIDING SET
Handy when chart marks 2-in. intervals on 6 to 18-in. diameter cakes. Triangle marker for precise spacing for stringwork, garlands, more. Includes instructions.
409-Z-800 **$8.99 set**

8. DECORATING COMB
Easy technique makes it look like you fussed. Makes ridges in icing. 12-in. long, plastic.
409-Z-8259 **$1.29 each**

9. DECORATING TRIANGLE
Each side adds a different contoured effect to icing. 5 X 5-in. plastic.
409-Z-990 **99¢ each**

10. DECORATOR'S BRUSHES SET
Perfect for smoothing icing, painting candy molds and colorful touches. Set of 3.
2104-Z-846 **$1.49 set**

STAINLESS STEEL & ROSEWOOD SPATULAS

11. 8 IN. TAPERED
409-Z-517 **$2.79 each**

12. 8 IN. SPATULA
409-Z-6043 **$2.79 each**

13. 11 IN. SPATULA
409-Z-7694 **$4.59 each**

14. 8 IN. ANGLED SPATULA
409-Z-738 **$2.79 each**

15. 12 IN. ANGLED SPATULA
409-Z-134 **$4.99 each**

1. FEATHERWEIGHT DECORATING BAGS

Lightweight, strong, flexible polyester bags are easy to handle, soft, workable and never get stiff. Specially coated so grease won't go through. May be boiled. Dishwasher safe. Instructions included.

Size	Stock No.	Each
8 in.	404-Z-5087	$2.39
10 in.	404-Z-5109	$3.69
12 in.	404-Z-5125	$4.69
14 in.	404-Z-5140	$5.99
16 in.	404-Z-5168	$7.29
18 in.	404-Z-5184	$7.89

2. DISPOSABLE DECORATING BAGS

Use and toss-no fuss, no muss. Perfect for melting Candy Melts™* in the microwave, too. Strong, flexible, and easy-to-handle plastic. 12 in. size fits standard tips and couplers.
*brand confectionery coating

2104-Z-358	$3.99 pack of 12
24-Count Value Pack	
2104-Z-1358	$6.29 pack of 24

3. PARCHMENT TRIANGLES

Make your own disposable decorating bags with our quality, grease-resistant vegetable parchment paper. Package of 100.

12in. 2104-Z-1206	$4.49 pack of 100
15in. 2104-Z-1508	$5.49 pack of 100

4. TIP SAVER

Reshape bent tips. Molded plastic.
414-Z-909 $2.79 each

5. TIP SAVER BOXES

Keep decorating tips clean and organized,
A. 26-Tip Capacity 405-Z-8773 $4.99 each
B. 52-Tip Capacity 405-Z-7777 $6.99 each

PLASTIC COUPLERS

Use to change tips without changing bags when using the same color icing.

6. LARGE COUPLER

Fits 14 in. to 18 in. Featherweight bags. Use with large decorating tips.
411-Z-1006 $1.19 each

7. ANGLED COUPLER

Reaches around sharp angles. Fits all bags and standard decorating tips.
411-Z-7365 79¢ each

8. STANDARD COUPLER

Fits all decorating bags, standard tips.
411-Z-1987 59¢ each

9. TIP COVER

Slip over tip and save to take filled bags of icing along for touch-ups. Plastic.
414-Z-915 Package of 4 99¢ pkg.

10. MAXI TIP BRUSH

Gets out every bit of icing fast and easy.
414-Z-1010 $1.79 each

11. TIP BRUSH

Plastic bristles clean tips thoroughly.
418-Z-1123 $1.19 each

12. DESSERT DECORATOR

Easy-to-control lever lets you decorate cakes, pastries, cookies with one hand. Includes 5 easy-to-change decorating nozzles.
415-Z-825 $10.99 each

13. CAKE LEVELER

Levels and tortes cakes up to 10 in. wide and 2 in. high.
415-Z-815 $2.99 each

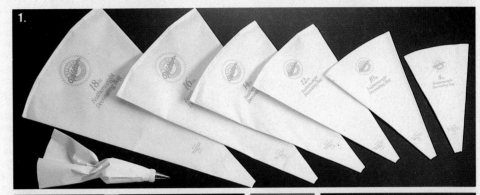

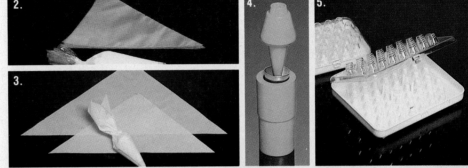

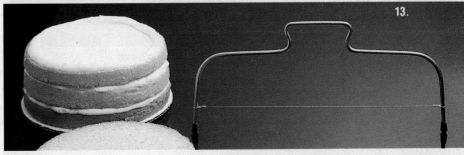

Decorating Essentials

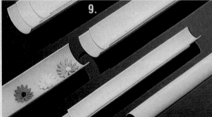

1. ROUND PARCHMENT CIRCLES
Non-stick parchment lines round pans, prevents sticking and withstands temperatures to 450°. Each package contains 25.
  8 in. 0000-Z-1024 $2.79 pack
  9 in. 0000-Z-1025 $3.49 pack
  10 in. 0000-Z-1026 $4.29 pack

2. PARCHMENT ROLLS
Professional grade, silicone-treated parchment. Ideal for cooking, baking and candy making. Double roll contains 41 square feet. (15 in. x 33 ft.)
0000-Z-1023 $4.69 roll

QUILON PARCHMENT ROLLS (not shown)
Withstands temperatures up to 450°. 20 1/2 square feet (15 in. x 16 1/2 in.)
0000-Z-1022 $2.99 roll

3. FLOWER NAIL NO. 9
1 1/4 in. diameter.
402-Z-3009 79¢ each

4. FLOWER NAIL NO. 7
1 1/2 in. diameter.
402-Z-3007 99¢ each

5. 2 IN. FLOWER NAIL
Use with curved and swirled petal tips, 116-123, to make large blooms.
402-Z-3002 $1.19 each

6. 3 IN. FLOWER NAIL
Has extra large surface, ideal with large petal tips.
402-Z-3003 $1.29 each

7. 1-PC. LILY NAIL
1 5/8 in. diameter.
402-Z-3012 89¢ each

8. LILY NAIL SET
Essential for making cup flowers, such as poinsettias and lilies. To use 2 pc. nails: Place aluminum foil in bottom half of nail and press top half in to form cup. Pipe flower petals. Set includes 1/2, 1 1/4, 1 5/8 and 2 1/2 in. diam. cups. Sturdy white plastic.
403-Z-9444 $1.99 8-pc. set

9. FLOWER FORMER SET
Plastic stands used to dry icing leaves and flowers in a convex or concave shape. Set of nine (11 in. long) in three widths: 1 1/2, 2, 2 1/2 in. (3 of each size.)
417-Z-9500 $5.99 set

10. TREE FORMER SET
Use to make icing pine trees and to dry royal icing or gum paste decorations. Set of four, 6 1/2 in. high.
417-Z-1150 $1.99 set

11. FLORIST WIRE
Medium weight for a multitude of projects. 175 white wires (18 in. long) per pack.
409-Z-622 $8.99 pack

12. STAMENS
Make flowers more realistic. 144 per pack.
Pearl White 1005-Z-102 $1.49 pack
Yellow 1005-Z-7875 $1.49 pack

13. EDIBLE GLITTER
Sprinkles sparkle on scores of things. 1/4 oz. plastic jar.
White 703-Z-1204 $2.29 each

14. GUM PASTE MIX
Easy to use! Just add water and knead. Results in a workable, pliable dough-like mixture to mold into beautiful flowers and figures. 1 lb. can.
707-Z-124 $4.99 each

15. GLUCOSE
Essential ingredient for making gum paste. 24 oz. plastic jar.
707-Z-109 $4.29 each

16. GUM-TEX™ KARAYA
Makes gum paste pliable, elastic, easy to shape. 6 oz. can.
707-Z-117 $6.99 each

17. GUM PASTE FLOWERS KIT
Make lifelike, beautiful gum paste flowers. Create bouquets or single blooms for cakes, centerpieces, favors and more. Full color how-to book contains lots of ideas and step-by-step instructions. Kit includes 24 plastic cutters, 1 leaf mold, 3 wooden modeling tools and 2 squares of foam for modeling. 30-pc. kit.
1907-Z-117 $14.99 kit
GUM PASTE FLOWERS BOOK ONLY
907-Z-117 $6.99 each

1. STARTER CAKE DECORATING SET

- 4 metal decorating tips
- Instruction booklet
- Six 12-in. disposable decorating bags
- Two tip couplers
- Five liquid color packets

2104-Z-2530 $6.99 set

2. BASIC CAKE DECORATING SET

- 5 professional quality metal tips
- Twelve 12-in. disposable bags
- Two tip couplers
- Flower nail no. 7
- Four ½ oz. icing colors
- Instruction booklet

2104-Z-2536 $9.99 set

3. DELUXE CAKE DECORATING SET

Contains 36 essentials!
- 10 nickel-plated metal tips
- Four ½ oz. icing colors
- Plastic storage tray
- Eighteen 12-in. disposable bags
- Two tip couplers
- No. 7 flower nail
- Cake Decorating, Easy as 1,2,3 book.

2104-Z-2540 $18.99 set

4. SUPREME CAKE DECORATING SET

52 tools in all!
- 18 metal tips
- Two tip couplers
- Five ½ oz. icing colors
- 8-in. angled spatula
- No. 9 flower nail
- Twenty-four disposable 12 in. bags
- Cake Decorating Easy as 1,2,3 book
- Storage Tray

2104-Z-2546 $26.99 set

5. TOOL CADDY

You can take it with you and keep it all beautifully organized. (Tools not included.) Holds 38 tips, 10 icing color jars, couplers, spatulas, books and more. Lightweight, stain-resistant molded polyethylene. 16⅝ x 11½ x 3 in.

2104-Z-2237 $19.99 each

6. DELUXE TIP SET

- 26 decorating tips
- 2 flower nails
- Tip coupler
- Tipsaver plastic box

2104-Z-6666 $18.99 set

7. MASTER TIP SET

- 52 metal tips
- Two flower nails
- Tipsaver box
- Two couplers

2104-Z-7778 $34.99 set

8. PRACTICE BOARD WITH PATTERNS

Practice is a must for decorating that gets an A+. Slip practice pattern onto board under wipe-clean vinyl overlay and trace in icing. Includes stand and patterns for flowers, leaves, borders and lettering-31 designs included.

406-Z-9464 $6.99 each

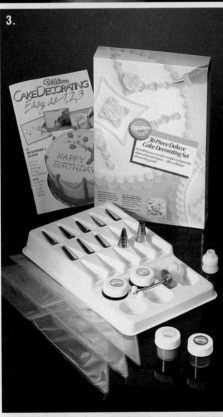

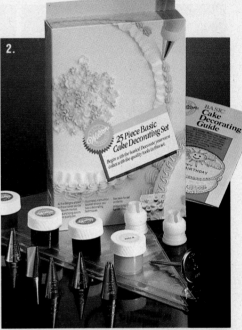

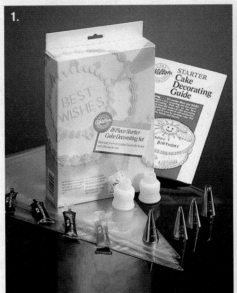

131

Beautiful Backdrops

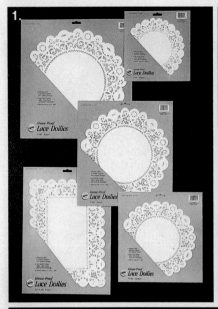

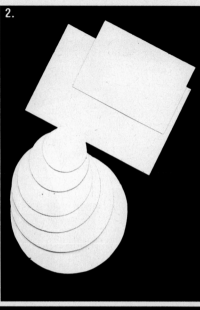

1. DOILIES
Grease-resistant, glassine-coated paper doilies are ideal for iced cakes. Round and rectangular shapes have lace borders sized to fit around your decorated cakes. Ideal for serving cookies and canapes, too!

8 in. Round	2104-Z-90004	$1.99 Pack of 16
10 in. Round	2104-Z-90000	$1.99 Pack of 12
12 in. Round	2104-Z-90001	$1.99 Pack of 8
14 in. Round	2104-Z-90002	$1.99 Pack of 8
10 x 14 in. Rectangle	2104-Z-90003	$1.99 Pack of 8

2. CAKE CIRCLES & BOARDS
Sturdy corrugated cardboard.

6 in.	2104-Z-64	$2.49 Pack of 10
8 in.	2104-Z-80	$3.69 Pack of 12
10 in.	2104-Z-102	$4.49 Pack of 12
12 in.	2104-Z-129	$4.49 Pack of 8
14 in.	2104-Z-145	$4.49 Pack of 6
16 in.	2104-Z-160	$5.49 Pack of 6
10 x 14 in.	2104-Z-554	$4.19 Pack of 6
13 x 19 in.	2104-Z-552	$4.69 Pack of 6

3. PROFESSIONAL CAKE STAND
Heavy-duty aluminum stand is 4 $^5/_8$ in. high with 12 in. rotating plate. Super strong; essential for decorating tiered wedding cakes.
307-Z-2501 $49.99 each

4. LAZY DAISY SERVER
Stationary stand. Sturdy white plastic with scalloped edges. 5 in. high with 12 in. plate.
307-Z-700 $8.99 each

5. TRIM 'N TURN CAKE STAND
Flute-edged. Plate turns smoothly on hidden ball bearings. Just turn as you decorate. White molded plastic; holds up to 100 lbs. 12 in. plate.
2103-Z-2518 $7.99 each

6. REVOLVING CAKE STAND
Now with easy, rotating ball bearings! Plate turns smoothly in either direction for easy decorating and serving; 3 in. high with 11 in. diameter plate in molded white plastic.
415-Z-900 $10.49 each

7. FANCI-FOIL WRAP
Serving side has a non-toxic grease-resistant surface. FDA approved for use with food.
Continuous roll: 20 in. x 15 ft. **$6.99 each**

Rose	804-Z-124
Gold	804-Z-183
Silver	804-Z-167
Blue	804-Z-140
White	804-Z-191

3.

4.

5.

6.

7.

Elegant Accents

All white board
. . . no brown edges!

8" 10" 12" 14" 16" 18"

1. RUFFLE BOARDS ™

Convenient, timesaving and ready to use. It's a cake board and ruffle in one. The Ruffle Board™ line features bleached white cake boards with all-white ruffling already attached. Creates an all-in-one, elegant presentation.

8" Ruffle Board™ 415-Z-950 **$1.99 each**
(for 6 in. round cake)

10" Ruffle Board™ 415-Z-960 **$2.49 each**
(for 8 in. round cake)

12" Ruffle Board™ 415-Z-970 **$2.99 each**
(for 10 in. round cake)

14" Ruffle Board™ 415-Z-980 **$3.49 each**
(for 12 in. round cake)

16" Ruffle Board™ 415-Z-990 **$4.39 each**
(for 14 in. round cake)

18" Ruffle Board™ 415-Z-1000 **$5.99 each**
(for 16 in. round cake)

2. TUK-N-RUFFLE

Attach to serving tray or board with royal icing or tape.

Pink	802-Z-702	$13.99 per 60 ft. bolt
Blue	802-Z-206	$13.99 per 60 ft. bolt
White	802-Z-1008	$13.99 per 60 ft. bolt
White 6 ft.	802-Z-1991	$2.89 per 6 ft. pkg.

3. SHOW 'N SERVE CAKE BOARDS

Scalloped edge. Protected with food-safe, grease-resistant coating.

8 in.	2104-Z-1125	$3.99 Pack of 10
10 in.	2104-Z-1168	$4.49 Pack of 10
12 in.	2104-Z-1176	$4.99 Pack of 8
14 in.	2104-Z-1184	$5.49 Pack of 6
14 X 20 in. Rectangle	2104-Z-1230	$5.99 Pack of 6

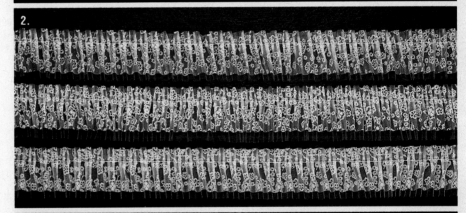

Decorating Tips Guide

ROUND

Outline, lettering, dots, balls, beads, stringwork, lattice, lacework.

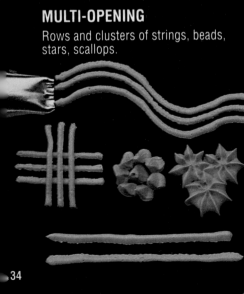

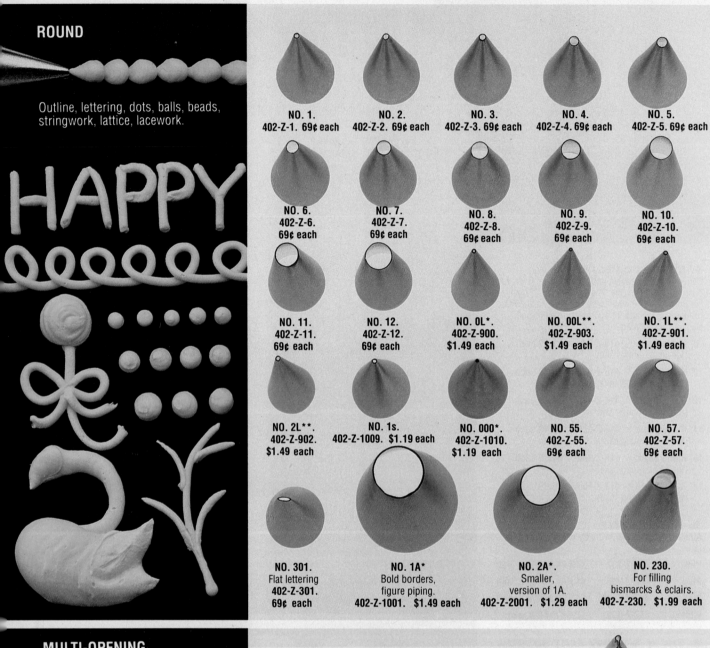

NO. 1. 402-Z-1. 69¢ each	**NO. 2.** 402-Z-2. 69¢ each	**NO. 3.** 402-Z-3. 69¢ each	**NO. 4.** 402-Z-4. 69¢ each	**NO. 5.** 402-Z-5. 69¢ each
NO. 6. 402-Z-6. 69¢ each	**NO. 7.** 402-Z-7. 69¢ each	**NO. 8.** 402-Z-8. 69¢ each	**NO. 9.** 402-Z-9. 69¢ each	**NO. 10.** 402-Z-10. 69¢ each
NO. 11. 402-Z-11. 69¢ each	**NO. 12.** 402-Z-12. 69¢ each	**NO. 0L*.** 402-Z-900. $1.49 each	**NO. 00L**.** 402-Z-903. $1.49 each	**NO. 1L**.** 402-Z-901. $1.49 each
NO. 2L**. 402-Z-902. $1.49 each	**NO. 1s.** 402-Z-1009. $1.19 each	**NO. 000*.** 402-Z-1010. $1.19 each	**NO. 55.** 402-Z-55. 69¢ each	**NO. 57.** 402-Z-57. 69¢ each

NO. 301. Flat lettering 402-Z-301. 69¢ each

NO. 1A* Bold borders, figure piping. 402-Z-1001. $1.49 each

NO. 2A*. Smaller, version of 1A. 402-Z-2001. $1.29 each

NO. 230. For filling bismarcks & eclairs. 402-Z-230. $1.99 each

MULTI-OPENING

Rows and clusters of strings, beads, stars, scallops.

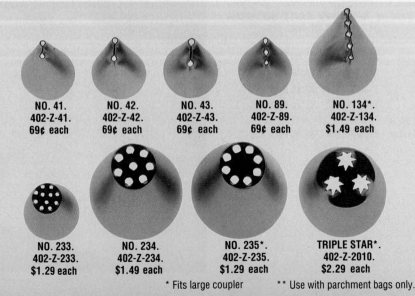

NO. 41. 402-Z-41. 69¢ each	**NO. 42.** 402-Z-42. 69¢ each	**NO. 43.** 402-Z-43. 69¢ each	**NO. 89.** 402-Z-89. 69¢ each	**NO. 134*.** 402-Z-134. $1.49 each

NO. 233. 402-Z-233. $1.29 each

NO. 234. 402-Z-234. $1.49 each

NO. 235*. 402-Z-235. $1.29 each

TRIPLE STAR*. 402-Z-2010. $2.29 each

34   * Fits large coupler   ** Use with parchment bags only.

Decorating Tips Guide

OPEN STAR

Star techniques and drop flowers; the finely-cut teeth of 199 thru 364 create decorations with many ridges; use 6B and 8B with pastry dough too.

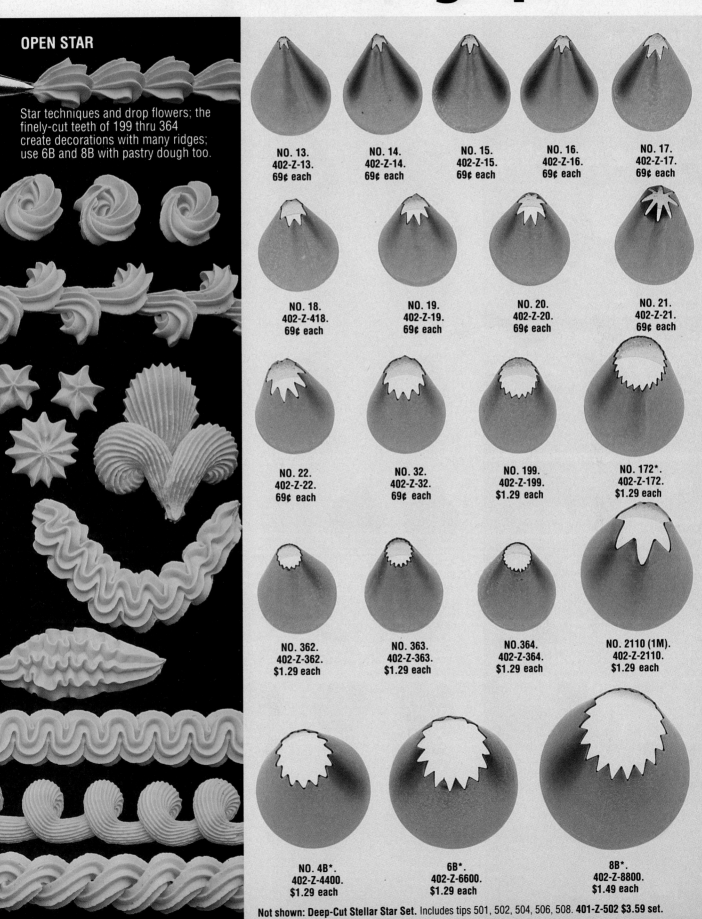

NO. 13.
402-Z-13.
69¢ each

NO. 14.
402-Z-14.
69¢ each

NO. 15.
402-Z-15.
69¢ each

NO. 16.
402-Z-16.
69¢ each

NO. 17.
402-Z-17.
69¢ each

NO. 18.
402-Z-418.
69¢ each

NO. 19.
402-Z-19.
69¢ each

NO. 20.
402-Z-20.
69¢ each

NO. 21.
402-Z-21.
69¢ each

NO. 22.
402-Z-22.
69¢ each

NO. 32.
402-Z-32.
69¢ each

NO. 199.
402-Z-199.
$1.29 each

NO. 172*.
402-Z-172.
$1.29 each

NO. 362.
402-Z-362.
$1.29 each

NO. 363.
402-Z-363.
$1.29 each

NO. 364.
402-Z-364.
$1.29 each

NO. 2110 (1M).
402-Z-2110.
$1.29 each

NO. 4B*.
402-Z-4400.
$1.29 each

6B*.
402-Z-6600.
$1.29 each

8B*.
402-Z-8800.
$1.49 each

Not shown: Deep-Cut Stellar Star Set. Includes tips 501, 502, 504, 506, 508. **401-Z-502** $3.59 set.

* Fits large coupler

Decorating Tips Guide

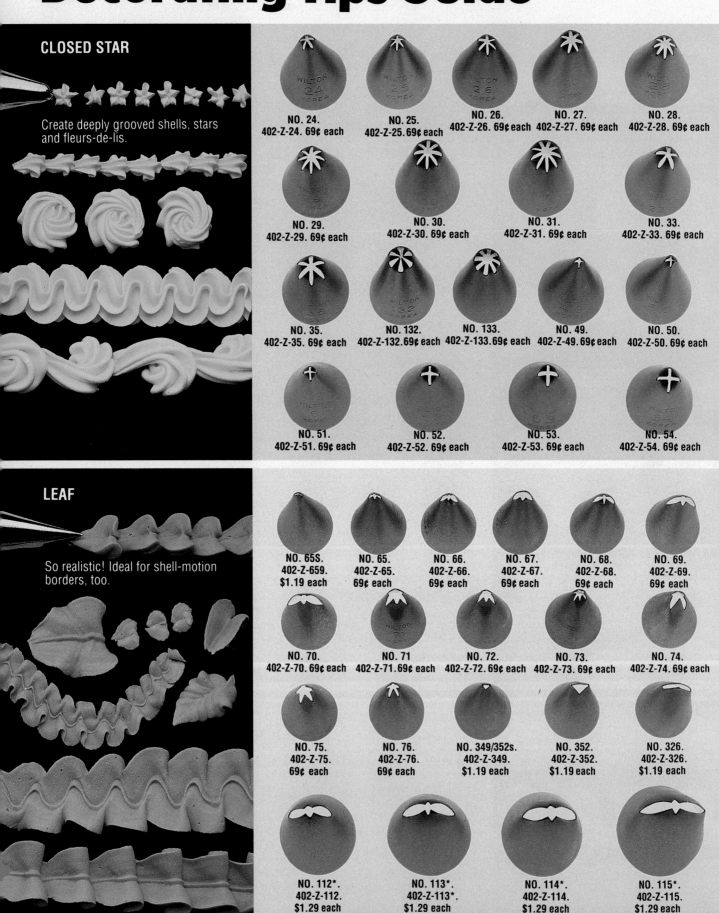

CLOSED STAR

Create deeply grooved shells, stars and fleurs-de-lis.

NO. 24. 402-Z-24. 69¢ each	NO. 25. 402-Z-25. 69¢ each	NO. 26. 402-Z-26. 69¢ each	NO. 27. 402-Z-27. 69¢ each	NO. 28. 402-Z-28. 69¢ each
NO. 29. 402-Z-29. 69¢ each	NO. 30. 402-Z-30. 69¢ each	NO. 31. 402-Z-31. 69¢ each		NO. 33. 402-Z-33. 69¢ each
NO. 35. 402-Z-35. 69¢ each	NO. 132. 402-Z-132. 69¢ each	NO. 133. 402-Z-133. 69¢ each	NO. 49. 402-Z-49. 69¢ each	NO. 50. 402-Z-50. 69¢ each
NO. 51. 402-Z-51. 69¢ each	NO. 52. 402-Z-52. 69¢ each	NO. 53. 402-Z-53. 69¢ each	NO. 54. 402-Z-54. 69¢ each	

LEAF

So realistic! Ideal for shell-motion borders, too.

NO. 65S. 402-Z-659. $1.19 each	NO. 65. 402-Z-65. 69¢ each	NO. 66. 402-Z-66. 69¢ each	NO. 67. 402-Z-67. 69¢ each	NO. 68. 402-Z-68. 69¢ each	NO. 69. 402-Z-69. 69¢ each
NO. 70. 402-Z-70. 69¢ each	NO. 71 402-Z-71. 69¢ each	NO. 72. 402-Z-72. 69¢ each	NO. 73. 402-Z-73. 69¢ each	NO. 74. 402-Z-74. 69¢ each	
NO. 75. 402-Z-75. 69¢ each	NO. 76. 402-Z-76. 69¢ each	NO. 349/352s. 402-Z-349. $1.19 each	NO. 352. 402-Z-352. $1.19 each	NO. 326. 402-Z-326. $1.19 each	
NO. 112*. 402-Z-112. $1.29 each	NO. 113*. 402-Z-113*. $1.29 each	NO. 114*. 402-Z-114. $1.29 each	NO. 115*. 402-Z-115. $1.29 each		

136

* Fits large coupler

DROP FLOWER

Small (106-225); medium (131-194); large (2C-1G) great for cookie dough too.

NO. 106.
402-Z-106.
$1.29 each

NO. 107.
402-Z-107.
$1.29 each

NO. 108**.
402-Z-108.
$1.29 each

NO. 109**.
402-Z-109.
$1.49 each

NO. 129.
402-Z-129.
$1.29 each

NO. 217.
402-Z-217.
$1.29 each

NO. 220.
402-Z-220.
$1.29 each

NO. 224.
402-Z-224.
$1.29 each

NO. 225.
402-Z-225.
$1.29 each

NO. 131.
402-Z-131.
$1.29 each

NO. 177.
402-Z-177.
$1.29 each

NO. 190**.
402-Z-190.
$1.49 each

NO. 191.
402-Z-191.
$1.29 each

NO. 193.
402-Z-193.
$1.29 each

NO. 194**.
402-Z-194. $1.49 each

NO. 135**.
402-Z-135. $1.49 each

NO. 140.
402-Z-140.
$1.49 each

NO. 195**.
402-Z-195.
$1.29 each

NO. 2C*.
402-Z-2003.
$1.29 each

NO. 2D*
402-Z-2004.
$1.29 each

NO. 2E*
402-Z-2005.
$1.29 each

NO. 2F*.
402-Z-2006.
$1.29 each

NO. 1B*.
402-Z-1002.
$1.49 each

NO. 1C.
402-Z-1003. $1.49 each

NO. 1E*
402-Z-1005.
$1.49 each

NO. 1F*
402-Z-1006.
$1.49 each

NO. 1G*
402-Z-1007.
$1.49 each

* Fits large coupler   ** Use with parchment bags only.

Decorating Tips Guide

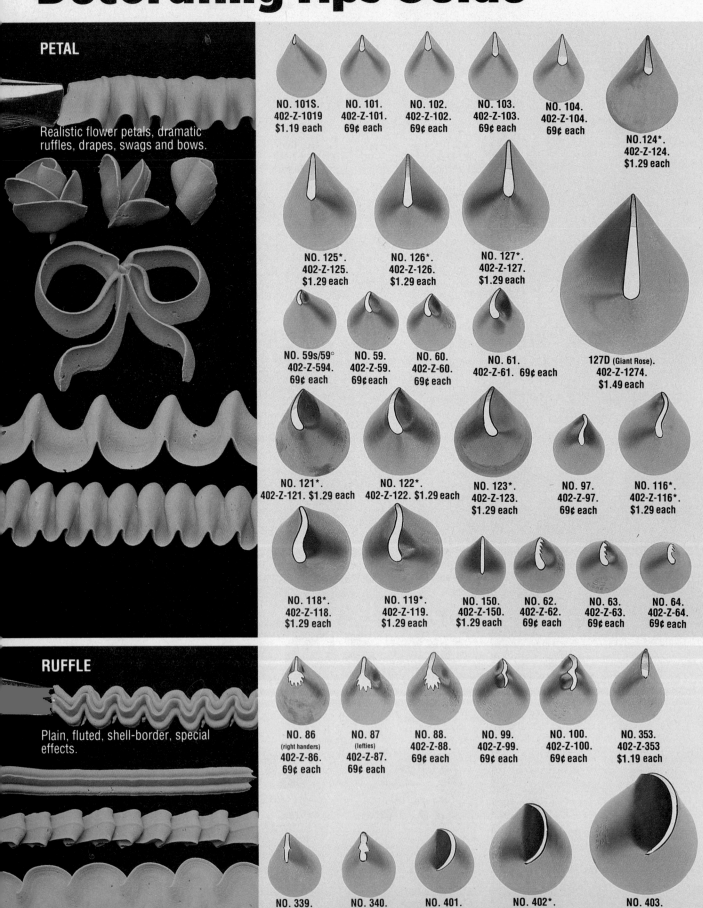

PETAL

Realistic flower petals, dramatic ruffles, drapes, swags and bows.

NO. 101S. 402-Z-1019 $1.19 each

NO. 101. 402-Z-101. 69¢ each

NO. 102. 402-Z-102. 69¢ each

NO. 103. 402-Z-103. 69¢ each

NO. 104. 402-Z-104. 69¢ each

NO.124*. 402-Z-124. $1.29 each

NO. 125*. 402-Z-125. $1.29 each

NO. 126*. 402-Z-126. $1.29 each

NO. 127*. 402-Z-127. $1.29 each

127D (Giant Rose). 402-Z-1274. $1.49 each

NO. 59s/59° 402-Z-594. 69¢ each

NO. 59. 402-Z-59. 69¢ each

NO. 60. 402-Z-60. 69¢ each

NO. 61. 402-Z-61. 69¢ each

NO. 121*. 402-Z-121. $1.29 each

NO. 122*. 402-Z-122. $1.29 each

NO. 123*. 402-Z-123. $1.29 each

NO. 97. 402-Z-97. 69¢ each

NO. 116*. 402-Z-116*. $1.29 each

NO. 118*. 402-Z-118. $1.29 each

NO. 119*. 402-Z-119. $1.29 each

NO. 150. 402-Z-150. $1.29 each

NO. 62. 402-Z-62. 69¢ each

NO. 63. 402-Z-63. 69¢ each

NO. 64. 402-Z-64. 69¢ each

RUFFLE

Plain, fluted, shell-border, special effects.

NO. 86 (right handers) 402-Z-86. 69¢ each

NO. 87 (lefties) 402-Z-87. 69¢ each

NO. 88. 402-Z-88. 69¢ each

NO. 99. 402-Z-99. 69¢ each

NO. 100. 402-Z-100. 69¢ each

NO. 353. 402-Z-353. $1.19 each

NO. 339. 402-Z-339. $1.19 each

NO. 340. 402-Z-340. $1.19 each

NO. 401. 402-Z-401. 89¢ each

NO. 402*. 402-Z-402. $1.29 each

NO. 403. 402-Z-403. $1.49 each

Decorating Tips Guide

BASKET-WEAVE

44, 45 make smooth stripes; rest of basket-weave tips make both smooth and ribbed stripes.

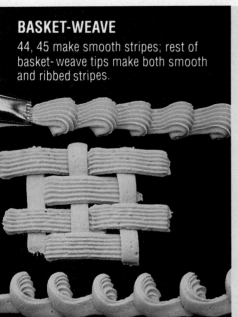

NO. 44.
402-Z-44.
69¢ each

NO. 45.
402-Z-45.
69¢ each

NO. 48.
402-Z-48.
69¢ each

NO. 327.
402-Z-327.
$1.19 each

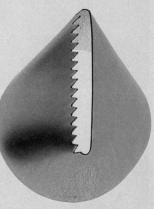

NO. 46.
402-Z-46.
69¢ each

NO. 47.
402-Z-47.
69¢ each

NO. 2B*.
402-Z-2002.
$1.29 each

NO. 1D*.
402-Z-1004.
$1.49 each

789 CAKE ICER.
For icing top and sides. Use with decorating bag 16-in. or larger.
409-Z-789 $1.99 each

SPECIALTY

Shells, ropes, heart, Christmas trees, ring candle holders!

NO. 320.
402-Z-320.
$1.29 each

NO. 347.
402-7-347.
$1.29 each

NO. 96.
402-Z-96.
69¢ each

NO. 98.
402-Z-98. 69¢ each

NO. 105.
402-Z-105. 69¢ each

NO. 110.
402-Z-110.
69¢ each

NO. 136.
402-Z-136.
$1.49 each

NO. 250*.
402-Z-250.
$1.49 each

NO. 252*.
402-Z-252. $1.49 each

NO. 77.
402-Z-77.
69¢ each

NO. 78.
402-Z-78.
69¢ each

NO. 79.
402-Z-79.
69¢ each

NO. 80.
402-Z-80.
69¢ each

NO. 81.
402-Z-81.
69¢ each

NO. 83.
402-Z-83.
69¢ each

NO. 95.
402-Z-95.
69¢ each

139

* Fits large coupler

Toppers

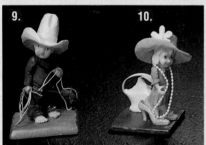

1. CLOWNS SET
2 1/4 to 2 1/4 in. high
2113-Z-9003 $2.99 set of 3

2. JUGGLER CLOWN
Jolly fellow in action. 4 in. high.
2113-Z-2252 $2.19 each

3. CIRCUS BALLOONS SET
12 in a bunch. 3 bunches per set.
6 1/2 in. high.
2113-Z-2366 $2.49 pack

4. COMICAL CLOWNS SET
Varied expressions. 2 in. to 3 in.
2113-Z-2635 $3.29 set of 4

5. DERBY CLOWNS SET
A quartet of gigglers. On picks. 2 in. high.
2113-Z-2333 $2.49 pack of 4

6. SMALL DERBY CLOWNS SET
Miniatures! Perfect for cupcakes. 2 in. high
with pick.
2113-Z-2759 $1.99 pack of 6

7. CLOWN SEPARATOR SET
Two big-footed clowns balance a 6 in. round
cake on top plate. Perfect to set atop a large
base cake (be sure to dowel rod). They can
stand on their hands or feet. Set includes two
7 in. scalloped-edge plates and two snap-on
clown supports. 4 in. high.
301-Z-909 $6.99 set

8. CAROUSEL SEPARATOR SET
Galloping ponies will add excitement for that
special little one. Contains: 2 brown and 2
white snap-on pony pillars, two 10 in. round
plates-one clear acrylic, one plastic. Two 10
in. cardboard circles to protect plates.
9 in. high.
2103-Z-1139 $10.99 set

9. LI'L COWPOKE
Wee buckaroo; 5 1/4 in. high.
2113-Z-2406 $2.69 each

10. DOLLY DRESS UP
High style; 4 1/2 in. high.
2113-Z-1485 $2.69 each

11. APPALOOSA ROCKING
HORSES SET
Four painted ponies; 2 1/2 in. high.
2113-Z-2015 $3.49 set

12. HONEY BEAR
Hand-painted. 3 3/4 in. high.
2113-Z-2031 $2.69 each

13. CAROUSEL CAKE TOP SET
A fast, easy, circus in seconds for 10 in. or
larger cakes. 9 in. high.
1305-Z-9302 $4.99 set

1. NUMERAL PICKS SET
Numbers 2 in. high. With picks, about
3 ½ in. high, 10 numbers in set.
1106-Z-7406 $1.39 set

2. TEEN DOLL PICK
6 ½ in. high without pick.
2815-Z-101 $2.99 each

3. FRECKLE-FACED DOLL PICK
4 in. high without pick.
2113-Z-2317 $2.99 each

4. MINI DOLL PICK SET
4 picks, 4 ¼ in. high with pick.
1511-Z-1019 $5.69 set

5. TELEPHONE TEENS SET
Get in on the conversation track with
these teens. 6 pieces - 3 girls, 3 boys,
1 ⅜ to 2 in. high.
1301-Z-706 $3.69 set

6. COMMUNION ALTAR
Tulle veil on girl. Each, 3 ½ in. high.
Boy 1105-Z-7886 $2.09 each
Girl 1105-Z-7878 $2.09 each

7. SHINING CROSS
Detachable pick. 3 ¾ in. high.
1105-Z-7320 $1.09 each

8. SLEEPING ANGELS SET
1 ½ in. high x 3 in. long.
2113-Z-2325 $1.99 set

9. 3 A.M. FEEDING
5 in. high.
2113-Z-3333 $3.99 each

10. CRYSTAL-CLEAR BOOTIES SET
Add ribbon laces.
2 in. high x 4 ¼ in. long.
1103-Z-9332 $1.69 set

11. BABY SHOES CAKE PICKS
3 in. high.
2113-Z-3811 $1.39 pack of 6

12. STORK CAKE PICKS
3 ¼ in. high.
2113-Z-3805 $1.39 pack of 6

13. BABY BRACELETS
1 in. diameter.
2111-Z-72 $1.69 pack of 4

14. TINY TODDLER
4 ¾ in. high.
Blue 1103-Z-7429 $2.09 each
Pink 1103-Z-7437 $2.09 each

15. BABY RATTLES
Great as gift trimmers, too!
3 ½ in. long,
2113-Z-3283 $1.09 pack of 2

16. MAMA STORK
4 in. high.
1305-Z-6303 $1.69 each

17. MR. STORK
5 in. high.
115-Z-1502 $6.00 each

18. PETITE LULLABY
4 ½ in. high.
115-Z-1987 $8.00 each

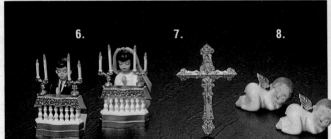

Toppers

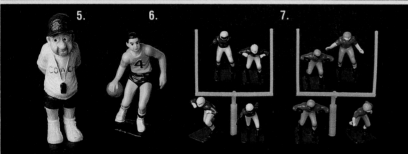

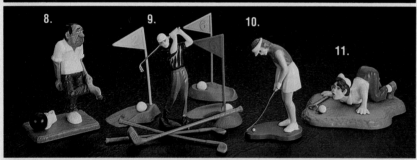

1. SOCCER CAKE TOP SET
9 pieces, 1¾ to 2 in. high.
2113-Z-9002 $2.49 9-pc. set

2. SOFTBALL PLAYER
4⅜ in. high.
2113-Z-3705 $3.29 each

3. BASEBALL SET
Batter, catcher, pitcher and 3 basemen. Handpainted. Each 2⅛-2¾ in. high.
2113-Z-2155 $2.99 6-pc. set

4. "NICE PLAY" BASEBALL SET
3 pieces, 1½ to 3⅛ in. high.
2113-Z-2473 $2.99 3-pc. set

5. GOOD SPORTS COACH
4½ in. high,
2113-Z-4140 $2.69 each

6. BASKETBALL PLAYER
3¾ in. high
2113-Z-9354 $1.99 each

7. FOOTBALL SET
Eight 1½-2 in. high players and two 4½ in. high goal posts.
2113-Z-2236 $2.99 10-pc. set

8. BUMBLING BOWLER
4½ in. high.
2113-Z-2783 $2.69 each

9. GOLF SET*
Includes 4½ in. high golfer plus 3 each: 2½ in. wide greens, 4 in. high flags, 5 in. clubs and golf balls.
1306-Z-7274 $2.09 13-pc. set

10. FEMALE GOLFER   4⅛ in. high.
2113-Z-9000 $1.79 each

11. COMICAL GOLFER
2 in. high, 4¼ in. wide, 5⅛ in. long.
2113-Z-2554 $2.09 each

12. FISHY SITUATION
5¼ in. high.   2113-Z-2074 $2.69 each

13. END OF DOCK FISHERMAN
5 in. high.
2113-Z-4832 $2.69 each

14. FRUSTRATED FISHERMAN
4½ in. high.
2113-Z-2384 $3.29 each

15. MESSAGE CAKE PICKS
Pipe on icing message. 4½ in. high.
1008-Z-726 $1.39 pack of 2

16. SHARP SHOOTER
5⅞ in. high.
2113-Z-2422 $2.99 each

17. JAUNTY JOGGER
4 in. high.
2113-Z-2066 $2.69 each

18. ARMCHAIR QUARTERBACK
Man 3½ in. high; TV 2¼ in. high
2113-Z-1302 $2.69 2-pc. set

19. LAZY BONES
3 in. high x 5½ in. long.
2113-Z-2414 $2.69 each

20. PARTY GUY   3 x 3¾ in. high.
2113-Z-3739 $2.69 each

21. BACKYARD GARDENER
4⅜ in. high.
2113-Z-1973 $2.09 each

22. ALL THUMBS   5 in. high.
2113-Z-2686 $2.09 each

23. OL' SMOKY
Man 5⅛ in. tall; grill 2⅜ in. tall.
2113-Z-2694 $2.09 2-pc. set

24. BIG BOSS
3½ in high x 2½ in. long.
2113-Z-3798 $2.69 each

*CAUTION: Contains small parts.
Not recommended for use by children 3 years and under.

Toppers

1. BATMAN ™ CAKE TOP
3 ½ in. high.
2113-Z-2902 $1.99 set

2. GARFIELD PICKS
3 ½ to 3 ⅞ in. high.
2113-Z-9007 $1.99 set of 6

3. SESAME STREET SET*
Big Bird 3 in., Oscar the Grouch 2 in., Cookie Monster 2¼ in., Bert 2 ¼ in., Ernie 2 in. high.
2113-Z-1728 $2.99 5-pc. set

4. BIG BIRD PICK
3 ½ in. high.
2113-Z-3815 $1.99 pkg. of 6

5. COOKIE MONSTER PICK
3 ¼ in. high.
2113-Z-3813 $1.99 pkg. of 6

6. BIG BIRD WITH AGE
Age indicator 1-6, 4 in. high.
2113-Z-1430 $2.09 each

7. THE SIMPSONS BIRTHDAY TOPPER
5 ⅜ in. diameter.
2113-Z-9005 $1.99 each

8. WACKY WITCH 5¼ in. high.
2113-Z-6118 $2.09 each

9. JACK-O-LANTERNS 2 in.
2113-Z-3135 $1.69 set of 4

10. BLACK CAT PICK 3 in. high.
2113-Z-4301 $1.39 pack of 6

11. JACK-O-LANTERN PICK
3 ½ in. high.
2113-Z-4328 $1.39 pack of 6

12. CHRISTMAS TREE PICK
3 ⅜ in. high.
2113-Z-4344 $1.39 pack of 6

13. SNOWMAN PICK
3 ⅝ in. high.
2113-Z-4360 $1.39 pack of 6

14. HEART CAKE PICK
2 in. high.
1502-Z-1011 $1.39 pack of 6

15. SHAMROCK PICK
3 ¼ in. high.
2113-Z-4387 $1.39 pack of 6

16. EASTER BUNNY PICK
3 ⅞ in. high.
2113-Z-4476 $1.39 pack of 6

17. GOOD LUCK KEY PICK
3 ¼ in. high.
2113-Z-3801 $1.39 pack of 6

18. GRADUATION CAKE PICK
3 in. high.
1½ in. on 1¾ in. pick.
2113-Z-3803 $1.39 pack of 6

19. SUCCESSFUL GRAD
4 ¼ in. tall.
2113-Z-4549 $1.69 each

20. GLOWING GRAD
4 ½ in. tall.
2113-Z-1833 $1.69 each

21. GLAD GRADUATE
4 ½ in. tall.
2113-Z-1817 $2.09 each

22. HAPPY GRADUATE
5 in. tall.
2113-Z-1818 $2.09 each

*CAUTION: Contains small parts.
Not recommended for use by children 3 years and under.

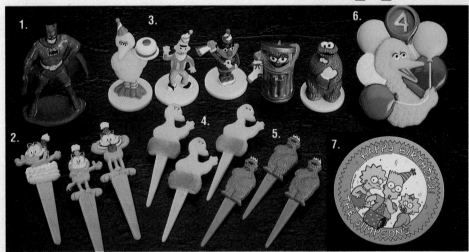

Cake Top Sets

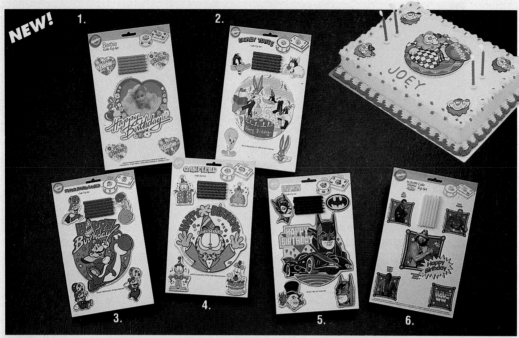

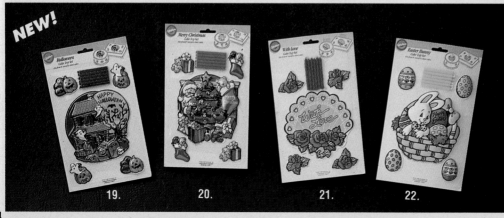

Fun and festive cake top sets for fast and easy decorating. Sets are designed to be used on 8 or 9 inch round or 9 x 13 inch sheet cakes. Each set includes 5 theme-oriented decorations that are food-safe, washable and reusable, plus 6 color-coordinating candles.

1. NEW! BARBIE®
2113-Z-2828 $2.49 set
(Available Sept. 1, 1992)
BARBIE and associated trademarks are owned by and used under license from Mattel, Inc. © 1992 Mattel, Inc. All Rights Reserved.

2. NEW! LOONEY TUNES
2113-Z-2826 $2.49 set
(Available Sept. 1, 1992)
TM and © Warner Bros. Inc. 1992. All Rights Reserved.

3. NEW! SUPER MARIO BROTHERS®
2113-Z-2827 $2.49 set
(Available Sept. 1, 1992)
©1992 Nintendo of America, Inc.

4. NEW! GARFIELD
2113-Z-2829 $2.49 set
(Available Sept. 1, 1992)
GARFIELD CHARACTERS: © 1978 United Features Syndicate, Inc.

5. NEW! BATMAN RETURNS
2113-Z-2830 $2.49 set
(Available Sept. 1, 1992)
TM & © 1992 DC Comics Inc.

6. NEW! WWF®
2113-Z-2831 $2.49 set
(Available Sept. 1, 1992)
© 1992 Titan Sports, Inc. All Rights Reserved.

7. BASEBALL STAR
2113-Z-2819 $2.49 set

8. SOCCER STAR
2113-Z-2815 $2.49 set

9. DINOSAUR PARTY
2113-Z-2825 $2.49 set

10. BIRTHDAY BEARS
2113-Z-2823 $2.49 set

11. PARTY! PARTY!
2113-Z-2821 $2.49 set

12. ROCK & ROLL PARTY
2113-Z-2814 $2.49 set

13. KING FOR A DAY
2113-Z-2822 $2.49 set

14. VICTORIAN HEARTS
2113-Z-2820 $2.49 set

15. BALLERINA BUNNY
2113-Z-2824 $2.49 set

16. LITTLE LOCOMOTIVE
2113-Z-2818 $2.49 set

17. CIRCUS FRIENDS
2113-Z-2816 $2.49 set

18. HAPPY CLOWNS
2113-Z-2817 $2.49 set

19. NEW! HALLOWEEN
2113-Z-3900 $2.49 set

20. NEW! CHRISTMAS
2113-Z-3901 $2.49 set

21. NEW! WITH LOVE
2113-Z-3903 $2.49 set

22. NEW! EASTER
2113-Z-3902 $2.49 set
(Available Dec. 1, 1992)

144

Candles

1. NEW! WWF®
3 ½ in. high.
2811-Z-762 $2.99 each
(Available Sept. 1, 1992)
© 1992 Titan Sports, Inc. All Rights Reserved. Hulk Hogan is a trademark of Marvel Entertainment Group, Inc.

2. NEW! BARBIE®
3 in. high.
2811-Z-763 $2.99 each
(Available Sept. 1, 1992)
BARBIE and associated trademarks are owned by and used under license from Mattel, Inc. © 1992 Mattel, Inc. All Rights Reserved.

3. BIG BIRD HAPPY BIRTHDAY CANDLE
3 in. high.
2811-Z-910 $2.79 each

4. BIG BIRD CANDLES
3 in. high. $2.79 each
2811-Z-911 Big Bird #1
2811-Z-912 Big Bird #2
2811-Z-913 Big Bird #3
2811-Z-914 Big Bird #4
Sesame Street Characters
©Jim Henson Productions, Inc. All rights reserved.

5. MAGGIE SIMPSON #1 3 in. high.
2811-Z-1991 $2.49 each

6. 5-PC. SIMPSON CANDLE SET 2 to 3 ½ in.
2811-Z-1990 $3.49 set
©MATT GROENING
TM & ©1990 Twentieth Century Fox Film Corporation. All Rights Reserved

7. JUMBO CRAYON CANDLES
8 candles color a birthday happy.
3 ½ in. high.
2811-Z-226 $1.49 pkg.

8. CRAYON CANDLES
10 candles for a big time party.
2 ½ in. high.
2811-Z-227 $1.49 pkg.

9. CELEBRATION CANDLES 2 ½ in. high.
24 in pkg. 59¢ per pkg.
Asst. 2811-Z-215
White 2811-Z-207
Yellow 2811-Z-208
Red 2811-Z-209
Blue 2811-Z-210
Green 2811-Z-211
Pink 2811-Z-213
Black 2811-Z-224
Neon 2811-Z-225 69¢ /pkg.

10. CELEBRATION JUMBO CANDLES
3 ¼ in. high.10 in pkg.
59¢ per pkg.
Asst. 2811-Z-222
Red 2811-Z-201
White 2811-Z-202
Green 2811-Z-203
Pink 2811-Z-204
Blue 2811-Z-205
Yellow 2811-Z-206
Black 2811-Z-223
Neon 2811-Z-221
(Ass't-Pink,Green,Yellow,Orange)
69¢ per pkg.

11. GOLD AND SILVER CANDLES
10 gold candles.
2811-Z-9122 $1.49 pkg.
10 silver candles.
2811-Z-9123 $1.49 pkg.
8 jumbo gold candles.
2811-Z-9124 $1.49 pkg.
8 jumbo silver candles.
2811-Z-9125 $1.49 pkg.

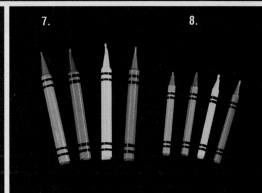
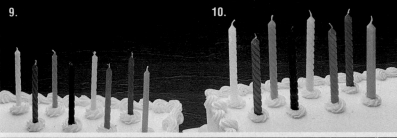

12. RELIGHTING CANDLES
2 ½ in. high. 10 in pkg.
2811-Z-220 99¢ pkg.

13. SLENDERS
6 ½ in. high.
2811-Z-1188 79¢ pkg.

14. SPARKLERS
6½ high, 24 per pkg.
2811-Z-1230 99¢ pkg.

15. CANDLE HOLDERS
Multi-color; 12 per pkg.
2811-Z-150 79¢ pkg.

145

Candles

NEW!

1.

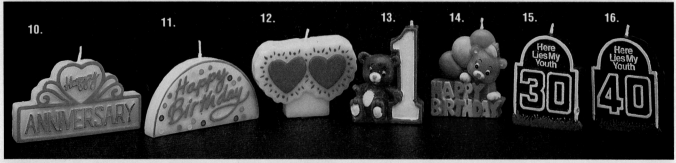

Great new novelty candles will make birthdays extra special and fun!

1. _NEW!_ ICE CREAM CONES
2 in. high.
2811-Z-758 $2.99 pkg. of 6

2. _NEW!_ MUSICAL NOTES
2 1/8 in. high.
2811-Z-753 $2.99 pkg. of 6

3. _NEW!_ PENCILS
2 1/2 in. high.
2811-Z-754 $2.99 pkg. of 6

4. _NEW!_ COLA BOTTLES
2 1/4 in. high.
2811-Z-751 $2.99 pkg. of 6

5. _NEW!_ BABY BOTTLES
2 1/4 in. high.
2811-Z-755 $2.99 pkg. of 6

6. _NEW!_ LIPSTICK
2 1/4 in. high.
2811-Z-756 $2.99 pkg. of 6

7. _NEW!_ FISH
2 1/2 in. high.
2811-Z-752 $2.99 pkg. of 6

8. _NEW!_ BASEBALL BATS
2 3/4 in. high.
2811-Z-750 $2.99 pkg. of 6

9. _NEW!_ TENNIS RACKETS
2 1/4 in. high.
2811-Z-759 $2.99 pkg. of 6

10. _NEW!_ FOOTBALLS
2 1/4 in. high.
2811-Z-757 $2.99 pkg. of 6

11. _NEW!_ BOWLING SET
6 pins, 1 ball; pins 2 in. high.
2811-Z-760 $2.99 set

Candle holder sets turn any cake into a party cake quickly. Sets include theme coordinating candle holders and candles.

12. RACE CARS
4 cars, 6 candles
2113-Z-1467 $1.99 set

13. SHIPS
6 ships, 6 candles
2113-Z-1468 $1.99 set

14. AIRPLANES
4 airplanes, 6 candles
2113-Z-1469 $1.99 set

15. HELICOPTERS
4 helicopters, 6 candles
2113-Z-1470 $1.99 set

16. TRUCKS
6 ships, 6 candles
2113-Z-1471 $1.99 set

17. TRAIN
All aboard! 6 train cars 1 1/4 in. to 1 5/8 in. high; 6 candles 2 1/2 in. high.
2113-Z-9004 $2.49 set

18. BALLERINAS
6 ballerinas, 6 candles.
2113-Z-1472 $2.49 set

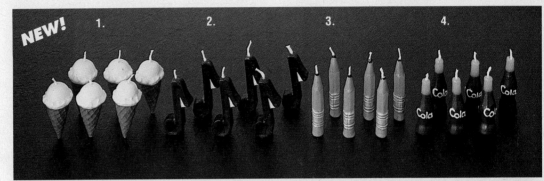

NEW! 1. 2. 3. 4.

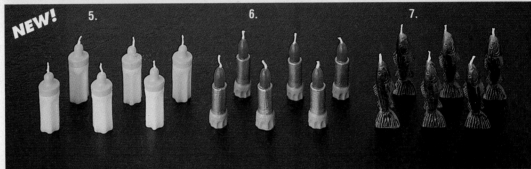

NEW! 5. 6. 7.

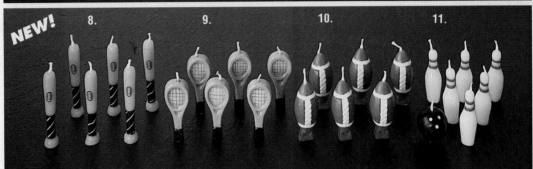

NEW! 8. 9. 10. 11.

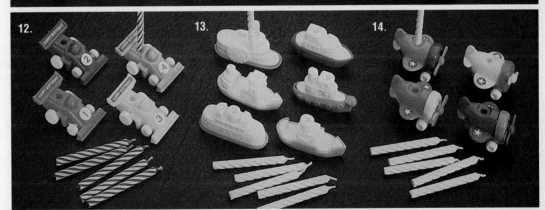

12. 13. 14.

15. 16. 17. 18.

There are as many types of favors as there are cake designs!
No matter what the style, each adds its own elegance to any occasion.
Below are several favors which accent cakes in this Yearbook—
we've grouped them according to style.
Find one that's perfect for your celebration!

CONTAINERS WITH PUFFS

Take a candy-filled tulle puff, finish with Instant Bow and a small trim, then place right inside any of our novelty containers. It couldn't be easier!

"Precious Cargo" shown p. 89

FAVOR BOXES

Fast and impressive. They fold or snap closed to make an easy candy container that works well with a variety of ribbon techniques.

"Treasured Forever" shown p. 82

HOLDING RIBBON FAVORS

A continuous double-sided pocket to hold candies or potpourri. It gives you flexibility to add on bows, puffs and other accents.

"Two Hearts As One" shown p. 83

WIRED SHAPING RIBBON FAVORS

For rich, deep color and full, lifelike shapes, this flexible wired ribbon is unsurpassed. Great for flowers; excellent for many bows.

"Sweet Remembrance" shown p. 78

POUCHING RIBBON FAVORS

Divided into trimmable segments, this ribbon is a pleasure to use. Simply cut at the seams to form a candy bag which can be tied off with Instant Bow and accented with other Bomboniere!™ pieces.

"Lovely Lamb" shown p. 88

DOUBLE-GATHERING RIBBON FAVORS

This "bon-bon" style may be the easiest ribbon to use. Strings on either side gather to form a middle pocket, then tie off.

"Wedded Bliss" shown p. 69

SAUCER-BASED FAVORS

These ideas use the favor saucer for support. Your favor stands on its own, for a better view of accessories and full puffs.

"Winning Formula" shown p. 86

A complete product selection from Wilton to help you make the most beautiful party favors your guests have ever seen. Bomboniere!™ Party Favor products cover every detail — elegant favor ideas, an easy-to-follow instruction book and a complete selection of products. Bomboniere!™ makes favors easy and fun!

You begin with brilliant ideas! The Bomboniere!™ Party Favors Book is your source for elegant, easy-to-make favors that make any special occasion unforgettable:

— Vivid floral creations for wedding and anniversary parties
— Romantic bridal shower ideas, using dramatic puffs of ribbon and tulle
— Adorable baby shower favors which focus on cute, fuzzy bears, milk bottles or other baby accessories in a candy-filled saucer.

Use these exquisite favors on cakes, at place settings — wherever you want to make an elegant impression. The Party Favors Book tells you how to create the look you want, with step-by-step instructions and color photographs of each favor.

On the following pages, you'll find the exclusive Bomboniere!™ products that make these ideas come to life. Brilliant ribbon and tulle in an array of colors and finishes to match to your party color scheme...creative accessories which capture the perfect mood for your event.

Make The Party Favors Book your first Bomboniere!™ purchase. It's filled with the ideas and expertise you need to create beautiful favors in a few easy steps. 40 color pages; over 100 ideas; complete product selection.

Party Favors Book   916-Z-825 $4.99 each

Make your own beautiful party favors!

Bomboniere!™
Party Favors

Ideas, instructions and products for all your special events

149

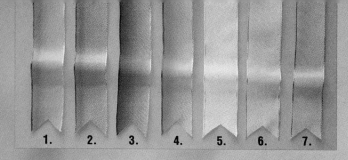

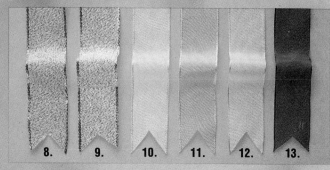

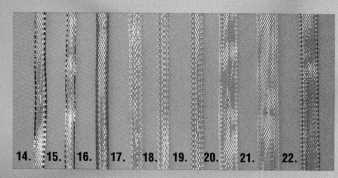

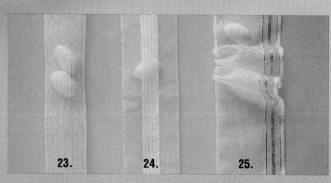

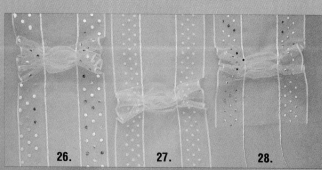

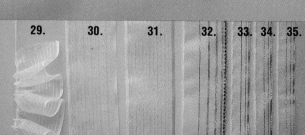

RIBBON

Discover the variety of Bomboniere!™ ribbon! You'll find exactly the color you need to match the occasion, in the proper width to enhance the size of your favors. Use the right ribbon for the job, to make shaping, gathering, tying bows and other favor-making tasks easy.

WIRED SHAPING RIBBON

Hidden wire along both edges makes this ribbon easy to work with, yielding exquisite bows and flowers. Each package contains 2 yards of 1 in. wide ribbon.

1.	PINK/GREEN	1003-Z-3103	$4.79 pk.
2.	BLUE/GREEN	1003-Z-3101	$4.79 pk.
3.	VIOLET/PINK	1003-Z-3104	$4.79 pk.
4.	LAVENDER/PINK	1003-Z-3102	$4.79 pk.
5.	WHITE	1003-Z-3107	$4.29 pk.
6.	PINK	1003-Z-3105	$4.29 pk.
7.	BLUE	1003-Z-3106	$4.29 pk.
8.	GOLD LAMÉ	1003-Z-3112	$4.79 pk.
9.	SILVER LAMÉ	1003-Z-3113	$4.79 pk.
10.	YELLOW	1003-Z-3111	$4.29 pk.
11.	LAVENDER	1003-Z-3108	$4.29 pk.
12.	PEACH	1003-Z-3110	$4.29 pk.
13.	TEAL	1003-Z-3109	$4.29 pk.

INSTANT BOW RIBBON

Woven-in pull strings help you create foolproof, perfectly-shaped iridescent bows in colors that complement every party theme. Each package contains 4 yards.

14.	$3/16$ IN. SILVER	1003-Z-3118	$3.19 pk.
15.	$3/16$ IN. GOLD	1003-Z-3117	$3.19 pk.
16.	$3/16$ IN. RED	1003-Z-3119	$3.19 pk.
17.	$3/16$ IN. WHITE	1003-Z-3114	$3.19 pk.
18.	$3/16$ IN. PINK	1003-Z-3115	$3.19 pk.
19.	$3/16$ IN. BLUE	1003-Z-3116	$3.19 pk.
20.	$5/16$ IN. WHITE	1003-Z-3120	$3.99 pk.
21.	$5/16$ IN. PINK	1003-Z-3121	$3.99 pk.
22.	$5/16$ IN. BLUE	1003-Z-3122	$3.99 pk.

23. HOLDING RIBBON

An exciting way to present candy, rice, potpourri - this continuous ribbon pouch lets you decide which way to showcase your favor. Ribbon is 1 1/2 in. wide; package contains 2 yards.

IRIDESCENT	1003-Z-3124	$3.99 pk.

24. POUCHING RIBBON

Segmented ribbon pouches make a fancy presentation of almonds, mints, rice, potpourri - but only you will know how simple they are to work with! Each pouch is 2 in. wide, 6 1/4 feet long. Each package contains 6 pouches.

LUREX STRIPE	1003-Z-3123	$3.19 pk.

25. POUCHED GATHERING RIBBON

Fill this ribbon with candy, rice or potpourri; then gather into the most beautiful ruffles you've ever seen. Ribbon is 2 3/8 in. wide; package contains 2 yards.

GOLD EDGE	1003-Z-3128	$4.99 pk.

26-28. DOUBLE GATHERING RIBBON

Use this ribbon to create bountiful ruffles and precise containers for almonds, mints, rice and potpourri! Ribbon is 4 3/4 in. wide; package contains 1 yard.

26.	SILVER DOTS	1003-Z-3126	$3.79 pk.
27.	WHITE DOTS	1003-Z-3125	$3.79 pk.
28.	GOLD DOTS	1003-Z-3127	$3.79 pk.

29-31. STRIPED GATHERING RIBBON

Begin your favors with shimmering striped ribbon to ruffle and form into fancy flowers! Ribbon is 2 1/4 in. wide; package contains 2 yards.

29.	IRIDESCENT WHITE	1003-Z-3133	$3.19 pk.
30.	PINK	1003-Z-3134	$3.19 pk.
31.	BLUE	1003-Z-3135	$3.19 pk.

32. GATHERING RIBBON WITH LUREX AND PICOT EDGE

Dramatic ruffles are easily executed using this unique ribbon. The decorative edge adds a special look. Ribbon is 2 in. wide; package contains 2 yards.

MULTICOLOR	1003-Z-3129	$3.19 pk.

33-35. GATHERING RIBBON

Beauty on a smaller scale! 7/8 in. wide ribbon makes dainty ruffles and flowers - but it's still easy to work with. Package contains 4 yards.

33.	PINK	1003-Z-3131	$3.19 pk.
34.	BLUE	1003-Z-3132	$3.19 pk.
35.	MULTICOLOR	1003-Z-3130	$3.19 pk.

Bomboniere!™ products are both imported and made in the United States.

Bomboniere!™
Party Favors

TULLE CIRCLES

Sheer mesh fabric for elegant puffs and pleated bows. Our wide assortment of colors gives you unmatched decorating options! 9 in. diameter.

Solid Tulle Circles come 25 per pkg.

1. WHITE	1005-Z-1	$4.29 pk.
2. PINK	1005-Z-2	$4.29 pk.
3. BLUE	1005-Z-3	$4.29 pk.
4. IVORY	1005-Z-4	$4.29 pk.
5. PEACH	1005-Z-5	$4.29 pk.
6. MINT	1005-Z-6	$4.29 pk.
7. LILAC	1005-Z-8	$4.29 pk.
8. YELLOW	1005-Z-14	$4.29 pk.
9. TEAL	1005-Z-13	$4.29 pk.
10. RASPBERRY	1005-Z-11	$4.29 pk.
11. ROYAL	1005-Z-9	$4.29 pk.
12. RED	1005-Z-10	$4.29 pk.
13. PURPLE	1005-Z-12	$4.29 pk.
14. EMERALD	1005-Z-15	$4.29 pk.
15. BLACK	1005-Z-7	$4.29 pk.

FANCY TULLE CIRCLES

Dotted Tulle Circles come 12 per pkg.

16. DOTTED WHITE	1005-Z-16	$6.49 pk.
17. DOTTED PINK	1005-Z-17	$6.49 pk.
18. DOTTED BLUE	1005-Z-18	$6.49 pk.
19. DOTTED YELLOW	1005-Z-19	$6.49 pk.

Lurex-Edge Tulle Circles come 12 per pkg.

20. LUREX-EDGE IRIDESCENT	1005-Z-20	$7.49 pk.
21. LUREX-EDGE GOLD	1005-Z-21	$7.49 pk.
22. LUREX-EDGE SILVER	1005-Z-22	$7.49 pk.

Organza Scalloped-Edge Tulle Circles come 12 per pkg.

23. ORGANZA SCALLOPED-EDGE WHITE	1005-Z-23	$5.39 pk.

Lace Scalloped-Edge Tulle Circles come 25 per pkg.

24. LACE SCALLOPED-EDGE WHITE	1005-Z-24	$5.39 pk.

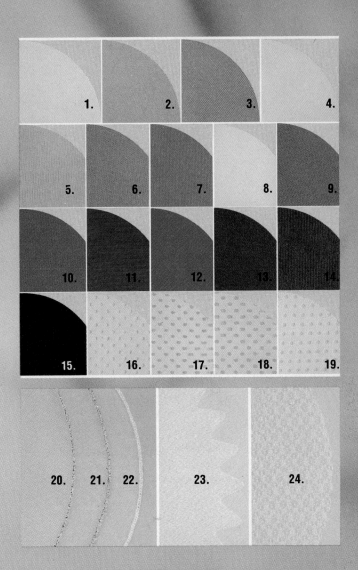

ACCESSORIES

Carry out your party theme perfectly with a wonderful accessory choice. Baby and wedding showers, anniversaries and milestone events will have a professional finish when you begin with the Bomboniere ™ selection.

25. PARTY FAVORS! BOOK
40 pgs, over 100 ideas.
916-Z-825 **$4.99 each**

26. MINI BABY BOTTLES
Assorted colors. 1 ¼ in. high.
1103-Z-25 **$1.59 pk. of 12**

27. PINK FUZZY BEARS
1 in. high.
1103-Z-14 **$2.15 pk. of 4**

28. BLUE FUZZY BEARS
1 in. high.
1103-Z-15 **$2.15 pk. of 4**

29. BABY LAMBS
1 ⅛ in. high.
1103-Z-17 **$2.15 pk. of 2**

30. WHITE BABY SHOES
1 ¾ in. high.
1103-Z-23 **$2.15 pk. of 2**

31. BLUE SMALL SAFETY PINS
1 ½ in. wide.
1103-Z-19 **$1.09 pk. of 12**

32. PINK SMALL SAFETY PINS
1 ½ in. wide.
1103-Z-18 **$1.09 pk. of 12**

33. BLUE LARGE SAFETY PIN RATTLE
4 ½ in. wide.
1103-Z-11 **$1.09 pk. of 2**

34. PINK LARGE SAFETY PIN RATTLE
4 ½ in. wide.
1103-Z-10 **$1.09 pk. of 2**

35. BABY CARRIAGE
3 ½ in. high.
1103-Z-22 **$1.39 pk. of 2**

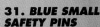

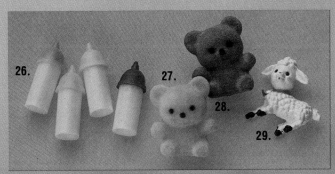

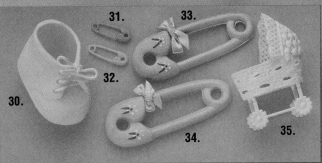

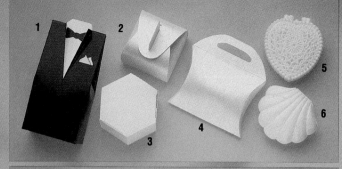
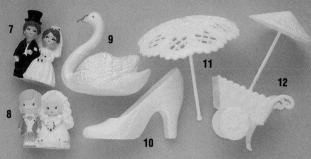
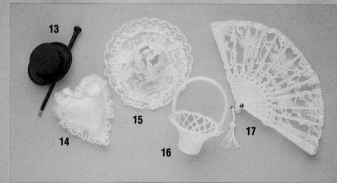

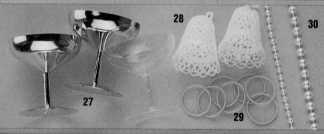
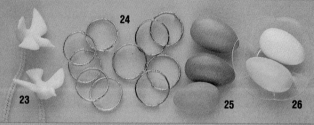

Bomboniere!™
Party Favors

ACCESSORIES

1. TUXEDO BOX
4 in. high 1006-Z-48 $2.59 pk. of 2

2. SQUARE PURSE BOX
1 7/8 in. sq.
1006-Z-50 $1.99 pk. of 2

3. HEXAGON BOX
1006-Z-49 $1.99 pk. of 2

4. SILK-LOOK PURSE BOX
3 in. high. 1006-Z-47 $1.99 pk. of 2

5. FILIGREE HEART BOX
2 1/4 in. high
1006-Z-21 $1.09 pk. of 4
2 1/4 in. high
1006-Z-107 $2.79 pk. of 12

6. SCALLOP SHELL
2 in. high 1006-Z-28 $1.79 pk. of 4

7. WEDDING COUPLE WITH BLACK TUXEDO
2 1/4 in. high 1006-Z-25 $1.99 pk. of 1

8. WEDDING COUPLE WITH GREY TUXEDO
1 7/8 in. high 1006-Z-14 $1.99 pk. of 1

9. 3" PEARL SWANS
1006-Z-12 $1.09 pk. of 2
1006-Z-108 $2.15 pk. of 4
1006-Z-109 $5.39 pk. of 12

10. HIGH HEELS 2 1/4 in. high
White
1006-Z-29 99¢ pk. of 2
Clear (not shown)
1006-Z-110 $1.59 pk. of 4
Clear (not shown)
1006-Z-111 $4.29 pk. of 12

11. PARTY PARASOLS
2 3/4 in. high
1006-Z-27 $1.79 pk. of 4

12. FLOWER CART
1 3/4 in. 1006-Z-24 $1.39 pk. of 2

13. TOP HAT AND CANE
1 in. high hat; 4 in. long cane
1006-Z-11 $1.09 pk. of 2

14. SATIN PILLOW
3 1/4 in. high
1006-Z-26 $1.89 pk. of 2

15. LACE BONNET
4 1/4 in. wide
1006-Z-51 $2.39 pk. of 1

16. ROUND BASKET
3 in. high 1006-Z-13 75¢ pk. of 2
3 in. high 1006-Z-113 $1.39 pk. of 4
3 in. high 1006-Z-112 $3.19 pk. of 12

17. FANCY FAN
4 in. high 1006-Z-34 $3.99 pk. of 1

18. STAMENS
1006-Z-30 $1.59 pk. of 12

19. PEARL SPRAYS
1006-Z-31 $2.15 pk. of 12

20. PEARL HEARTS
4 1/2 in. high
1006-Z-35 $1.49 pk. of 6

21. WHITE FROSTED BELLS
5/8 in. high
1006-Z-36 $1.69 pk. of 6

22. IRIDESCENT LEAVES
1 in. 1006-Z-32 $1.59 pk. of 12
2 in. 1006-Z-33 $1.59 pk. of 12

23. DOVES ON STEM
1 1/4 in. wide
1006-Z-18 99¢ pk. of 6

24. ANNIVERSARY BANDS
Gold. 3/4 in. diam.
1006-Z-19 55¢ pk. of 12
Silver. 3/4 in. diam.
1006-Z-20 55¢ pk. of 12
Gold. 3/4 in. diam.
1006-Z-100 $1.59 pk. of 48
Silver. 3/4 in. diam.
1006-Z-101 $1.59 pk. of 48

25. JORDAN ALMONDS
White. 12 oz. pkg.
1006-Z-74 $5.39 pk.
Assorted. 12 oz. pkg.
1006-Z-75 $5.39 pk.

26. FAVOR SAUCERS
1006-Z-39 $1.39 pk. of 12
1006-Z-114 $3.79 pk. of 48

27. CHAMPAGNE GLASSES
Gold. 2 in. high.
1006-Z-16 75¢ pk. of 2
Silver. 2 in. high.
1006-Z-17 75¢ pk. of 2
Clear. 2 in. high.
1006-Z-15 45¢ pk. of 2
Gold. 2 in. high.
1006-Z-104 $1.49 pk. of 4
Silver. 2 in. high.
1006-Z-103 $1.49 pk. of 4
Clear. 2 in. high.
1006-Z-105 85¢ pk. of 4
Clear. 2 in. high.
1006-Z-106 $2.49 pk. of 12

28. OPENWORK BELLS
1 3/4 in. high
1006-Z-10 75¢ pk. of 6
1 3/4 in. high
1006-Z-102 $1.79 pk. of 24

29. RUBBER BANDS
1006-Z-72 $1.69 pk. of 50

30. PEARL BEADS
4 mm. 211-Z-1989 $2.69 pk./5 yd.
6 mm. 211-Z-1990 $3.19 pk./5 yd.

31. 25 TAGS
1006-Z-45 $1.99 pk. of 12

32. HEART TAGS
1006-Z-44 $1.99 pk. of 12

33. DOVES TAGS
1006-Z-43 $1.99 pk. of 12

34. BRIDAL COUPLE TAGS
1006-Z-42 $1.99 pk. of 12

35. BABY TAGS
1103-Z-34 $1.99 pk. of 12

The Ellen Williams Tier Top Collection provides many designs to mix and match with any of her wedding ornaments. These delicate poufs complement a cake beautifully when used between the tiers and on side cakes. Lovely as party favors and table decorations, too.

1. MINI-BOUQUET
Soft floral bouquet set on field of cameo lace. Base diameter 4 inches; approx. 2 inches high. Exciting look attached to pillars or cakes as well as placed between tiers.
211-Z-604 $18.00 pack of 3

2. BLOSSOM TIER TOP
Contemporary spray with tulle and "pearl"-decked flowers. Base diameter 4 7/8 inches; approx. 3 1/2 inches high. Beautiful with Masterpiece, Dreams Come True and Glorious.
211-Z-1991 $10.00 each

3. PEARL TIER TOP
"Pearl" wisps decorate blooms and flower sprays. Base diameter 4 inches; approx. 2 1/2 inches high. For a dramatic cake use with Crowning Glory, Timeless and Classique.
211-Z-1992 $12.50 each

4. PEARL LEAVES TIER TOP
Delicate pearl leaves peek through tufts of tulle and "pearl"-trimmed blossoms. Base diameter 4 7/8 inches; approx. 3 1/2 inches high. An exciting match for Opulence, Beautiful and True Love.
211-Z-1994 $15.00 each

Designer Series by Ellen Williams

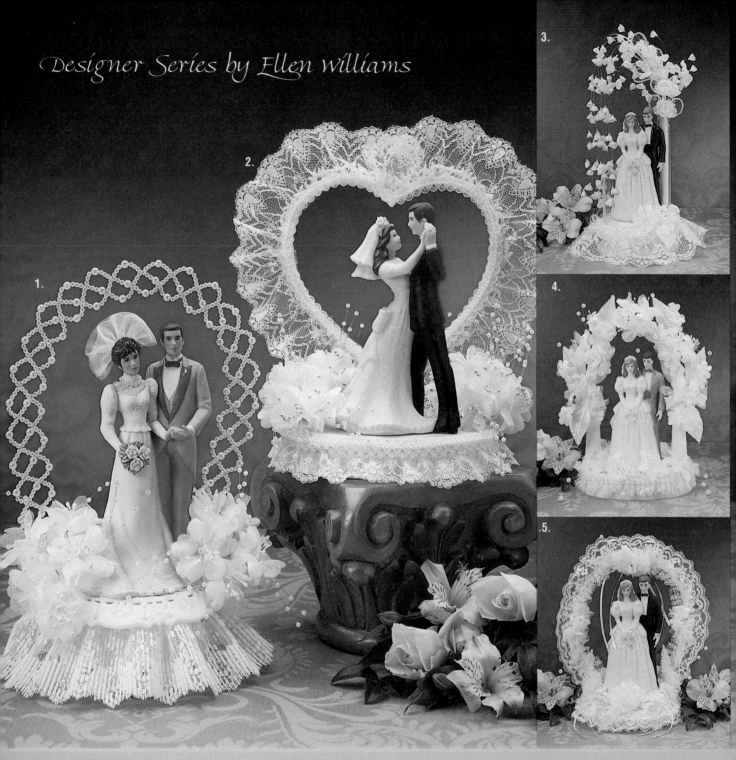

An incomparable treasury of keepsake ornaments exquisitely created by noted giftware designer, Ellen Williams. A cherished collection of fine bisque porcelain figurines accented with flowers, satin ribbons and "pearls".

For an inspiring bridal cake, coordinate these magnificent ornaments with Tier Tops and Mini-Bouquets featured on page 153. Designed to accent the lower cake tiers, these charming cake tops match or mix perfectly with the ornaments shown on these pages.

1. HEAVENLY

A lovely African-American couple beneath a lattice arch of "pearls" on an accordion-pleated base of lace. Hand-painted and hand-crafted porcelain bisque couple. 10 1/2 in. high.

Grey Tux	118-Z-603	$85.00 each
Black Tux	118-Z-604	$85.00 each

2. SWEETHEARTS

Graceful hand-painted porcelain bisque couple under an arched lace heart trimmed with "pearl" sprays. Hyacinths bloom atop lace-edged base. 9 1/4 in. high.

Grey Tux	118-Z-605	$85.00 each
Black Tux	118-Z-606	$85.00 each

3. GLORIOUS

Charming porcelain bisque figurine afloat on a lace-veiled base punctuated with floral bouquet. Lucite-look backdrop holds a spray of softly cascading lily of the valley. 12 1/2 in. high.

Grey Tux	118-Z-425	$60.00 each
Black Tux	118-Z-420	$60.00 each

4. CLASSIQUE

Timeless romantic porcelain bisque couple between two Gothic pillars edged with soft blooms, "pearls" and crisp pleats of lace. 11 in. high.

Grey Tux	118-Z-410	$50.00 each
Black Tux	118-Z-415	$50.00 each

5. DREAMS COME TRUE

Graceful arch of ribbons, lace and "pearl" dotted posies frame our loving couple. Lace-edged base is trimmed with flowers and ribbons. 10 1/2 in. high.

Grey Tux	118-Z-400	$60.00 each
Black Tux	118-Z-405	$60.00 each

© 1991 EHW Enterprises, Inc
Licensee Wilton Enterprises
Figurines Crafted by *Roman, Inc.*

6. ROSE GARDEN
A glorious floral arch of roses, ribbons and "pearl" sprays frame a loving porcelain bisque couple. 11 in. high; includes 6 ½ in. high couple.

White Setting/Black Tux	118-Z-475	$75.00 each
Ivory Setting/Black Tux	118-Z-465	$75.00 each

7. BEAUTIFUL
Joyous porcelain couple in a mist of tulle, "pearl" leaves, flowers and lace. On a base of leaves trimmed in "pearls". 7 ½ in. high; includes 6 ½ in. high couple.

Grey Tux	118-Z-440	$70.00 each
Black Tux	118-Z-445	$70.00 each

8. TIMELESS
A radiant porcelain bisque couple under a lattice arch of "pearls". Adorned with lovely floral and "pearl" bursts on a lace and "pearl"-trimmed base. 10 in. high; includes 6 ½ in. high couple.

Grey Tux	118-Z-450	$75.00 each
Black Tux	118-Z-455	$75.00 each

9. DELICATE JOY
Solitary tiny porcelain couple on a lacy ruffled base dotted with lovely floral blooms and streamers. 6 in. high; includes 4 ½ in. in. high couple.

Grey Tux	108-Z-640	$40.00 each
Black Tux	108-Z-645	$40.00 each

10. SWEET BEGINNINGS
Lacy heart frames a tiny, joyous porcelain couple. Lace and rose-dotted base is edged with a soft blossom. 9 in. high; includes 4 ½ in. high couple.

Grey Tux	118-Z-495	$60.00 each
Black Tux	118-Z-490	$60.00 each

11. EVERLASTING
A dramatic gazebo is the setting for this glorious tiny porcelain couple. Tulle sprays tied with ribbons and flowing lily of the valley. 11½ in. high; includes 4 ½ in. high couple.

Grey Tux	118-Z-500	$60.00 each
Black Tux	118-Z-505	$60.00 each

© 1991 EHW Enterprises, Inc
Licensee Wilton Enterprises
Figurines Crafted by *Roman, Inc.*

Designer Series by Ellen Williams

1. ALLURE
An enchanting gazebo adorned with a profusion of tulle and satin bows enhances this lovely wedding setting. 11 in. high. Exquisitely detailed matte resin Lasting Love and Happiest Day couples.

White/Ivory White Couple/Grey Tux 101-Z-1782
White/Ivory White Couple/Black Tux 101-Z-1783
White/Ivory Black Couple/Grey Tux 101-Z-1784
White/Ivory Black Couple/Black Tux 101-Z-1785
$45.00 each

2. TRUE LOVE
Pearl-adorned swooning doves rest on a pair of "pearl" studded wedding bands. Tufts of tulle and soft roses. 8 1/4 in. high.
103-Z-410 $40.00 each

3. CROWNING GLORY
Two fluttering doves in flight on a lace and "pearl" trimmed heart and satiny bell. Lace also underscores base. 9 1/2 in. high.
103-Z-405 $40.00 each

4. HEART'S DESIRE
Delicate lace, flowers and ribbons encircle a sweetheart backdrop for a happy beautifully detailed matte resin Sweethearts couple. 8 in. high.
White Couple/Grey Tux 101-Z-1790 $22.00 each
White Couple/Black Tux 101-Z-1791 $22.00 each

5. LOVE'S DELIGHT
Flowers, ribbons and lace provide a lovely setting for a radiant, finely detailed matte resin Sweethearts couple. 8 1/2 in. high.
White Couple/Grey Tux 101-Z-1786 $22.00 each
White Couple/Black Tux 101-Z-1787 $22.00 each

6. I DO
Double lucite-look hearts and bells highlighted with blossoms, satin ribbons and "pearls" witness this blessed exchange. Features painstakingly detailed matte resin Lasting Love and Happiest Day couples. 9 in. high.
White/Ivory White Couple/Grey Tux 101-Z-1778
White/Ivory White Couple/Black Tux 101-Z-1779
White/Ivory Black Couple/Grey Tux 101-Z-1780
White/Ivory Black Couple/Black Tux 101-Z-1781
$40.00 each

7. GARDEN DELIGHT
Breathtaking spiral holds a topiary of blooms and long streamers of ribbons and "pearls" accenting lovely detailed matte resin Lasting Love and Happiest Day couples. Lucite-look backdrop adds drama to the scene. 10 in. high.

White Couple/Grey Tux 101-Z-1774
White Couple/Black Tux 101-Z-1775
Black Couple/Grey Tux 101-Z-1776
Black Couple/Black Tux 101-Z-1777
$40.00 each

8. WEDDING DREAM
A lacy-adorned arch, golden rings and ribbon bows for a sweet, gorgeously detailed matte resin Sweethearts couple. 9 in. high.
White Couple/Grey Tux 101-Z-1788 $22.00 each
White Couple/Black Tux 101-Z-1789 $22.00 each

9. REJOICE
Our beautiful bells toll the joyous message of love and wedding good wishes. Decked with bows, blooms and pearl sprays. 7 ½ in. high.
103-Z-415 $35.00 each

10. MASTERPIECE
Ornately-trimmed bells toll out the happiest of wedding messages. Tied with ribbon and set in a lace-trimmed heart. 9 ½ in. high.
Ivory   103-Z-425 $40.00 each
White   103-Z-430 $40.00 each

11. OPULENCE
"Pearl"-adorned wedding bands shimmer on a base of "pearl" leaves and accordion-pleated lace. 6 ½ in. high.
103-Z-420 $40.00 each

12. INSPIRATION
The gilded cross is highlighted on a petal base flowing with tulle bursts. A soft bouquet of posies drapes cross and base. 6 ½ in. high.
106-Z-355 $16.00 each

13. BLESSED EVENT
Two satin and "pearl" trimmed bells toll this most sacred union. "Gold" cross crowns the bloom-filled ornament. 9 in. high.
103-Z-845 $40.00 each

14. EXUBERANCE
Two graceful swans float on a lace-trimmed base. Both glide under a shower of flowing tulle and "pearl" decked buds. 7 in. high.
103-Z-440 $25.00 each

15. LOVE FOREVER
A pair of elegant swans carry bouquets of blossoms on a base of lace ruffles. Open-heart backdrop is treated with lace and "pearl" stamens. 6 ¼ in. high.
103-Z-435 $25.00 each

NEW!

Introducing the most life-like collection of wedding musicals and figurines in sturdy, matte-finished plastic and porcelain. Delicately detailed with tulle veiling, hand-painted facial features, and softly-blooming flowers. A keepsake-quality collection from noted giftware designer, Ellen Williams.

1. NEW! SWEET TOGETHER
Charming porcelain couple is encircled in heart-shaped lace, trimmed with flowers and "pearls". 6 1/4 in. high.

Grey Tux/African American Couple	118-Z-701	$35.00 each
Grey Tux/White Couple	118-Z-700	$35.00 each

2. NEW! HOPES AND DREAMS
Precious porcelain couple on a base covered with lavish lace, and a spray of blooming flowers and "pearls". 6 1/4 in. high.

Grey Tux/White Couple	118-Z-703	$30.00 each

3. NEW! LITTLE DARLINGS AFRICAN AMERICAN COUPLE
Solemn duo await their nuptial celebration. Porcelain. 3 3/4 in. high.

Grey Tux	214-Z-900	$25.00 each

4. NEW! TENDER TWOSOME WHITE COUPLE
Happy bride and groom in porcelain. 3 3/4 in. high.

Grey Tux	214-Z-901	$25.00 each

5. HAPPIEST DAY AFRICAN AMERICAN COUPLE
Sweetly poised couple with lifelike resin bouquets and headpiece. 4 1/2 in. high.

Black Tux	202-Z-306	$6.99 each
White Tux	202-Z-305	$6.99 each
Grey Tux	202-Z-304	$6.99 each

6. SWEETHEARTS WHITE COUPLE
Soft tulle veil on modern bride flows over lacy dress. Plastic. 4 1/2 in. high.

Grey Tux	202-Z-307	$4.99 each
Black Tux	202-Z-308	$4.99 each
White Coat	202-Z-309	$4.99 each

7. LASTING LOVE WHITE COUPLE
Lovely bride has a flowing tulle veil. Plastic, with lifelike resin bouquets. 4 1/2 in. high.

White Tux	202-Z-303	$6.99 each
Black Tux	202-Z-302	$6.99 each
Grey Tux	202-Z-301	$6.99 each

8. SWEET SYMPHONY*
A delightful musical couple. Plays "The Wedding March". Hand-painted detail adds life-like quality to this delicately hand-crafted and hand-painted resin piece. 7 3/4 in. high.

Grey Tux	215-Z-775	$50.00 each
Black Tux	215-Z-776	$50.00 each

*musical

Why not add to the magic of that wonderful day with enchanted figurines and musical ornaments? Handcrafted and hand-painted fine porcelain bisque figurines of keepsake quality, often with "pearl" accents.

9. MARY AND CHARLES*
This musical creation echoes fond memories of the past. Turn-of-the-century couple stands on a base of bells and flowers. Plays "Clair de Lune." 8 in. high.
215-Z-772 $75.00 each

10. ASHLEY AND STEVEN*
Lovely musical ornament makes a perfect wedding keepsake. Modern couple on a base of bells and flowers. Plays "Through the Eyes of Love". 8 ½ in. high.
215-Z-773 $75.00 each

11. PERFECT HARMONY*
Engaging modern African-American couple created with a keen eye for detail. Bride radiates with "pearl" necklace and beautiful handcrafted rose bouquet. Plays "The Wedding March". 8 in. high.
215-Z-771 $110.00 each

12. TOGETHER FOREVER*
Traditional wedding couple. "Pearl"-accented bride has graceful tulle veil and bouquet with satin and "pearl" ribbons. Plays "The Wedding March". 8 in. high.
215-Z-770 $110.00 each

13. ONE DREAM COUPLE
Loving Ellen Williams couple stands ready to exchange wedding vows. In fine porcelain. 6 in. high.
214-Z-420 Grey Tuxedo $25.00 each
214-Z-425 Black Tuxedo $25.00 each

14. TOGETHER FOREVER COUPLE
Romantic Ellen Williams porcelain couple in a traditional bridal pose. 6 ½ in. high.
214-Z-400 Grey Tuxedo/Ivory Dress $35.00 each
214-Z-405 Black Tuxedo/Ivory Dress $35.00 each
214-Z-410 Grey Tuxedo/White Dress $35.00 each
214-Z-415 Black Tuxedo/White Dress
$35.00 each

15. PERFECT HARMONY COUPLE
Avant garde couple in fine porcelain from Ellen Williams. African-American pair hold hands while exchanging vows. 6 ½ in. high.
214-Z-603 Grey Tuxedo $39.50 each
214-Z-604 Black Tuxedo $39.50 each

16. ADORING COUPLE
Dainty Ellen Williams pair dance their all-important first waltz with stars in their eyes. 5 ⅞ in. high.
214-Z-605 Grey Tuxedo $45.00 each
214-Z-606 Black Tuxedo $45.00 each

17. PETITE TOGETHER FOREVER COUPLE
Dainty Ellen Williams porcelain figure is perfect for cakes and table settings. 4 ½ in. high.
214-Z-437 Grey Tuxedo $30.00 each
214-Z-439 Black Tuxedo $30.00 each

*musical

1. DESIGNER BRIDESMAID
So many beautiful jewel and soft tones available to match many bridal color themes; plastic. 4 1/2 in. high. Packaged in sets of 2.

NEW! Dark Pink	203-Z-9119	Light Blue	203-Z-9106
Amethyst	203-Z-9107	Sapphire	203-Z-9109
Pink	203-Z-9103	*NEW!* White	203-Z-9111
Black	203-Z-9110	Raspberry	203-Z-9108
Emerald	203-Z-9104	Light Mauve	203-Z-9105

$3.99 pkg. of 2

2. *NEW!* AFRICAN-AMERICAN DESIGNER BRIDESMAIDS
Dramatic, life-like bridesmaids dressed in a beautiful variety of shades that will coordinate well with many wedding color motifs. In plastic, 4 1/2 in. high. Packaged in sets of 2.

Sapphire	203-Z-9112	Emerald	203-Z-9115
Pink	203-Z-9113	White	203-Z-9114

$3.99 pkg. of 2

3. DESIGNER GROOMSMEN
Handsome groomsman. In attractive matte finish; plastic. 4 1/2 in. high. Packaged in sets of 2.

White Coat	203-Z-9100
Grey Tux	203-Z-9102
Black Tux	203-Z-9101

$3.99 pkg. of 2

4. *NEW!* AFRICAN-AMERICAN DESIGNER GROOMSMEN
At last, groomsmen have the option of exactly matching their tuxedo to that of the groom. Three most popular shades. Sold in packaged sets of 2. Plastic, 4 1/2 in. high.

White Coat	203-Z-9117
Black Tux	203-Z-9116
Grey Tux	203-Z-9118 $3.99 pkg. of 2

5. *NEW!* JOYFUL DEBUT ORNAMENT WITH LA QUINCEAÑERA
Lavish lace , ribbon, and "pearls" encircle the lovely young lady in celebration of her 15th birthday. 9 in. high, base diameter 4 5/8 in.
203-Z-306 $22.00 each

6. *NEW!* LA QUINCEAÑERA FIGURINE
Sweetly poised figurine is a beautiful remembrance of her 15th birthday jubilee. In matte resin, 4 1/2 in. high.
203-Z-305 $3.49 each

© 1991, 1992 EHW Enterprises, Inc
Licensee Wilton Enterprises

Cake Decorating! Classes Near You!

Attend a Wilton Method Cake Decorating Class Near Your Home!

Convenient Wilton Method of Cake Decorating Classes are now being held in area department and craft stores and cake decorating specialty shops close to your home. You'll learn exciting basic decorating techniques in 4 easy lessons.* For a complete list of the classes nearest you, send us this coupon right away or call toll free 1-800-323-1717, Operator 440. (In Illinois, call 1-800-942-8881, Operator 440.)

Name _____

Address _____

City _____ State _____ Zip _____

Daytime Phone No. (____) _____
area code

*Four 2-hour lessons include course book and personalized instruction. Class program available in continental United States only.

Cake Decorating! Home Study Course

$17.99 Per Lesson*!
Learn cake decorating the easy Wilton way!
Order Lesson 1 today! Just fill in and mail this card.

☐ Yes! Send me Lesson One of the Wilton Home Study Course of Cake Decorating for only $17.99 including tax, plus $3.50 for shipping and handling. I understand that if I'm not completely satisfied, I can return both the instruction manual and materials within 30 days for a full refund or credit. I understand that the other four lessons will be sent to me for the same low price of $17.99 plus $3.50 for shipping and handling. Any lesson can be returned within 30 days for a full refund or credit if I'm not completely satisfied.

Enclosed is a check or money order payable to Wilton Home Study Course or charge my Visa, MasterCard or Discover Card :

☐ Visa
MasterCard
Discover
(Circle one)

☐☐☐☐☐☐☐☐☐☐☐☐☐☐☐ (card number) ☐☐☐☐ (Exp. date)

Name _____
(Please print)

Signature (for credit card only) _____

Address _____

City _____ State _____ Zip _____

Daytime Phone No. (____) _____
area code

*Plus shipping and handling   Dept. No. **LV**

Cake Decorating! Home Video Course

$29.99 Per Lesson*!
On Wilton Video Home Study Course of Cake Decorating!

☐ Yes! Send me Lesson One of the Wilton Video Home Study Course of Cake Decorating for only $29.99 including tax, plus $3.50 for shipping and handling. I understand that if I'm not completely satisfied, I can return the video, instruction manual and materials within 30 days for a full refund or credit. I understand that the other two lessons will be sent to me-- one each month through Lesson 3 -- for the same low price of $29.99 plus $3.50 for shipping and handling.

Enclosed is a check or money order payable to Wilton Home Study Course or charge my Visa, MasterCard or Discover Card :

☐ Visa
MasterCard
Discover
(Circle one)

☐☐☐☐☐☐☐☐☐☐☐☐☐☐☐ (card number) ☐☐☐☐ (Exp. date)

Name _____
(Please print)

Signature (for credit card only) _____

Address _____

City _____ State _____ Zip _____

Daytime Phone No. (____) _____
area code

*Plus shipping and handling   Dept. No. **LW**

Wilton®

2240 W. 75th Street
Woodridge, IL 60517-9985

Attention: Retail CS, MS #9C

Enclose in envelope provided on Order Form or call (708) 963-7100

Enclose in envelope provided on Order Form or call (708) 963-7100

Make that once-in-a-lifetime wedding day unforgettable with lace-lavished keepsakes from the Loving Traditions™ Collection.

Discover a gathering of cherished wedding mementos created with close attention to detail. Find ring bearer's pillows, bride's purses, garters and glassware embellished with laces, pearls, flowers, bows and much more. A very romantic series that will sweetly enhance this magical day.

1. TOASTING GLASSES SET
Fluted leaded crystal glasses etched with beautiful roses. 8 3/8 in. high.
Bride & Groom Set 120-Z-200 $24.00 set
Anniversary Set 120-Z-202 $24.00 set

2. SHERBET GLASSES SET
Enhanced with satin ribbons. 4 1/2 in. high.
Bride and Groom 120-Z-203 $14.00 set
Anniversary Wishes
120-Z-205 $14.00 set

3. RING BEARER'S PILLOW
Choose from tailored look with classic or embellished treatments. Square pillows approximately 10 1/2 x 10 1/2 in .
Lacy Square-Ivory 120-Z-107 $20.00 each
Lacy Square-White 120-Z-106 $20.00 each
Ribbon Heart-White
120-Z-100 $16.00 each
Ribbon Square-White
120-Z-104 $16.00 each

4. BRIDE'S PURSE
Dainty satin drawstring bag punctuated with fabric flowers and pearl trim. 11 x 13 in.
120-Z-601 $15.00 each

5. BRIDE'S HANDKERCHIEF
Lacy cotton handkerchief to tuck into handbag.
White 120-Z-500 $5.00 each

6. BRIDE'S GARTER
Traditional feminine accessory. Delicate and lacy garter is trimmed with satin band, ribbons.
Blue 120-Z-402 $5.00 each
Pink 120-Z-400 $5.00 each
White 120-Z-401 $5.00 each
Ivory 120-Z-403 $5.00 each
Black 120-Z-404 $5.00 each

7. NEW! ACRYLIC CAKE & KNIFE SERVERS
Shining stainless with beautifully detailed handles. Tied with sprays of flowers, ribbons and "pearls".
Cake Knife 120-Z-704 $13.50 each
Cake Server 120-Z-705 $13.50 each
Knife & Server Set 120-Z-703 $24.00 set

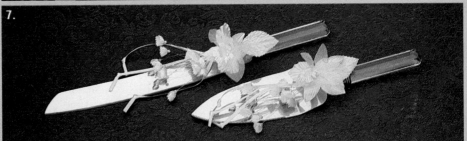

Wedding Ornaments

1. LUSTROUS LOVE
A burst of tulle peeks from behind lace leaves; dotted with forget-me-nots and rimmed with gleaming "pearls". Satiny roses bloom while "pearls" are suspended on transparent strings around the happy glazed porcelain couple. 8 in. high.
White   117-Z-621 $35.00 each

2. SPLENDID
Sweeping curve of lucite-look surrounds adoring glazed porcelain pair. Cylindrical vase holds a matching spray of flowers that accents base. Add real flowers if you wish. 10 ½ in. high.
White   117-Z-506 $28.00 each
Pink   117-Z-507 $28.00 each
Peach   117-Z-450 $28.00 each

3. GARDEN ROMANCE
Charming porcelain couple stands in a gazebo decked with flowery vines. Clusters of tulle and ribbons complete this romantic hideaway. 10 ½ in. high.
White Iridescent   117-Z-711 $35.00 each

4. RHAPSODY
Contemporary belled arch is dotted with flowers and tulle. Stylized porcelain couple stands on crystal-look base, trimmed with tulle puff and floral spray. 9 ½ in. high.
Pink   117-Z-305 $25.00 each
White   117-Z-301 $25.00 each

5. REFLECTIONS
Sleek, streamlined and sophisticated. Dramatic lucite-look backdrop reflects porcelain couple, tulle burst, "pearl" sprays and florals. 8 in. high.
Blue   117-Z-130 $25.00 each
White   117-Z-268 $25.00 each
Pink   117-Z-297 $25.00 each

6. ECSTASY
Sprays of flowers and leaves surround the romantic porcelain pair. Delicate tulle forms a lovely base. 9 ½ in. high.
White   117-Z-831 $40.00 each

7. PROMISE
Simple beauty. Dramatic lucite-look heart frames dainty white porcelain couple. Crystal-look base is covered with tulle, ribbons and fabric flowers. 9 ⅝ in. high.
White   117-Z-315 $25.00 each
Pink   117-Z-311 $25.00 each

8. DEVOTION
Lucite-look arch is framed with gathered tulle and lace. Glazed porcelain couple stands on pedestal base in burst of tulle, blooms and pearl strands. 9 ½ in. high.
White   117-Z-425 $25.00 each

Wedding Ornaments

9. EVERLASTING LOVE
Graceful arches of lace and filigree heart, dotted with tulle and wedding bands, surround floral-filled bell. 10 in. high.
103-Z-236 $18.00 each

10. SPRING SONG
Perching lovebirds sing their romantic love songs in a garden of posies and tulle. 9 ½ in. high.
111-Z-2802 $18.00 each

11. VICTORIAN CHARM
Graceful ribbon loops and fantasy florals layer over romantic satin five-bell cluster. 7 ½ in. high.
Ivory   **103-Z-1586 $20.00 each**
White   **103-Z-1587 $20.00 each**

12. CIRCLES OF LOVE
Symbolic double rings and doves in a hideaway of flowers and "pearl" sprays. 10 in. high.
White   **103-Z-9004 $25.00 each**

13. HEARTS TAKE WING
Romantic beak-to-beak birds perched on a setting of heart-shaped branches and tulle. 10 ½ in. high.
103-Z-6218 $12.00 each

14. WEDDING BELLS
Filigree bell clusters in a generous spray of tulle and lace. 10 ½ in. high.
103-Z-1356 $18.00 each

15. SATIN ELEGANCE
Lace-edged satin heart bursting with "pearls", flowers and tulle bears a pair of wedding rings. 7 in. high.
Ivory
 on ivory base **109-Z-1002 $20.00 each**
White
 on white base **109-Z-1001 $20.00 each**

Wedding/Anniversary

1. PETITE BELLS OF JOY
Cluster of white filigree bells with fabric roses, lace-covered arches and tulle. 7 in. high. 3 1/4 in. base diameter.
White   106-Z-2658 $12.00 each

2. NATURAL BEAUTY
Lovebirds beneath filigree heart trimmed with lily of the valley and a smooth satin bow. 6 in. high.
Peach   106-Z-1104 $10.00 each
Pink   106-Z-1120 $10.00 each
White   106-Z-1163 $10.00 each

3. PETITE DOUBLE RING
Graceful doves land on simple wedding bands on heart base. Adorned with tulle puff. 5 1/2 in. high.
106-Z-4316 $7.00 each

4. LA BELLE PETITE
Tolling bell surrounded by tulle glimmers with iridescence. 5 1/2 in. high.
White   106-Z-248 $9.00 each

5. PETITE SPRING SONG
A dainty song bird duet arched in flowers, "pearls" and tulle. 7 in. high.
White   106-Z-159 $11.00 each
Pink   106-Z-160 $11.00 each
Peach   106-Z-161 $11.00 each

6. SWEET CEREMONY
Seed pearl hearts frame glistening bell. Bride and heart frame are accented with tulle. 10 in. high.
White Coat   101-Z-22028 $14.00 each
Black Coat   101-Z-22011 $14.00 each
Grey Coat   101-Z-22045 $14.00 each

7. PETITE LOVERS IN LACE
Glowing couple beneath a double arch of lace. 7 in. high.

Coat	Couple	Stock No.	Each
Grey	White	104-Z-834	$10.00
Black	Black	104-Z-302	$10.00
Black	White	104-Z-818	$10.00

8. MORNING ROSEBUD
Doves in flight above open gate. Soft fabric flowers dot landscape. 8 in. high.
White Coat   101-Z-44020 $10.00 each
Black Coat   101-Z-44013 $10.00 each

9. 25 OR 50 YEARS OF HAPPINESS
In gold or silver, the number tells the happy story. Accented with blooms and shimmering leaves. 10 in. high.
25th   102-Y-207 $16.00 each
50th   102-Y-223 $16.00 each

10. GOLDEN/SILVER JUBILEE
Say it in gold or silver tulle. Couple is on numeral wreath with orchids and ferns. 8 1/2 in. high.
Gold   102-Z-1250 $16.00 each
Silver   102-Z-1225 $16.00 each

11. PETITE DOUBLE RING DEVOTION
Celebrating couple surrounded by rings and the shimmer of pearls and ferns. 5 in. high.
25th Silver 105-Z-4613 $10.00 each
50th Gold   105-Z-4605 $10.00 each

12. PETITE ANNIVERSARY YEARS
The addition of beautiful blooms adds appeal to this versatile favorite. Embossed wreath holds snap-on numbers—5, 10, 15, 20, 40. 5 3/4 in. high.
105-Z-4257 $7.00 each

13. PETITE ANNIVERSARY
Shining numeral wreath is highlighted by two fluttering doves. 5 1/2 in. high.
25th   105-Z-4265 $6.00 each
50th   105-Z-4273 $6.00 each

Couples & Accessories

1. STYLIZED COUPLE
Wedded happiness holds them in a longing gaze.
4 5/8 in. high. Glazed porcelain.
202-Z-218 **$15.99 each**

2. TOUCH OF ROSE *
Porcelain, musical base plays "Evergreen". 6 in. high.
215-Z-774 **$32.50 each**

3. FIRST KISS COUPLE
Sweet porcelain couple. A lovely remembrance.
4 3/4 in. high.
214-Z-440 **$35.00 each**

4. SIDE-BY-SIDE-COUPLE
Lovely bisque porcelain. 4 3/4 in high.
White Coat   214-Z-202   **$12.99 each**

5. DANCING COUPLE
A sweet romance. 4 3/4 in. high.
White Coat   214-Z-320   **$12.99 each**

6. LIBERATED BRIDE
Plastic, 4 1/2 in. high.
2113-Z-4188 **$3.99 each**

7. RELUCTANT GROOM COUPLE
Plastic, 4 1/2 in. high.
1316-Z-9520 **$4.99 each**

8. ANNIVERSARY COUPLE
Gold or silver gown. Plastic. 3 1/2 in. high.
25th Silver   203-Z-2828   **$3.99 each**
50th Gold   203-Z-1821   **$3.99 each**

9. CLASSIC COUPLE
Plastic, 4 1/2 in. high.

Coat	Couple	Stock No.	Each
White	White	202-Z-8121	$4.69
Black	White	202-Z-8110	$4.69
Grey	White	202-Z-300	$4.69

Plastic, 3 1/2 in. high. Petite.

Coat	Couple	Stock No.	Each
White	White	203-Z-8221	$3.99
Grey	White	203-Z-304	$3.99
Black	Black	203-Z-302	$3.99

10. BRIDESMAIDS
Plastic, 3 1/2 in. high. 2 per package.

White	203-Z-0279	$1.99 pkg. of 2
Pink	203-Z-0281	$1.99 pkg. of 2
Blue	203-Z-0278	$1.99 pkg. of 2
Yellow	203-Z-0280	$1.99 pkg. of 2

11. GROOMSMEN
Plastic, 3 1/2 in. high. 2 per package.

All White	203-Z-0277	$1.99 pkg. of 2
Black Coat	203-Z-0282	$1.99 pkg. of 2
White Coat	203-Z-0283	$1.99 pkg. of 2

12. PEARL LEAF PUFF
5 1/2 in. tulle puff with "pearls".
White   211-Z-1125   **$4.69 each**

13. FLORAL PUFF ACCENT
5 1/2 in. tulle puff with soft flowers and "pearl" sprays.
White   211-Z-1011   **$2.99 each**
Pink   211-Z-1013   **$2.99 each**

14. FLOWER BASKET
Plastic basket ready to decorate.
3 x 2 x 2 3/4 in.
White   1008-Z-299   **99¢ each**

15. ARTIFICIAL LEAVES
Green or white cloth; gold or silver foil.
(Add 1005 -Z- prefix before number.)

Color	#Per pkg.	1 7/8"	Per pkg.	1 1/4"	Per pkg.
Gold	144	6518	$2.59	6712	$2.29
Silver	144	6526	$2.59	6720	$2.29
Green	72	7555	$2.59	7570	$2.29
White	72	7565	$2.59	N/A	

16. PEARL LEAVES
2 per package. 2 1/4 in. long.
211-Z-1201 **$2.99 per pkg.**

*Musical

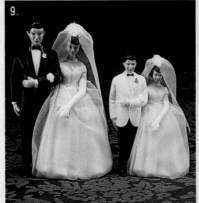

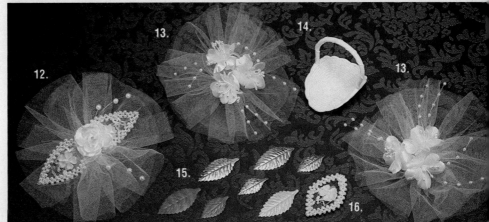

Bases & Trims

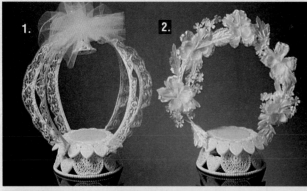

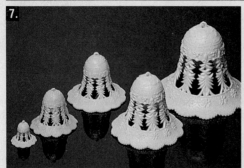

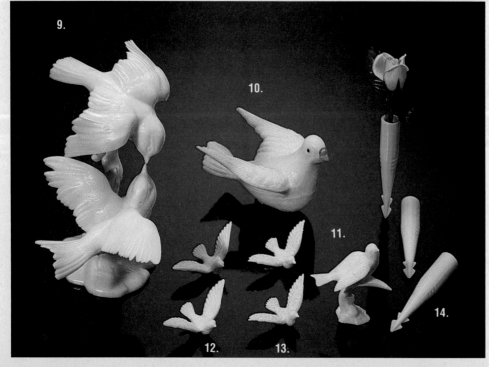

1. CIRCLES OF LACE
10 in. high.
210-Z-1986 **$8.99 each**

2. FLORAL ARCH
10-in. high.
210-Z-1987 **$8.99 each**

3. FLORAL BASE
White, 1 ½ in. high, 4 ⅞ in. diameter.
201-Z-1815 **$1.99 each**

4. CRYSTAL-LOOK BASE
1 ¾ in. high, 4 ½ in. diameter.
201-Z-1450 **$2.99 each**

5. ROMANTIC HEART BASE
White openwork, 2 pcs. 1 ½ in. high.
4 ⅝ in. 201-Z-7332 **$2.99 each**
3 ¼ in. 201-Z-7847 **$2.69 each**

6. FLORAL SCROLL BASE
Victorian Charm. 4 ½ x 2 ½ in. 2 pcs.
White 201-Z-1303 **$2.99 each**
Ivory 201-Z-305 **$2.99 each**

7. FILIGREE BELLS

Height	Stock No.	Price	Pack
1 in.	1001-Z-9447	$1.79	12
1 ⅞ in.	1001-Z-9422	$1.79	6
2 ¼ in.	1001-Z-9439	$2.29	6
2 ⅝ in.	1001-Z-9404	$1.59	3
3 ½ in.	1001-Z-9411	$1.89	3

8. GLITTERED BELLS

Height	Stock No.	Price	Pack
1 in.	1007-Z-9061	$2.99	12
1 ⅜ in.	2110-Z-9075	$1.09	6
1 ⅞ in.	1007-Z-9088	$2.49	6
2 ½ in.	2110-Z-9090	$2.49	6
4 ¼ in.	1007-Z-9110	$2.99	1

9. KISSING LOVE BIRDS
Beak-to-beak romantics. 5 ½ in. high.
1002-Z-206 **$4.99 each**

10. LOVE DOVES
4 x 2 ¾ in.
1002-Z-1806 **$2.99 pack of 2**

11. PETITE SONG BIRDS
2 ¼ in.
1316-Z-1210 **$2.99 pack of 4**

12. SMALL DOVES
2 x 1 ½ in.
1002-Z-1710 **$1.99 pack of 12**

13. GLITTERED DOVES
2 x 1 ½ in. Coated with non-edible glitter.
1006-Z-166 **$1.69 pack of 12**

14. FLOWER SPIKES
Fill with water, push into cake and add
flowers. 3 in. high.
1008-Z-408 **$2.49 pack of 12**

Backdrops & Accents

1. WHITE PEARL BEADING
One of the most innovative creations to happen to cake decorating in years. With just one continuous row of lustrous pearls you can transform a beautiful cake into a glorious work of art. Stunning and easy to work with, these pearls will be a must for all serious decorators. The pearls are easy to use as they are molded on one continuous 5 yard strand and can be easily cut to size.
To use: Work with long, continuous strands. Position before icing crusts. Trim after pearls are in position to insure exact measure. Do not trim smaller than 6" lengths. Remove pearls before cutting and serving cake.

Size	Stock No.	Price
6 mm	211-Z-1990	$3.19 each
4 mm	211-Z-1989	$2.69 each

2. CRYSTAL-LOOK HEARTS
Can be background for many varied settings.
5 1/2 in. 205-Z-1674 $1.99 each
4 1/4 in. 205-Z-1672 $1.79 each

3. FORMAL RAILINGS
2 5/8 in. posts, 1 in. pegs, 144 snap-together links.
1107-Z-8326 $2.49 set

4. DOUBLE WEDDING BANDS
3 1/2 in. diameter.
White 201-Z-1008 $1.99 each

5. CURVED GOTHIC WINDOW
Pretty stand for flowers, couple, more!
5 x 9 in. 2 pcs.
205-Z-3059 $3.99 set

6. GAZEBO
5 x 9 in. Easy to assemble.
205-Z-8298 $4.69 set

7. IRIDESCENT DOVES
2" wide.
1002-Z-509 $3.49 pack of 6

8. IRIDESCENT GRAPES
2" high.
1099-Z-200 $3.79 pack of 4

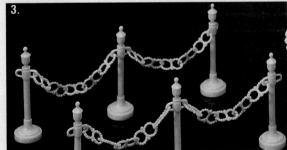

Angelic Additions

1. ARCHED TIER SET
Quite dramatic when used with Kolor-Flo Fountain. Includes: Six 13 in. arched columns, two super strong 18 in. round Decorator Preferred Separator Plates, and six angelic cherubs to attach to columns with royal icing or glue.
301-Z-1982 **$44.99 set**
18 in. DECORATOR PREFERRED PLATE
302-Z-18 **$11.49 each**
13 in. PILLARS
303-Z-9719 **$3.99 each**
SAVE $4.95 on pack of six.
301-Z-9809 **$18.99 pack of 6**

2. HARVEST CHERUB SEPARATOR SET
Includes four 7 in. Harvest Cherub pillars, two 9 in. separator plates (lower plate has 12 in. overall diameter).
301-Z-3517 **$11.99 set**

3. DANCING CUPID PILLARS
5 1/2 in. high.
303-Z-1210 **$7.99 pack of 4**

4. CHERUB SNAP-ONS
Accent 5 and 7 in. Grecian pillars. (Pillars not included). 3 1/2 in. high.
305-Z-4104 **$1.29 pack of 4**

5. FROLICKING CHERUB
Animated character. 5 in. high.
1001-Z-244 **$2.79 each**

6. ANGEL DUET
Fluttering fancies. A pair per package. 2 1/2 x 2 in.
1001-Z-457 **$1.80 pack of 2**

7. MUSICAL TRIO
Setting just the right mood. Each 3 in. high.
1001-Z-368 **$2.29 pack of 3**

8. KNEELING CHERUB FOUNTAIN
Beautiful when accented with tinted piping gel and flowers. 4 in. high.
1001-Z-9380 **$1.99 each**

9. ANGELINOS
Heavenly addition to wedding, birthday and holiday cakes. 2 x 3 in.
1001-Z-504 **$3.29 pack of 6**

10. CHERUB CARD HOLDER
What neat place makers, too. (Cards not included). 1 5/8 x 3 3/8 in.
1001-Z-9374 **$3.49 pack of 4**

11. HEAVENLY HARPISTS
Striking the perfect chord. 3 1/2 in. high.
1001-Z-7029 **$4.49 pack of 4**

Fountains, Stairs & More

1. CRYSTAL BRIDGE AND GRACEFUL STAIRWAY SET
Create a dramatic masterpiece. Includes two stairways (16 ³/₄ in. long) and one platform (4 ³/₄ in. X 5 in.). Plastic.
205-Z-2311 $14.99 set
ONE STAIRWAY ONLY
205-Z-2315 $7.99 each

2. FILIGREE PLATFORM AND STAIRWAY SET
Bridge the gap between lavish tiers. Includes two stairways (16 ³/₄ in. long) and one platform (4 ³/₄ in. x 5 in.). White plastic.
205-Z-2109 $11.99 set
ONE STAIRWAY ONLY
205-Z-1218 $4.99 each

3. THE KOLOR-FLO FOUNTAIN
Cascading waterfall with shimmering lights is the most dramatic way to underscore elegant formal tiers. Water pours from three levels. Top levels can be removed for smaller fountain arrangement. Intricate lighting system with two bulbs for extra brilliance. Use with 14 in. or larger plates, 13 in. or taller pillars for tallest cascade. Plastic fountain bowl is 9 ³/₄ in. diameter. 110-124v. A.C. motor with 65 in. cord. Pumps water electrically. Directions and replacement part information included.
306-Y-2599 $99.99 each

Replacement Parts

Pump	306-Z-1002	$39.99 each
Piston	306-Z-1029	$ 2.99 each
Pump/Bulb Bracket	306-Z-1037	$ 3.39 each
Lamp Socket	306-Z-1045	$ 4.99 each
Light Bulb	306-Z-1053	$ 3.29 each
Cascade/Pump Connector	306-Z-1088	$ 2.59 each
Floater Switch	306-Z-1096	$12.99 each
Upper Cascade	306-Z-1118	$ 6.99 each
Middle Cascade	306-Z-1126	$ 7.99 each
Lower Cascade	306-Z-1134	$ 8.99 each
Bowl	306-Z-1142	$13.99 each
Bottom Base	306-Z-1169	$ 8.39 each

4. FOUNTAIN CASCADE SET
Dome shapes redirect water over their surface in nonstop streams. Set includes 4 pieces; 2 ¹/₂, 4 ¹/₂, 8 and 11 ¹/₂ in. diam. (Kolor-Flo Fountain sold separately.)
306-Z-1172 $14.99 set

5. FLOWER HOLDER RING
White plastic. 12 ¹/₂ in. diam. x 2 in. high. Put at base of Kolor-Flo Fountain.
305-Z-435 $4.99 each

6. FILIGREE FOUNTAIN FRAME
Perfect around the Kolor-Flo Fountain. Eight white plastic scallops snap together. 9 in. diameter. 3 ¹/₂ in high.
205-Z-1285 $2.99 each

7. CRYSTAL-LOOK BOWL
Perfect for blooms. 4 ¹/₂ x 1 ¹/₂ in. deep
205-Z-1404 $2.69 each

8. FILIGREE GAZEBO
4 pcs. 4 ¹/₄ x 8 ¹/₂ in.
205-Z-4100 $4.69 each

9. SEED PEARL HEART
7 x 6 ¹/₂ in.
205-Z-1006 $3.69 pack of 3

10. FANCY FILIGREE HEART
7 x 6 ³/₄ in.
1004-Z-2208 $3.79 each

11. FILIGREE HEART FRAMES
4 IN. 205-Z-1527 $1.69 pack of 3
7 IN. 205-Z-1501 $2.69 pack of 3

12. FILIGREE SWIRLS
Variations on a delicate theme. Leaf-framed scrollwork. 4 in. high.
1004-Z-2100 $2.49 pack of 12

13. SCROLLS
Graceful flowing decorations. 2 ³/₄ x1¹/₄ in.
1004-Z-2801 $2.29 pack of 24

14. LACY HEARTS
What delicate beauty. 3 ³/₄ x 3 ¹/₂ in.
1004-Z-2306 $2.49 pack of 12

15. CURVED TRIANGLE
Dramatic addition. 3 x 3 ¹/₂ in.
1004-Z-3001 $2.49 pack of 12

Cake Stands

1. FLOATING TIERS CAKE STAND

Display three tiers on this graceful white metal cake stand. Fast and easy to use! Set includes stand and 8 in., 12 in., 16 in., smooth-edged separator plates and instructions.

307-Z-825 $62.99 set
Additional plates available (same plates as Crystal-Clear Cake Divider Set).

Plates	Number	Price
8 in.	302-Z-9749	$3.99 each
12 in.	302-Z-9765	$6.99 each
16 in.	302-Z-9780	$10.99 each

2. CRYSTAL-CLEAR CAKE DIVIDER

White plastic separator plates; 1/2 in. diameter 7 1/2 in. high; clear plastic twist legs penetrate cake and rest on plate below (dowel rods not needed). Includes 6 in., 8 in., 10 in., 12 in., 14 in., 16 in. plates plus 24 legs.

SAVE 25% ON SET.
301-Y-9450 $47.99 set

Plates	Number	Price
6 in.	302-Z-9730	$2.99 each
8 in.	302-Z-9749	$3.99 each
10 in.	302-Z-9757	$4.99 each
12 in.	302-Z-9765	$6.99 each
14 in.	302-Z-9773	$8.99 each
16 in.	302-Z-9780	$10.99 each

7 1/2 in. TWIST LEGS
303-Z-9794 $3.99 pack of 4

9 in. TWIST LEGS Add more height.
303-Z-977 $3.99 pack of 4

Our Ruffle Boards™ work beautifully with the two sets above or the spiked pillars on facing page.

3. TALL TIER STAND SET

Five twist-apart columns 6 1/2 in. high with 1 bottom and 1 top bolt; 18 in. footed base plate; 16 in., 14 in., 12 in., 10 in., 8 in. separator plates (interchangeable, except footed base plate). White plastic.

SAVE 25% ON SET.
304-Z-7915 $45.99 set

Plates	Number	Price	Columns	Number	Price
8 in.	302-Z-7894	$3.99 each	6 1/2 in.	303-Z-7910	$1.59 each
10 in.	302-Z-7908	$4.99 each	7 3/4 in.	304-Z-5009	$2.59 each
12 in.	302-Z-7924	$5.99 each	13 1/2 in.	303-Z-703	$4.49 each
14 in.	302-Z-7940	$8.99 each			
16 in.	302-Z-7967	$11.99 each			
18 in.	302-Z-7983	$14.99 each			

TOP COLUMN CAP NUT	304-Z-7923	79¢ each
GLUE-ON PLATE LEGS	304-Z-7930	59¢ each
BOTTOM COLUMN BOLT	304-Z-7941	99¢ each

4. TALL TIER 4-ARM BASE STAND

Replace Tall Tier Base Plate (See No. 3) with this heavy-duty white plastic support; add separator plates up to 12 in. For proper balance, add up to 3 graduated tiers to center column. Includes base bolt.

304-Z-8245 $11.99 each
BASE BOLT ONLY
304-Z-8253 59¢ each

5. CAKE CORER TUBE

Prepare tiers quickly and neatly for the Tall Tier Stand column. Serrated edge removes cake centers with one push. Ice cake before using. 7 in. long solid center fits into 6 1/2 in. long hollow corer to eject cake bits. Cleans easily.

304-Z-8172 $1.99 each

6. CATHEDRAL CAKE KIT

Transform basic wedding cakes into dramatic masterpieces. Kit includes: 5 easy-to-assemble white church pieces, 4 white plastic cake supports and a church window that can be illuminated from within.

2104-Z-2940 $13.99 kit

7. STAIRSTEPS SET

Twenty-four 1 in. high stairs with 3 in. candleholders.
1107-Z-8180 $5.49 set

8. SUPER STRONG CAKE STAND

Holds up to 185 pounds of cake! High impact polystyrene and underweb of ribbing make stand super strong. 2 3/4 in. high. 18 in. diameter for larger cakes.
307-Z-1200 $13.49 each

GRECIAN SPIKED PILLARS

Eliminates need for separator plates on cake tier tops. Push into cake to rest on separator plate or cake circle beneath. Wide diameter bottom for increased stability.
5 in. 303-Z-3708 $2.09 pk/4
7 in. 303-Z-3710 $3.19 pk/4
9 in. 303-Z-3712 $4.19 pk/4

GRECIAN PILLARS

Elegantly scrolled and ribbed.
3 in. 303-Z-3606 $2.09 pk/4
5 in. 303-Z-3703 $3.19 pk/4
7 in. 303-Z-3705 $4.19 pk/4

SWAN PILLARS

Grecian pillars with romantic swan bases add grace to your masterpiece. 4 in. high.
303-Z-7725 $2.99 pack of 4

ROMAN COLUMNS

Handsome pillars may be used with Kolor-Flo Fountain.
10¼ in.
303-Z-8135 $2.59 ea.
13¾ in.
303-Z-2129 $2.99 ea.

SIX-COLUMN TIER SET

Includes six 13 ¾ in. Roman columns and two super strong 18-in. round Decorator Preferred® Separator Plates. A lovely set to use with the Kolor-Flo Fountain. White plastic.
301-Z-1981 $34.99 set

"HIDDEN" PILLARS

Designed to separate cake tiers slightly and create a floating illusion — adapted from the English method of cake decorating. Pushed into cake tiers as dowel rods, hidden pillars fit onto all white separator plates except Tall Tier. Trimmable, white hollow plastic.
6 in. 303-Z-8 $1.99 set of 4

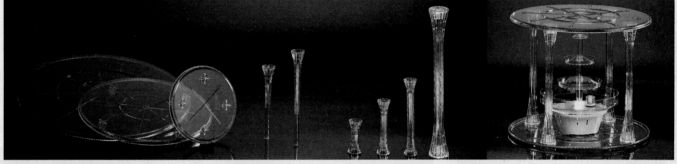

CRYSTAL-LOOK PLATES

Use with crystal-look pillars.

7 in.	302-Z-2013	$2.99 each
9 in.	302-Z-2035	$3.99 each
11 in.	302-Z-2051	$4.99 each
13 in.	302-Z-2078	$6.99 each
*17 in.	302-Z-1810	$13.99 each

*(Use only with 13 ¾ in. crystal pillars.)

CRYSTAL-LOOK SPIKED PILLARS

Push into cake to rest on separator plate or cake circle beneath. Double cake circles for extra support.
7 in. 303-Z-2322 $4.19 pk/4
9 in. 303-Z-2324 $5.19 pk/4

CRYSTAL-LOOK PILLARS

Combine with crystal-look plates and Crystal Bridge and Stairway Set.

3 in.	303-Z-2171	$3.19 pk/4
5 in.	303-Z-2196	$4.19 pk/4
7 in.	303-Z-2197	$4.69 pk/4
*13¾ in.	303-Z-2242	$3.99 each

*(Use only with 17" crystal plate.)

CRYSTAL-LOOK TIER SET

Teams with the Kolor-Flo Fountain. Plastic. Two 17 in. plates; four 13 ¾" pillars.
301-Z-1387 $41.99 set

PLASTIC PEGS

Insure that cake layers and separator plates atop cakes stay in place. These pegs do not add support, so dowel rod cake properly before using. 4 in. long.
399-Z-762 $1.44 set of 12

FILIGREE PILLAR

Airy, lacy look open designs on these square pillars. Just add ribbons or fabric to coordinate with bride's color scheme. 12-in. high.
3 in. 303-Z-8071 $2.09 pk/4
5 in. 303-Z-7717 $3.19 pk/4
12 in. 303-Z-8976 $2.99 ea

ARCHED PILLARS

Grecian-inspired with arched support
4½ in. 303-Z-452 $2.99 pk/4
6½ in. 303-Z-657 $4.99 pk/4

ARCHED TIER SET

Quite dramatic when used with Kolor-Flo Fountain. Includes: Six 13 in. arched columns, two super strong 18 in. round Decorator Preferred Separator Plates, and six angelic cherubs to attach to columns with royal icing or glue. (Cherubs not shown above; shown on p. 168)
301-Z-1982 $44.99 set
18 in. Decorator Preferred Plate
302-Z-18 $11.49 each
13 in. Pillars 303-Y-9719 $ 3.99 each
13 in. Pillars Save $4.95 on pack of six.
301-Z-9809 $18.99 pack

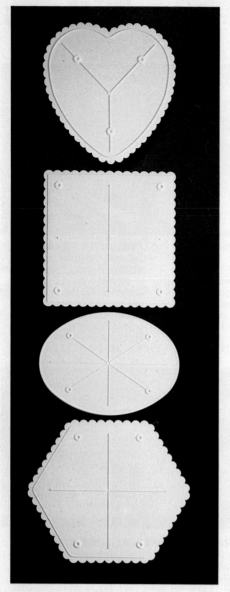

- •**Complete** Size Selection
- •**Scalloped** Edges
- •**Smooth** Back
- •**Easy** Identification

SEPARATOR PLATES

No better way to get your baked masterpieces off to a great foundation! Sturdy, yet beautiful, separator plates bring wedding, shower, anniversary, birthday and even Valentine's Day cakes to new decorating heights. Square, heart and hexagon shapes are edged with delicate scallops; oval has a clean, streamlined beauty.

HEART SEPARATOR PLATES

8 in.	302-Z-2112	$2.99 each
11 in.	302-Z-2114	$3.99 each
14 1/2 in.	302-Z-2116	$7.99 each
16 1/2 in.	302-Z-2118	$8.99 each

SQUARE SEPARATOR PLATES

7 in.	302-Z-1004	$2.99 each
9 in.	302-Z-1020	$3.99 each
11 in.	302-Z-1047	$4.99 each
13 in.	302-Z-1063	$5.99 each

OVAL SEPARATOR PLATES

8 1/2 in. x 6 in.	302-Z-2130	$3.99 each
11 1/2 in. x 8 1/2 in.	302-Z-2131	$4.99 each
14 1/2 in. x 10 3/4 in.	302-Z-2132	$5.99 each

HEXAGON SEPARATOR PLATES

7 in.	302-Z-1705	$2.99 each
10 in.	302-Z-1748	$3.99 each
13 in.	302-Z-1764	$5.99 each
16 in.	302-Z-1799	$7.99 each

DISPOSABLE SINGLE PLATE SYSTEM

The Baker's Best® Disposable Separator system features sturdy plates, pillars and adjustable pillar rings. All made of recyclable plastic.

DISPOSABLE PLATES

6 in. Plate	302-Z-4000	$1.49 each
7 in. Plate	302-Z-4001	$1.69 each
8 in. Plate	302-Z-4002	$1.99 each
9 in. Plate	302-Z-4003	$2.49 each
10 in. Plate	302-Z-4004	$2.89 each
12 in. Plate	302-Z-4006	$3.79 each
14 in. Plate	302-Z-4008	$4.39 each

DISPOSABLE PILLARS WITH RINGS

7 in. Pillar w/Rings (4 each)
303-Z-4000 $2.59 pack of 4
9 in. Pillar w/Rings (4 each)
303-Z-4001 $2.69 pack of 4

DOWEL RODS

Essential for supporting stacked cakes and tiers. Complete assembling instructions on page 106.

PLASTIC DOWEL RODS

Heavy-duty hollow plastic provides strong, sanitary support for all tiered cakes. Can be cut with serrated knife to desired length.
12 3/4 in. long x 3/4 in. diameter
399-Z-801 $2.29 pack of 4

WOODEN DOWEL RODS

Cut and sharpen with strong shears and knife.
12 in. long, 1/4 in. wide.
399-Z-1009 $2.29 pack of 12

Guaranteed
Non-Breakable

Decorator Preferred.®

• Circles of Strength™
Construction

The best, strongest separator plates –
with features important to cake decorators:

CIRCLES OF STRENGTH™ CONSTRUCTION
An exclusive Wilton design distributes the cake weight evenly. Round indentations accommodate plastic pegs (if desired). Plastic "knobs" help secure cardboard cake circle to plate.

GUARANTEED NON-BREAKABLE
High impact resin composition means maximum strength. Guaranteed non-breakable under normal use.

TRADITIONAL WILTON SCALLOPED EDGES
Lovely scalloped-edge design so they are completely compatible with all Wilton plates and pillars.

EASY IDENTIFICATION
Sizes are clearly marked on each plate for fast, easy identification.

SMOOTH BACK
Reverse side of plates have no printing, so there is nothing to hide. Plain back complements the most elegant decorating.

6 in.	302-Z-6	$2.09 each
7 in.	302-Z-7	$2.29 each
8 in.	302-Z-8	$2.59 each
9 in.	302-Z-9	$3.19 each
10 in.	302-Z-10	$3.59 each
11 in.	302-Z-11	$4.19 each
12 in.	302-Z-12	$4.69 each
13 in.	302-Z-13	$5.49 each
14 in.	302-Z-14	$5.79 each
15 in.	302-Z-15	$6.99 each
16 in.	302-Z-16	$7.79 each
18 in.	302-Z-18	$11.49 each

When the success of your baked masterpiece depends upon its foundation, you'll be glad you've chosen the undisputable best, Wilton.

CLASSIC SEPARATOR SETS
Stately Grecian pillars and scalloped-edged plates create beautiful settings for all tiered cakes. Sets include 2 Decorator Preferred® Plates, 4 pillars and 4 pegs.

6 in. Plate Set with 3 in. Pillars	2103-Z-639	$6.49 set
8 in. Plate Set with 5 in. Pillars	2103-Z-256	$7.49 set
10 in. Plate Set with 5 in. Pillars	2103-Z-108	$9.49 set
12 in. Plate Set with 5 in. Pillars	2103-Z-124	$11.49 set

54-PC. GRECIAN PILLAR AND PLATE SET
(not shown)
A deluxe collection for the serious cake decorator. Features Decorator Preferred® scalloped-edged separator plates and 5 inch pillars. Includes: two each 6, 8, 10, 12 and 14-inch plates; 20 Grecian pillars and 24 pegs.
301-Z-8380 $45.99 set

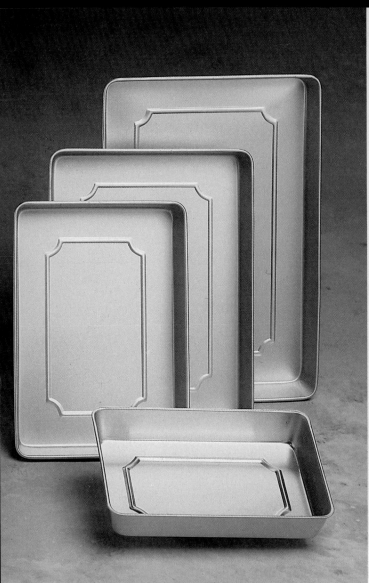

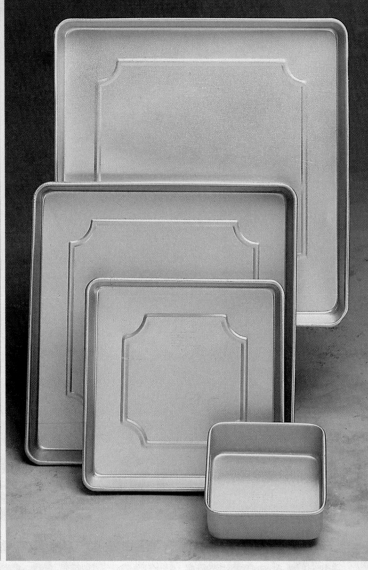

SHEET PANS
2 in. deep.

A priceless collection for any baker or cook. These multi-use pans will be in constant use for everything from special occasion cakes to Sunday dinner. The versatility and high quality of these pans make them invaluable for any kitchen.

7 x 11 in.	2105-Z-2304	$5.99 each
9 x 13 in.	2105-Z-1308	$7.49 each
11 x 15 in.	2105-Z-158	$10.99 each
12 x 18 in.	2105-Z-182	$12.99 each

SQUARE PANS
2 in. deep.

Square . . .the shape that offers an extensive variety of baking and cooking options. Can be used in cake designs from simple to fancy. A great collection to have close at hand.

6 in.	507-Z-2180	$4.99 each
8 in.	2105-Z-8191	$6.49 each
10 in.	2105-Z-8205	$8.49 each
12 in.	2105-Z-8213	$10.99 each
14 in.	2105-Z-8220	$13.99 each
16 in.	2105-Z-8231	$15.99 each

9 X 13 CAKE COVER

Just the protection you need when transporting decorated cakes. Designed for use with the Wilton 9 X 13 in. Performance Pan*, this cover has a raised dome lid which allows you to cover decorated cakes with ease. Keeps cakes and other foods fresh in the pan, even after slicing.
415-Z-903 $4.49 each
*Cake pan not included

CAKE SAVER - 2 PIECE

Designed to carry most elaborately decorated cakes. Generous size accommodates borders and top decorations easily. Use to carry or store all types of cakes, including fancy ring, angel food, cheese cakes, even pies, as well as layer cakes. Maintains freshness. Wide enough for a 10 in. cake with borders or a 12 in. cake without borders. Includes one 14 in. round base and one 6 in. high cover.
415-Z-905 $10.99 set

PERFORMANCE PANS™

You'll achieve repeated success with these professional quality anodized aluminum pans. Not only are they durable, they're dishwasher safe. An unequaled variety of sizes and shapes gives you countless possibilities. Whether you're creating tall-tiered cakes or roasting prime rib, you can depend on Performance Pans™ for the finest results.

ROUND PANS 2 in. deep.

Bake everything from a cake for two to a wedding cake to serve hundreds. You'll find it easy with a varied collection of round-sized pans.

Size	Item	Price
6 in.	2105-Z-2185	$4.99 each
7 in.	2105-Z-2190	$5.49 each
8 in.	2105-Z-2193	$5.49 each
10 in.	2105-Z-2207	$6.49 each
12 in.	2105-Z-2215	$8.99 each
14 in.	2105-Z-3947	$11.99 each
16 in.	2105-Z-3963	$15.99 each
9 in. 2-Pan Set	2105-Z-7908	$9.99 each

ROUND PANS 3 in. deep.

Bake impressive high cakes. Perfect for tortes, fruit and pound cakes, and cakes to be covered with fondant icing.

Size	Item	Price
8 in.	2105-Z-9104	$6.99 each
10 in.	2105-Z-9945	$8.99 each

BAKE-EVEN STRIPS

At last, an innovative way to bake perfectly level, moist cakes. Avoid high-rise centers, cracked tops or crusty edges. Just dampen strips and wrap around the pan before baking. Each band is 1 1/2 in. wide x 30 in. long, with 1 in. overlap.

SMALL SET
Contains 2 bands, enough for two 8 or 9 in. round pans.
415-Z-260 $5.49 set

LARGE SET
Contains 4 bands. enough for one of each of the following: 10, 12, 14 and 16 in. round pans.
415-Z-262 $13.99 set

Non-Stick Bakeware

Excelle®

PREMIUM NON-STICK BAKEWARE

- **DOUBLE NON-STICK COATING**
- **HEAVY GAUGE STEEL CONSTRUCTION**
- **QUICK, EVEN HEATING**
- **RECIPE ON EVERY LABEL**

Two layers of non-stick coating make Excelle® Bakeware superior. The double coated surface has a slicker feel than other non-stick bakeware — meaning food release is easy and clean-up is a breeze. Excelle® Bakeware also feels heftier — its heavy-gauge steel construction assures more durable performance and a longer life. And Excelle® Bakeware is designed to conduct heat quickly and effectively, without burning your baked goods. You'll love the results from the complete Excelle® line!

COOKIE SHEET
10 1/4 x 15 1/4 in.	2105-Z-100	$10.99 each
11 1/4 x 17 1/4 in.	2105-Z-101	$11.99 each

SHEET PAN
9 x 13 x 2 in.	2105-Z-103	$10.99 each

MUFFIN PAN
12 Cup Standard	2105-Z-105	$13.99 each

SQUARE CAKE PAN
8 1/2 x 8 1/2 in.	2105-Z-108	$7.99 each

FLUTED MOLD PAN
9 in.	2105-Z-111	$13.99 each

SPRINGFORM PAN
Waffle-texture bottom supports heavy cakes!
6 x 3 in.	2105-Z-106	$8.99 each
9 x 3 in.	2105-Z-107	$11.99 each

ROUND CAKE PAN
8 7/8 x 1 3/8 in.	2105-Z-102	$6.99 each

PIE PAN
9 in.	2105-Z-119	$6.99 each

LOAF PAN
9 x 5 x 2 1/2 in.	2105-Z-104	$6.99 each

NON-STICK COOLING GRID
Tight grid pattern won't let cookies fall thru!
10 x 16 in.	2305-Z-0228	$7.99 each
14 1/2 x 20 in.	2305-Z-0229	$11.99 each

Even-Bake®

BROWNS WITHOUT BURNING!

Quality that can be warranted for life—Even-Bake® Insulated Bakeware promises years of baking excellence and uniform browning. The difference is an insulating layer of air between two sheets of high-quality aluminum. The bottom layer protects the top from the intense heat of your oven. Our expanded selection of sizes and styles lets all your baked goods benefit from the Even-Bake® design.

UNIFORM BAKING
Designed to prevent hot spots — a layer of insulating air protects baked goods from burning. On cookie sheets, the bottom sheet touches the top only on the perimeter, for completely even baking.

IMMERSIBLE AND DISHWASHER SAFE
Exclusive patent-pending design allows cookie sheets and pans to be totally immersed and drains the water for immediate use.

EASY GRIP LIP
Exclusive ribbed edge lets you handle Even-Bake® pans more easily. Grip lip on cookie sheets is on the wide edge for easier oven removal.

NEW! JELLY ROLL PAN WITH COVER
Clear cover fits tightly for safe transport of desserts.
10 ½ x 15 ½ x 1 ⅛ in.
2105-Z-2620 **$22.99 each**

JELLY ROLL
10 ½ x 15 ½ x 1 ⅛ in.
2105-Z-2650 **$17.99 each**

SHEET PAN WITH COVER
See-thru cover displays what's inside at a glance!
9 x 13 x 2 in.   2105-Z-2667 **$20.99 each**

SHEET PAN
9 x 13 x 2 in.   2105-Z-2661 **$16.49 each**

BISCUIT/BROWNIE
7 x 11 x 1 ⅛ in.   2105-Z-2664 **$12.99 each**

COOKIE SHEET
13 x 17 x ¼ in.   2105-Z-2644 **$14.99 each**
10 ¼ x 15 ½ x ¼ in.
2105-Z-2646 **$12.99 each**

HEART PAN (one cake mix)
12 ½ x 12 x 1⅞ in.
2105-Z-2663 **$14.99 each**

ROUND
8 x 1 ⅞ in.   2105-Z-2669 **$12.99 each**
9 x 1 ⅞ in.   2105-Z-2666 **$14.49 each**

SQUARE
8 x 8 x 1 ⅞ in.   2105-Z-2665 **$12.99 each**

MUFFIN PAN
4-Cup Jumbo   2105-Z-2662 **$14.99 each**
NEW! 6- Cup Standard
2105-Z-2672 **$14.99 each**
NEW! 12-Cup Mini
2105-Z-2671 **$14.99 each**

NEW! LOAF PAN
9 x 5 x 2 ⅔ in.   2105-Z-2670 **$14.99 each**

Insulated Bakeware

Selected *Jeff* by *Smith*

The Frugal Gourmet

"I have tried them and they work!"

Pizza Pans

Selected by Jeff Smith

The Frugal Gourmet

"I've tried the best... this is better!"

Introducing Wilton pizza pans and serving trays. Exclusive patent pending dual action baking design lifts pizza dough from the surface, so that heat circulates and browns the crust. It crisps the crust by eliminating moisture through the vent holes.

Extra wide rim keeps hot mitts and fingers safely away from pizza. Smooth bottom trays have skid stop rims and keep pizza warm while serving.

Included with each pan or pan/tray set is a 6-page recipe book developed by the Wilton Kitchen.

14 ½ in. pan with red tray	2105-Z-3902	$19.99 each
14 ½ in. pan with black tray	2105-Z-3908	$19.99 each
16 ½ in. pan with red tray	2105-Z-3904	$24.99 each
16 ½ in. pan with black tray	2105-Z-3909	$24.99 each
14 ½ in. pan	2105-Z-3901	$10.99 each
16 ½ in. pan	2105-Z-3903	$12.99 each

NEW! Deep Dish Pizza Pan
13 in. round x 1 ⅝ in. deep
	2105-Z-3921	$12.99 each

PIZZA ACCESSORIES
The Wilton pizza accessory collection gives you the ideal way to dish up piping hot pizza with ease. Each piece is heavy-gauge stainless steel that will not rust or pit. The cutters have a double-sided cutting wheel for a cleaner cut.

2 ½ in. cutter	2105-Z-3905	$4.99 each
3 ¾ in. cutter	2105-Z-3906	$5.99 each
Spatula Server	2105-Z-3907	$6.99 each

Lean-Loaf Pan

NEW! THE LEAN-LOAF PAN
Makes a healthier meat loaf! The 2 in. deep drip rack drains into the 2 ½ in. deep loaf pan so your meat loaf won't bake in and absorb fat. The loaf pan is perfect for breads, too. Crafted of quality aluminum for even heating and uniform baking. Dishwasher safe.
2105-Z-5251 $11.49 each

OVENCRAFT™
Professional Bakeware

PROFESSIONAL-QUALITY desserts and cakes begin with the finest bakeware. Ovencraft Bakeware is the professional's choice—every pan is built to the highest standards for consistent, superior baking results.

— EXTRA-THICK ALUMINUM means Ovencraft pans provide the best heat distribution and will never warp. Compare our square sheet pans (.060-.065" thick) to ordinary bakeware (.015" thick on average) and you'll see why Ovencraft pans can last for a lifetime.

— DESIGNED FOR PRECISION: each pan with special features which enhance its performance. Extra depth versus ordinary bakeware to reduce overflow...perfectly straight sides and 90° corners on squares and sheets for exact results...welded corners for strength.

— A PROFESSIONAL FINISH. Anodized aluminum finish will not rust, discolor, chip or peel—it's the best finish for your baked goods. Smooth finish cleans easily, releases food quickly and evenly.

2 IN. DEEP ROUND PANS
Ideal for two-layer cakes and tier cakes.

		Each
6 in.	2105-Z-5601	$4.99
8 in.	2105-Z-5602	$5.49
9 in.	2105-Z-5619	$5.99
10 in.	2105-Z-5603	$6.49
12 in.	2105-Z-5604	$8.99
14 in.	2105-Z-5605	$11.99
16 in.	2105-Z-5606	$14.99

3 IN. DEEP ROUND PANS
Bake beautiful, tall cakes.

		Each
6 in.	2105-Z-5620	$4.99
8 in.	2105-Z-5607	$6.99
10 in.	2105-Z-5608	$8.99
12 in.	2105-Z-5609	$10.99
14 in.	2105-Z-5610	$12.99

3 IN. DEEP HALF-ROUND PAN
Use to bake an 18 in. round cake in conventional size oven.

18 in.	2105-Z-5622	$12.99 each

SQUARE PANS
Perfectly square corners and 2 3/16 in. depth produce professional quality cakes.

8 in.	2105-Z-5611	$7.99 each
10 in.	2105-Z-5612	$10.99 each
12 in.	2105-Z-5613	$13.99 each
14 in.	2105-Z-5614	$17.99 each

SHEET PANS
Discover endless options with this multi-use pan. 2 3/16 in. depth.

9 x 13 in.	2105-Z-5616	$11.99 each
11 x 15 in.	2105-Z-5617	$14.99 each
12 x 18 in.	2105-Z-5618	$17.99 each

179

Tier Pan Sets

1. CLASSIC ROUND PAN SET
Set includes 6, 8, 10 and 12 in. aluminum pans. 2 in. deep.
2105-Z-2101 $22.99 set

2. 3 IN. DEEP ROUND PAN SET
Set includes 8, 10, 12, 14 in. aluminum pans.
2105-Z-2932 $31.99 set

3. ROUND TIER SET
The perfect choice for engagement parties, anniversaries, religious occasions and more. Set includes 5 x 2 1/2 in., 7 1/8 x 2 1/2 in. and 9 5/16 x 2 5/8 in. aluminum rounds; eight 5 in. Grecian Spiked Pillars; 6 and 8 in. scallop-edged round white plastic separator plates; instructions. Takes 2 cake mixes.
2105-Z-2531 $22.99 set

4. ROUND MINI TIER SET
Takes one cake mix. Set includes 5, 6 and 8 in: round, 1 in. deep aluminum pans; 5, 7 in. separator plates; 8 clear plastic twist legs; decorating instructions.
2105-Z-98042 $11.99 set
ROUND MINI-TIER PLATE SET ONLY
301-Z-9817 $2.99 set

5. 4 PC. OVAL PAN SET
Set includes four 2 in. deep aluminum pans. Sizes are 7 3/4 x 5 5/8 in.; 10 3/4 x 7 7/8 in.; 13 x 9 7/8 in.; 16 x 12 3/8 in.
2105-Z-2130 $23.99 set

6. 2 PC. OVAL PAN SET
Set includes two 9 x 6 3/4 x 1 3/4 in. aluminum pans.
2105-Z-1553 $9.99 set

7. PETAL PANS
9 in. x 2 in. 2105-Z-5109 $6.99 each
12 in. x 2 in. 2105-Z-5117 $8.99 each

8. 4 PC. HEXAGON PAN SET
Set includes 6, 9, 12, 15 in. aluminum pans, 2 in. deep.
2105-Z-3572 $26.99 set

Individual hexagon pans available.

9 in. x 2 in. 2105-Z-5125 $6.99 each
12 in. x 2 in. 2105-Z-5133 $8.99 each

9. 4 PC. PETAL PAN SET
Set includes 6, 9, 12 and 15 in., 2 in. deep aluminum pans.
2105-Z-2134 $26.99 set

Basic Bakeware

1. MINI MUFFIN PAN
Create mini-muffins, fruitcakes, cupcakes, cheesecakes. Aluminum.
7 3/4 x 10 x 3/4 in. deep.
2105-Z-2125 **$7.49 each**

2. NEW! 6-CUP POPOVER/ MUFFIN PAN
Its unique, stepped design bakes cupcakes and muffins in a crown shape design. Even-heating performance for uniform browning every time. Aluminum. 13 1/2 x 9 1/4 x 1 3/4 in. deep.
2105-Z-5252 **$12.99 each**

3. SIX-CUP MUFFIN PAN
Perfect size for morning muffins, after school treats and desserts. Aluminum.
7 3/8 x 10 3/4 x 1 in. deep.
2105-Z-5338 **$7.49 each**

4. JUMBO MUFFIN PAN
Bake super-size cupcakes and muffins. Aluminum.
13 1/2 x 9 1/4 x 2 in. deep.
2105-Z-1820 **$12.99 each**

5. SHELL PAN
Simple elegance. A pan you'll reach for occasion after occasion. Aluminum.
11 x 12 x 1 7/8 in. deep.
2105-Z-8250 **$9.99 each**

6. VIENNESE SWIRL PAN
The foundation for elegant continental style desserts. Aluminum.
11 1/2 diameter x 1 7/8 in. deep.
2105-Z-8252 **$9.99 each**

7. MINI-LOAF PAN
Great for individual-sized nut breads, cakes. Individual loaves are 4 1/2 x 2 1/2 in. Pan is 10 3/4 x 12 1/4 x 1 1/2 in. deep. Aluminum.
2105-Z-9791 **$9.99 each**

8. LOAF PAN
Perfect for sandwich loaves, cakes and breads. Aluminum.
8 3/4 x 4 1/4 x 2 3/4 in. deep.
2105-Z-3688 **$5.99 each**

9. LONG LOAF PAN
Bake classic cakes or angel food delights. Legs provide proper cooling for angel food cakes. Aluminum. 16 x 4 x 4 1/2 in. deep.
2105-Z-1588 **$9.99 each**

10. SHORTCAKES 'N TREATS PAN
Decorate these single-serving desserts with in-season fruit and whipped cream. Aluminum. 12 1/2 x 8 x 1 in. deep.
2105-Z-5966 **$6.99 each**

Basic Bakeware

1. JELLY ROLL/COOKIE PANS
Two sizes come in handy for bar cookies, jelly rolls and more. Aluminum.
10 1/2 x 15 1/2 in.   2105-Z-1269 $8.99 each
12 x 18 x 1 in.   2105-Z-4854 $9.99 each

2. COOKIE SHEETS
Dependable, even-browning sheets in two convenient sizes. Aluminum.
10 x 15 in.   2105-Z-1265 $5.99 each
12 1/2 x 16 1/2 in.   2105-Z-2975 $8.49 each

3. RING MOLD PANS
Turn out beautiful cakes, gelatin molds and more. Two convenient sizes, each 3 in. deep. Aluminum.
8 in.   2105-Z-190 $6.49 each
10 1/2 in.   2105-Z-4013 $7.99 each

4. CONTINENTAL FLAN PAN
Create international recipes with elan. Aluminum. 11 diam. x 1 3/4 in. deep.
2105-Z-2046 $7.99 each

5. FANCY RING MOLD PAN
Beautiful bundt-style pan, ideal for pound cakes, mousse, more! 3 inch deep pan. Takes one standard bundt-type mix. Aluminum. 10 in. diameter; 3 in. deep.
2105-Z-5008 $9.99 each

6. PETITE FANCY RING MOLD PAN
Serve impressive desserts in dramatic individual servings. Aluminum.
12 1/2 x 8 x 1 in. deep.
2105-Z-2097 $16.99 each

7. NON-STICK SPRINGFORM PANS
Quality non-stick finish on heavy-gauge steel. Waffle-textured surface provides extra strength. 3 in. deep.
6 in.   2105-Z-218 $6.99 each
9 in.   2105-Z-219 $9.99 each

8. 2-PC. SPRINGFORM PANS
Waffle bottom for stronger support. Release springlock, remove sides and serve. 3 in. deep. Aluminum.
6 in.   2105-Z-4437 $7.99 each
9 in.   2105-Z-5354 $10.99 each

9. MINI ANGEL FOOD PAN
Create delicate, single serving desserts with easy 6-mold pan. 15 x 10 1/4 x 2 1/4 in. deep. Tinned steel.
0000-Z-2338 $20.69 each

10. 2-PC. ANGEL FOOD PAN
2-piece, 10 x 4 in. deep. Cooling legs. Removable inner core sleeve. Aluminum.
2105-Z-2525 $13.99 each

1. HEART ANGEL FOOD PAN
Cooling legs make it easy to properly cool an angel food cake. With removable bottom for easy release. Aluminum pan takes one angel food or chiffon mix. 10 $\frac{5}{8}$ x 10 $\frac{1}{8}$ x 4 in.
2105-Z-6509 $12.99 each

2. HEART RING PAN
Fill with fresh fruit, whipped cream, shaved chocolate. A heart's delight. Two-mix aluminum pan is 11 x 2 $\frac{5}{8}$ in. deep.
2105-Z-3219 $12.99 each

3. HEART FLAN PAN
Choose pudding, ice cream, fruit, even chocolates. It can also be trimmed with icing or whipped cream. One-mix aluminum pan is 11 x 10 $\frac{1}{2}$ x 2 in.
2105-Z-3218 $7.99 each

4. HEART DESSERT PAN
Great for cakes, pudding desserts, ice cream, mousse. Removable bottom makes it easy to remove delicate desserts. Aluminum pan is 10 x 9 $\frac{3}{4}$ x 2 $\frac{1}{2}$ in.
2105-Z-3217 $12.99 each

5. HEART MINI-CAKE PAN
Sweet gestures of love for bridal showers and kids' parties. Each heart of this 8 x 11 $\frac{1}{8}$ in. aluminum pan is 3 $\frac{1}{2}$ x 1 $\frac{1}{4}$ in. deep. One cake mix makes 12 hearts.
2105-Z-11044 $7.99 each

6. HEART MINI-TIER PAN SET
Make a petite masterpiece using any one cake mix in three sweetheart tiers. Set includes 5, 7 $\frac{1}{2}$ and 9 in. pans, two scallop-edged white separator plates and six crystal clear twist legs.
2105-Z-409 $11.99 set

SEPARATOR PLATE SET
Includes one 5 $\frac{1}{2}$ in. and one 8 in. Heart Separator Plate with 6 crystal clear twist legs.
301-Y-09728 $2.99 set

7. HEART PANS
The perfect cake for the most romantic occasions-anniversaries, bridal showers, birthdays and weddings. The 2-in. deep aluminum pans are sold separately in three essential sizes, 6, 9, 12 in.
  6 in. Heart   **2105-Z-4781 $3.99 each**
  9 in. Heart   **2105-Z-5176 $5.99 each**
 12 in. Heart   **2105-Z-5168 $8.99 each**

8. HAPPINESS HEART PAN SET
It takes just one mix to fill both aluminum pans; each 9 x 1 $\frac{1}{2}$ in. deep.
2105-Z-956 $7.99 set

9. HEART PAN SET
Celebrate showers, weddings and more with the ultimate heart-shaped cake. Set includes 6, 9, 12 and 15 $\frac{1}{2}$ in. diameter aluminum pans.
504-Z-207 $24.99 set

10. DOUBLE TIER HEART PAN
The perfect show of affection for birthdays, Mother's or Father's Day, wedding showers and much more. Instructions show 4 delightful ways to decorate. One-mix aluminum pan is 11 $\frac{1}{2}$ x 11 x 2 $\frac{1}{4}$ in. deep.
2105-Z-1699 $9.99 each

Halloween Pans

1. NEW!

2. YOU'RE BEWITCHING

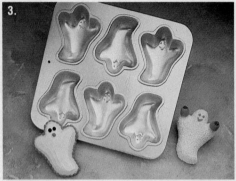

3.

4.

5.

6.

7.

1. NEW! SCARY CAT PAN
Here's one cat you'll want to cross your path on Halloween! And this fancy feline can be decorated in so many different ways. One-mix aluminum pan is 13 5/8 x 11 3/4 x 2 1/8 in.
2105-Z-5207 $7.99 each

2. WICKED WITCH PAN
Invite this not-so-wicked witch to your Halloween bash. This fun-loving lady will bring hearty laughs to the party. Can also turn into other characters. One-mix aluminum pan is 11 3/4 x 13 x 1 3/4 in.
2105-Z-4590 $7.99 each

3. MINI GHOST PAN
Create gobs of goblins at a time with this newest pan. Children will love customizing these creatures with candies and coconut. One cake mix makes 12-16 ghosts. Aluminum pan is 13 1/8 x 12 1/8 x 1 1/2 in.
2105-Z-3845 $7.99 each

4. BOO GHOST PAN
This giggling ghoul puts his message right up front for your celebration. It's a fun way to add all the extras to a party. Your goblins will love him. One-mix aluminum pan is 14 1/4 x 11 3/4 x 1 7/8 in.
2105-Z-1031 $7.99 each

5. MINI-PUMPKIN PAN
It's so easy to make little treats for all your favorite goblins. Or create kid-pleasing party cakes year 'round. Even try the fun alternate ideas shown. One cake mix makes 12-16 pumpkins. Each mold of this 12 1/4 x 8 x 1 3/8 in. aluminum pan takes 1/2 cup of cake batter.
2105-Z-1499 $7.99 each

6. JACK-O-LANTERN PAN
Carve out this toothless grin for that next Halloween party. It's a quick and easy way to brighten up your celebration. One-mix aluminum pan is 12 1/4 x 11 5/8 x 2 in.
2105-Z-3068 $7.99 each

7. SCARECROW PAN
Our timid little scarecrow will be happy to join all your autumn celebrations. From Halloween to Thanksgiving, you'll be keeping this little guy busy. Many alternate decorating schemes. One-mix aluminum pan is 15 x 11 1/2 x 1 7/8 in.
2105-Z-801 $7.99 each

Candy Molds, p.115
Candy Melts™*, p. 116
*brand confectionery coating

Pumpkin Mix Sprinkle Decorations, p. 127
Cats and Bats Icing Decorations, p.126
Halloween Baking Papers, p.127

This Halloween, try some Wilton tricks on your treats! Create creepy cookies with our haunting collection of cutters, then top them with icing decorations in scary shapes. Or concoct hair-raising candies in your laboratory, using Candy Melts™ and our exclusive molds and kits. Wilton has so many ways to get everyone into the Halloween spirit!

Halloween Favorites Cookie Cutters, p. 122

1. SNOWMAN PAN
This jolly man packs lots of winter fun. Sprinkled with coconut and decorated with candies, this cake makes a tasty Christmas treat. Inventive ideas to adapt for all seasons included on the label. One-mix aluminum pan is 15 1/4 x 10 1/4 x 2 in.
2105-Z-803 $7.99 each

2. NEW! MINI-SNOWMAN PAN
Build a blizzard of snowmen, 6 at a time with this newest pan. Kids love to decorate 'em; what a treat at holiday parties! One-mix makes approximately 15-18 snowmen. Aluminum pan is 11 1/2 x 10 1/2 x 1 7/8 in.
2105-Z-472 $7.99 each

3. SANTA BEAR PAN
Two childhood favorites in one. This santa bear has a bag load of good holiday wishes and cheer to distribute. One-mix aluminum pan is 13 7/8 x 11 1/4 x 2 in.
2105-Z-4432 $7.99 each

4. TREELITEFUL PAN
Here's holiday decorating made quick and easy. Just cover with one squeeze, add simple garlands and candy or cookie ornaments. Instructions include several ideas to use throughout the year. One-mix aluminum pan is 15 x 11 x 1 1/2 in.
2105-Z-425 $7.99 each

5. MINI CHRISTMAS TREE PAN
Trees, trees and more trees make the holiday merrier. Serve little ones individually or use them to decorate each guest's place setting. Label includes alternate ideas for year 'round versatility. One mix makes approximately 15-18 cakes. Aluminum pan is 13 x 10 1/2 x 1 1/4 in.
2105-Z-1779 $7.99 each

6. HOLIDAY HOUSE KIT
Create this enchanted cozy cottage of cake and icing. Can be as simple or elaborate as you wish. One-mix aluminum pan is 8 5/8 x 9 x 3 in.
2105-Z-2282 $11.99 kit

7. MINI GINGERBREAD BOY PAN
Populate your holiday fare with half a dozen of these fun-loving little fellows. The little ones will just love having their own individualized ginger boy at Christmas dinner. One mix makes approximately 12-15 cakes. Aluminum pan is 12 1/2 x 11 1/4 x 1 1/4 in.
2105-Z-6503 $7.99 each

8. GINGERBREAD BOY PAN
Find this happy-go-lucky guy popping up at all your yuletide get-togethers. Simple decorating creates great effects with this easy pan. One-mix makes approximately 12-15 gingerbread boys. Aluminum pan is 14 x 10 1/2 x 2 in.
2105-Z-2072 $7.99 each

9. JOLLY SANTA PAN
Send the sweetest season's greetings with the smiling face of old St. Nick. He's great fun for the whole family to decorate! One-mix aluminum pan is 13 1/4 x 11 1/2 x 2 in.
2105-Z-1225 $7.99 each

10. RUDY REINDEER PAN
It's Rudy, our irresistible reindeer. He'll soon be leading the fun at all holiday festivities. One-mix aluminum pan is 10 3/4 x 16 3/4 x 1 3/4 in.
2105-Z-1224 $7.99 each

Easter Pans

1. _NEW!_ MINI-BUNNY PAN
Hop to it! Make six bunny-shaped treats in no time flat, and have great fun, too! One mix makes about 12-16 bunnies. Aluminum pan is 12 3/4 x 11 3/4 x 1 1/2 in.
2105-Z-4426 $7.99 each

2. _NEW!_ PEEK-A-BOO BUNNY PAN
A little shy and oh-so-cute, this bunny will help you celebrate springtime and other hoppy occasions! Four different decorating ideas on label. One-mix aluminum pan is 16 x 8 3/4 x 2 in.
2105-Z-4395 $7.99 each
(Available January, 1993)

3. _EGG MINI-CAKE PAN_
Use them as colorful place markers at the holiday table. The label includes a variety of decorating ideas. One cake mix yields about 24 cakes. Each oval well is 3 1/2 x 2 3/8 in. Pan is 12 x 8 3/8 x 1 3/4 in.
2105-Z-2118 $7.99 each

4. _EGG PAN SET_
This cake makes a great holiday centerpiece. Two-piece aluminum pan takes just one cake mix. Each half is 8 3/4 x 5 3/8 in. and includes a ring base for level baking.
2105-Z-700 $10.99 set
EGG PAN RING ONLY
503-Z-954 $1.49 each

5. _LITTLE LAMB PAN SET_
A beautiful centerpiece for your Easter table. Two-piece aluminum pan is 10 x 7 in. tall and takes 6 cups of pound cake batter. Baking and decorating instructions included.
2105-Z-2010 $10.99 set

6. _SUNNY BUNNY PAN_
His big feet, big ears and big heart make him a most welcomed Easter guest and more. See label for ideas. One-mix aluminum pan is 12 5/8 x 10 1/4 x 2 in.
2105-Z-2435 $7.99 each

7. _COTTONTAIL BUNNY PAN_
This fluffy-tailed favorite is an adorable addition to birthdays and baby showers. The label includes a bunny-quick way to decorate. One-mix aluminum pan is 14 x 12 x 2 in.
2105-Z-2015 $7.99 each

8. _GENTLE LAMB PAN_
Invite this delicate little lamb to grace your Easter table. One-mix aluminum pan is 13 5/16 x 10 1/2 x 1 7/8 in.
2105-Z-2515 $7.99 each

9. _SPECIAL DELIVERY BUNNY PAN_
This little cottontail has a basketful of Easter wishes. Alternate decorating ideas included. One-mix aluminum pan is 14 x 11 1/4 x 2 in.
2105-Z-9001 $7.99 each

10. _CROSS PAN_
Bake and decorate this meaningful cake for holidays, christenings and other religious occasions. Instructions include a birthday and family reunion cake. One-mix aluminum pan is 14 1/2 x 11 1/8 x 2 in.
2105-Z-2509 $8.99 each

Novelty Pans

1. BASEBALL GLOVE PAN
The home team will love this mitt that can be customized with names and team colors. Can also be used for many occasions. One-mix aluminum pan is 12 x 12 1/4 x 1 3/4 in.
2105-Z-1234 $9.99 each

2. NEW! HOME RUN HITTER PAN
Decorate a cake that's always a hit, in any season! Celebrate opening day, birthdays, special occasions, the World Series! One-mix aluminum pan is 15 x 10 1/4 x 1 7/8 in.
2105-Z-2020 $9.99 each

3. MINI-BALL PAN
These little treats are perfect in any championship season. Ice mini-balls and push together for a 3-D effect. One cake mix will yield 12 to 15 balls. Aluminum pan is 11 1/2 x 7 1/2 x 1 1/2 in.
2105-Z-1760 $9.99 each

4. SPORTS BALL PAN SET
This multi-function ball can go from basketball to soccer and volleyball with ease. Many more uses in store. Set includes two 6-in. diameter half ball aluminum pans and two metal baking stands. Each pan half takes 2 1/2 cups batter.
2105-Z-6506 $9.99 set
BALL PAN BAKE STAND ONLY
503-Z-881 $1.49 each

5. FIRST AND TEN FOOTBALL PAN
From little guys to Monday morning quarterbacks, they'll score with this cake. Perfect for Super Bowl parties, homecomings, award dinners and much more. One-mix aluminum pan is 12 x 7 3/4 x 3 in.
2105-Z-6504 $9.99 each

6. BOWLING A "STRIKE" PAN
Unique ball and pins in action design is sure to strike a happy chord with that bowler in the family. One-mix aluminum pan is 14 3/4 x 11 3/4 x 2 in.
2105-Z-6505 $9.99 each

7. T-SHIRT PAN
This universal casual standby will be the most welcome attire at many occasions— birthdays, baby showers and any other celebration you can imagine. One-mix aluminum pan is 13 1/4 x 12 1/2 x 2 in.
2105-Z-2347 $9.99 each

8. HORSESHOE PAN
A horseshoe by any other name still means "good luck." Whether it's a good omen for graduations, bon voyage or a Christmas stocking, it's a style you'll be glad to have. One-mix aluminum pan is 12 x 1 3/4 in. deep.
2105-Z-3254 $9.99 each

9. STAR PAN
What better way to honor the celebrity in your life! Brighten birthdays, opening nights, even law enforcement occasions. New possibilities always emerging. One-mix aluminum pan is 12 3/4 in. across x 1 7/8 in. deep.
2105-Z-2512 $9.99 each

10. DOUBLE-TIER ROUND PAN
Special effects are simple to achieve. Use just one 2-layer cake mix in one pan to create two classic tiers-6 and 10 inch. Decorate this unique shape quite formally or with creative whimsy. A year-round party pleaser. Aluminum pan is 9 3/4 x 3 in.
2105-Z-1400 $9.99 each

Novelty Pans

1. _NEW!_ BALLERINA BEAR PAN
Always on her toes and ready to please kids and adults alike with her fancy designs. One-mix aluminum pan is 15 3/4 x 9 1/2 x 1 15/16 in.
2105-Z-2021 $9.99 each

2. MINI BEAR PAN
These petite bears will have little time to hibernate once kids find out just how much fun they are. Make six individual servings at once. One cake mix will yield 12-16 bears. Aluminum pan is 13 1/8 x 12 x 1 3/4 in.
2105-Z-4497 $9.99 each

3. HUGGABLE TEDDY BEAR PAN
He'll bring his happy mood to any occasion. Ideas for birthdays and baby showers included. One mix aluminum pan is 13 1/2 x 12 1/4 x 2 in.
2105-Z-4943 $9.99 each

4. TEDDY BEAR STAND-UP PAN
Great for birthdays, baby showers, school parties and just warm wishes. Two-piece one-mix aluminum pan is 9 1/2 x 8 1/2 x 5 in. Core, stand and clips.
2105-Z-2325 $15.99 set
BAKING CORE ONLY*
503-Z-504 $4.49 each
*although slightly smaller than the core included with the pan, this works as well.

5. PANDA PAN
This 3-D Panda is a hit at all sorts of happy events. Two-piece aluminum pan takes 6 1/2 cups of firm textured batter. Includes 6 clips, heat conducting core and instructions. Pan is 9 1/2 x 8 5/8 in. tall
2105-Z-603 $16.99 each
BAKING CORE ONLY
503-Z-504 $4.49 each

6. PANDA MOLD
Aluminum 2-pc. mold/pan is perfect for baking cakes and molding candy, ice cream, and sugar. About 4 3/4 in. high.
518-Z-489 $5.99 each

7. WONDER MOLD KIT
Use the mold alone or as a part of another design. Aluminum pan (8 in. diam., 5 in. deep) takes 5-6 cups of firm-textured batter. Heat-conducting rod assures even baking. Kit contains pan, rod, stand, 7 in. doll pick and instructions.
2105-Z-565 $11.99 kit
TEEN DOLL PICK
7 in. tall, same as in kit.
2815-Z-101 $2.99 each

8. PETITE DOLL PAN
Couple this aluminum pan with Small Doll Picks for a quartet of party treats. Alone, it lends itself to all sorts of inventive cake ideas. Great assembled with Wonder Mold kit as a color-coordinated bridal party centerpiece. One cake mix yields 4 to 6 cakes.
508-Z-302 $9.99 each
SMALL DOLL PICKS
4 1/2 in. high.
1511-Z-1019 $5.69 pack of 4

9. BOOK PAN
This open book details every one of life's important chapters-birthdays, baby showers, graduations and much more. Five ways to decorate included. One-mix aluminum pan is 13 x 9 1/2 x 2 in.
2105-Z-972 $9.99 each

10. TWO-MIX BOOK PAN
This great volume serves up to 30 guests. The story unfolds as the crowd gathers to celebrate most any occasion. Aluminum pan is 11 1/2 x 15 x 2 3/4 in.
2105-Z-2521 $12.99 each

Novelty Pans

1. _NEW!_ HANDSOME GUY PAN
This good-looking guy wants to attend your next party! And he'll dress for the occasion—formal, sports, even in uniform. One-mix aluminum pan is 16 ¾ x 11 x 2 in.
2105-Z-2023 **$9.99 each**

2. _NEW!_ PRETTY LADY PAN
She's a beauty! Dress her for success, either sophisticated or casual, and she'll be the center of attention at your next celebration. One-mix aluminum pan is 15 ¾ x 9 ⅝ x 2 in.
2105-Z-2022 **$9.99 each**

3. SUPER RACE CAR
Spinning out of the turn and headed right for birthday celebrations galore. This fast-paced automobile will travel from party to party all year long. One-mix aluminum pan is 18 ⅛ x 7 ⅝ x 2 in.
2105-Z-6508 **$9.99 each**

4. LITTLE FIRE TRUCK
This little engine can make any occasion a five-alarm event. Birthdays, school parties, even a retirement party can be fun with this creative pan. One-mix aluminum pan is 16 x 9 ⅛ x 2 in.
2105-Z-9110 **$9.99 each**

5. LITTLE TRAIN PAN
The new little birthday and all-occasion train packs a cargo-load of fun for party guests and the guest of honor. Lots of laughter on board. One-mix aluminum pan is 8 ¾ x 15 ¾ x 2 in.
2105-Z-6500 **$9.99 each**

6. CHOO CHOO TRAIN PAN
Here's the little 3-D engine that could–pulling through again with a trainload of uses. All aboard! Two-part aluminum pan snaps together. Pan is 10 x 6 x 4 in. Takes 6 cups of firm-textured batter.
2105-Z-2861 **$10.99 each**

7. 18-WHEELER TRUCK PAN
It's easy to deliver a special greeting on Dad's Day, moving day and life's major milestones. One-mix aluminum pan is 8 ¾ x 17 x 2 in.
2105-Z-0018 **$9.99 each**

8. UP 'N AWAY BALLOON PAN
This cake successfully transports greetings of "congratulations" and "bon voyage". Four ways to decorate included on label. One-mix aluminum pan is 14 ½ x 10 ½ x 1 ⅞ in.
2105-Z-1898 **$9.99 each**

9. PRECIOUS PONY PAN
Create a colt or a filly to prance about with happy birthday wishes. Captivating alternate ways to decorate are included. One-mix aluminum pan is 16 x 11 x 2 in.
2105-Z-2914 **$9.99 each**

10. GUITAR PAN SET
From Country & Western to Heavy Metal, music fans will go wild over this cake. Just ice, place plastic trims and pipe simple borders. Strings (not included) can be added for even more musical effect. Includes plastic neck, bridge and pick guard. One-mix aluminum pan is 17 ¾ x 8 ½ x 2 in.
501-Z-904 **$9.99 set**

GUITAR ACCESSORY KIT ONLY
503-Z-938 **$1.59 set**

PLEASE NOTE: All prices, certain products and services reflect the U.S. domestic market and do not apply in Australia and Canada.

Novelty Pans

1. NEW!

2.

3.

4.

Have a "SUPER" Birthday MARIO!

HAPPY BIRTHDAY SAM

5.

6. NEW!

7.

1. NEW! WWF® SUPERSTARS PAN
Team up with the mighty Hulk Hogan™, Big Boss Man™, and Macho Man Randy Savage™! All three decorating instructions are included. Aluminum one-mix pan is 13 1/2 x 12 3/4 x 2 in.
2105-Z-2552 $9.99 each
(Available Sept. 15, 1992)
©1992 TitanSports, Inc. Hulk Hogan™, is a trademark of Marvel Entertainment Group, Inc. All Rights Reserved.

2. SUPER MARIO BROTHERS® PAN
This non-stop character will make sure everyone has a super celebration. One-mix aluminum pan is 14 1/2 x 9 1/2 x 2 in.
2105-Z-2989 $9.99 each
©1989 Nintendo of America, Inc.

3. TEENAGE MUTANT NINJA TURTLE® HEAD PAN
Change his colors to make your favorite fighter. One-mix aluminum pan is 12 5/8 x 11 3/8 x 2 in.
2105-Z-4436 $9.99 each
® & © 1990 Mirage Studios, U.S.A. Exclusively licensed by Surge Licensing, Inc.

4. TEENAGE MUTANT NINJA TURTLES® PAN
It's those crazy crime-stopping amphibians. One-mix aluminum pan is 15 x 9 1/2 x 2 in.
2105-Z-3075 $9.99 each
® & © 1990 Mirage Studios, U.S.A. Exclusively licensed by Surge Licensing, Inc.

5. BATMAN PAN
It's everyone's favorite crime-fighting caped crusader. One-mix aluminum pan is 13 x 13 1/2 x 2 in.
2105-Z-6501 $9.99 each
TM and © 1992 DC Comics Inc. All Rights Reserved.

6. NEW! SUPERMAN PAN
Super fun for birthdays, parties, Father's Day! Includes plastic facemaker. One-mix aluminum pan is 13 x 13 x 2 in.
2105-Z-2555 $9.99 each
(Available Sept. 1, 1992)
TM and © 1992 DC Comics Inc. All Rights Reserved.

7. SUPER HEROES PAN
Set includes aluminum one-mix 13 x 13 x 2 in. pan, Superman, Batman plastic face masks, chest emblems.
2105-Z-8507 $9.99 set
Trademarks licensed by DC Comics Inc. © 1978

Novelty Pans

1. *NEW!* BUGS BUNNY PAN
This silly wabbit is ready to party! He'll help you celebrate birthdays, holidays, fun times together. One-mix aluminum pan is 13 ³/₄ x 7 ¹/₂ x 2 in.
2105-Z-2553 $9.99 each
(Available Sept. 15, 1992)
TM and © Warner Bros. Inc. 1992. All Rights Reserved.

2. *NEW!* BARBIE® PAN
She's a real doll and a cake the special birthday girl will remember forever! Decorating instructions included for three fun Barbie Fashions. Includes plastic facemaker. One-mix aluminum pan is 14 x 10 ¹/₄ x 2 in.
2105-Z-2551 $9.99 each
(Available Sept. 15, 1992)
BARBIE and associated trademarks are owned by and used under license from Mattel, Inc. © 1992 Mattel, Inc. All Rights Reserved.

3. COOKIE MONSTER PAN
He loves cookies and birthdays, too. This googly-eyed monster makes a great happy birthday surprise. Alternate designs turn his cake into other great ideas. One-mix aluminum pan is 14 ¹/₂ x 11 ¹/₂ x 1 ⁷/₈ in.
2105-Z-4927 $9.99 each
Sesame Street Characters ©Jim Henson Productions, Inc. All Rights Reserved.

4. BIG BIRD WITH BANNER PAN
Now lovable Big Bird will print your good wishes right up front for all to see. One-mix aluminum pan is 13 ¹/₈ x 12 x 12 ¹/₄ in.
2105-Z-3654 $9.99 each
Sesame Street Characters ©Jim Henson Productions, Inc. All Rights Reserved.

5. GARFIELD PAN
Count this mischievous cat to be on his best party behavior for birthdays, holidays and more. Five ways to decorate are included. The plastic face maker is a super decorating timesaver. One-mix aluminum pan is 11 ¹/₂ x 12 ¹/₂ x 2 in.
2105-Z-2447 $9.99 each
GARFIELD: © 1978 United Features Syndicate, Inc.

6. *NEW!* MINI-GARFIELD PAN
Multiple mischief! Here's fun and laughs for parties and snacks at every fun occasion. One-mix makes about 12-14 little Garfield cakes. Aluminum pan is 15 ⁷/₈ x 10 ¹/₈ x 1 in. Each cavity is 4 ¹/₄ x 4 x 1 in.
2105-Z-2550 $9.99 each
(Available Sept. 1, 1992)
GARFIELD: © 1978 United Features Syndicate, Inc.

NOTE: LICENSED CHARACTER PANS CANNOT BE SOLD FOR COMMERCIAL USE.

Novelty Pans

NEW!

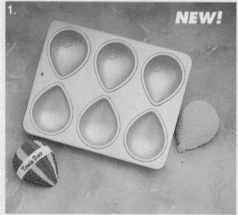

1. _NEW! MINI-BALLOON PAN_
Create a bright bunch of balloons for birthday fun! There are more great decorating ideas on the label. One-mix makes about 12-15 balloons. Aluminum pan is 11 1/4 x 8 3/4 x 1 3/8 in.
2105-Z-2024 $9.99 each

2. _HAPPY CLOWN PAN_
Color kids' parties happy. This circus funny man brings smiles to kids of all ages. His alternate looks can entertain at many occasions. One-mix aluminum pan is 12 x 12 x 2 in.
2105-Z-802 $9.99 each

3. _ROCKING HORSE PAN_
Indulge your hobby for decorating with this perennial favorite. A Wild West carnival or Christmas-time are just a few of the themes to give this lovable cake. It's a winner for birthdays and baby showers. One-mix aluminum pan is 13 1/2 x 13 1/2 x 2 in.
2105-Z-2388 $9.99 each

4. _LITTLE MOUSE PAN_
What trick does this little guy have up his sleeve? Nothing but the happiest of birthday wishes for every boy and girl. One-mix aluminum pan is 15 3/4 x 9 1/2 x 2 in.
2105-Z-2380 $9.99 each

5. _KITTY CAT PAN_
The reigning king is basking in the glow of being named the most popular house pet. Why not immortalize him in buttercream? Create sleek or long-haired breeds. One-mix aluminum pan is 9 x 15 x 2 in.
2105-Z-1009 $9.99 each

6. _CAROUSEL HORSE PAN_
This galloping horse on a brass pole will find itself the center of attention at baby showers, children's birthdays and more. One-mix aluminum pan is 14 x 13 x 1 7/8 in.
2105-Z-6507 $9.99 each

7. _PUPPY DOG PAN_
Finally, you can say "yes" when they ask for a puppy. Our frisky four-legged friend would just love a home for birthdays and kids' get-togethers. Make him your party mascot. One-mix aluminum pan is 17 3/4 x 8 7/8 x 1 7/8 in.
2105-Z-2430 $9.99 each

8. _PARTYSAURUS PAN_
Back from extinction and ready to party. The continued celebrity of dinosaurs makes our prehistoric party animal a must-have at all sorts of fun fests. One-mix pan is 16 x 10 x 1 7/8 in.
2105-Z-1280 $9.99 each